Recrudescence of Violence in Indian North-East States

RECRUDESCENCE OF VIOLENCE IN INDIAN NORTH-EAST STATES

Roots in Environmental Scarcity Induced Migration from Bangladesh

Narottam Gaan

Sudhansubala Das

Publications

KALPAZ PUBLICATION

DELHI - 110052

Recrudescence of Violence in Indian North-East States : Roots in Environmental Scarcity Induced Migration from Bangladesh

Rs. 790

ISBN : 81-7835-285-0

Published in 2004 in India by
Kalpaz Publication,
C-30, Satyawati Nagar,
Delhi-110 052
Email : kalpaz@hotmail.com

Lasertype Setting by: Tact Computer Graphics, Delhi
Printed at: Mehra Offset Press, Delhi

Dedication

To

Our two loving beautiful divine flower

Tattawamasi

and

Mokshayaprada

Contents

	Preface	11
1.	Introduction	13
2.	Environmental Scarcity and Degradation of Resources.	49
3.	Social Effects	87
4.	Environmental Conflict : Intra-Inter State.	123
5.	Future Sea Level Rise : Exacerbating Migration and Conflict.	161
6.	Floods and Cyclones in Bangladesh : Implications and Consequences, Intra and Interstate.	171
7.	International Intervention : Questions of Equity, Ethics and Political Will	237
8.	Conclusion	249
	Bibliography	273
	Index	293

List of Acronyms

ADA	Association of Development Agencies
ADAB	Association of Development Agencies Bangladesh
ADB	Asian Disaster Preparedness Centre
BBS	Bangladesh Bureau of Statistics
BDP	Bangladesh Development Programme
BIDS	Bangladesh Institute of Development Studies
BMD	Bangladesh Meteorological Department
BWDB	Bangladesh Water Development Board
CARDMA	Coastal Area Resources Development and Management Association
CARE	Cooperative Agency for Relief Everywhere
DANIDA	Danish International Development Agency
DIA	Disaster Impact Assessment
ENA	Estimate Not Available
FCFC	Flood Control and Forecasting Centre
FFWS	Flood Forecasting and Warming System
GDP	Gross Domestic Product
GIS	Geological Information System
HYV	High Yielding Variety
IDNDR	International Decade for Natural Disaster Reduction
NDMAC	National Disaster Management Advisory Committee
SPARRSO	Bangladesh Space Research and Remote Sensing Organization
UNDAP	Union Disaster Action Plan
UNCHS	United National Centre of Human Settlements
UNDRO	United Nations Disaster Relief Organisation
UNEP	United Nations Environment Organisation

WAPRO	Water Resources Planning Organisation
WCHNR	World Conference for Natural Disaster Reduction
WCNDR	World Conference on Natural Disaster Reduction
WDR	World Development Report
WMO	World Meteorological Organisation

Preface

In recent years with the end of the Cold War the realist understanding of national security becomes redundant. With the degradation and scarcity of resources, the need for redefining security was seriously felt, because of their disastrous effects on society in terms of global warming, sea level rise, desertification, land degradation, poverty and decline in economy being a threat to the very survival of the people. Thus environmental degradation has been perceived as an equal even if a greater threat to humanity than a military threat. The term security was broadened to include the environmental components. Environmental security came to the centre stage of political analysis.

A number of analysts have argued that human induced environmental degradation and pressures might seriously affect national and international security. The topic 'environmental security' encompasses an almost unmanageable array of subissues, especially if security is defined broadly to include general, physical, social and economic well-being.

The scope of the problem has been narrowed by focusing on how environmental stress affects conflict, rather than security. Still the topic is too vast. Environmental stress might contribute to conflict as diverse as war, terrorism, or diplomatic and trade disputes. Moreover, it might have a great range of causal roles, in some cases, it might be a proximate and powerful cause of conflict, whereas in others it might be a distant or minor player in a tangled conflict involving political, economic and physical factors.

The scope has been further narrowed by focusing on how environmental stress affects violent national and international conflict. The connection between environmental scarcity and degradation of resources and violent conflict has been well established in the present study which focuses on causes and problems of environmental scarcity and degradation of resources in Bangladesh. The various social effects in terms of economic decline and poverty, and growing incapability of the state have been studied which ultimately have led to migration of Bangladeshi people to Indian states. This study remains significant in that it well establishes the link between environmental scarcity and conflict between Bangladesh and India. In chime with the current development and prediction of science this study has focused on the future sea level rise in Bangladesh and predicted migration to India which could exacerbate the conflict more intensely within Bangladesh and between India and Bangladesh, with serious security implications on India.

Keeping in mind the disastrous consequences of environmental scarcity of resources, the study has suggested a broader comprehensive security in South Asia on environmental dimension as a major part of the solution to the crisis as well to the other outstanding issues bedeviling their bilateral relation. This study assumes importance in global context, as global warming due to the industrialised North's emission of CO_2 to the atmosphere has a great bearing on Bangladesh and other countries like Egypt and Maldives. The present study posits a challenge to the western pattern of development being imitated by the South at the cost of their own environment, society and economy. What it suggests is to rethink the very concept of development and inordinate life style that could come as a greater security threat for the entire humanity especially the poor people in the South.

We are extremely grateful to Dr. Thomas F.Homer Dixon, of Toronto University, Canada, Dr. Arthur H.Westing, and European Center for Peace Studies, Austria for having provided us materials and suggestions from time to time. We remain extremely grateful to JNU Library, Centre for Science and Environment and UN Library, New Delhi for having provided us the opportunity to collect the materials and prepare the manuscript. Our unbounded thanks go to Prof. Kanti Bajpai of JNU, New Delhi, Prof. Benudhar Pradhan, and Prof. Asha Hans for having encouraged us always to work on this subject

Finally, we always remain indebted to our Gurudev Paramhamsa Hariharananda, and also to Paramhamsa Prajnanananda for being the sole doer in us and present in our every breath. We offer at Their Lotus Feet flowers of gratitude with our unswerving love and devotion from the core of our heart.

–Narottam Gaan

Sudhansubala Das

1

Introduction

Environment, Scarcity and Conflict

The concept 'national security' has eluded many theorists to define it in precise terms. Security is tied closely to the categories of sovereignty and political community understood in territorial exclusiveness. Stephen Krasner defined the conventional meaning of national security as the defense to territorial and political integrity which was understood as the fundamental, the immutable objective of states in the international system".[1] The dominant paradigm in international relations realism has seen the role of states as the exercise of sovereignty and development of state power to protect states from external threats violating their territorial integrity. The concern with national security has presumed hostile, or potentially hostile, interstate relations and a more or less permanent danger to states of organised, intentional, state directed violence through military means.[2] Thus the realist model of understanding national security provides the rationale for putting exclusive reliance on military force as the sine qua non of statehood. The Cold War during its conflict ridden turbulent years seemed to validate and buttress many of the postulates and predictions that realists envisaged prior to and in the wake of World War I. With the winding down of Cold War swift changes took place in the international system casting doubts about human safety in future and marking an uncertainty about its unfolding and direction in which it is heading. The end of the Cold War encouraged new thinking about threats to international security. The dominant realist framework to understand the current realities seemed to be inadequate. According to Charles W.Kegley, Jr. "the questions realism asks and the answers it provides may become increasingly less relevant".[3] In a similar vein, Holsti states that realism in short, is increasingly perceived to have "become an anachronism that has lost much of its explanatory and prescriptive power.[4] In other words, realism may not be an adequate guide for the future of international politics".[5]

Even much before realism struck deep roots in the international system many scholars rejected realism as incomplete, misdirected, non-rigorous, inconsistent with scientific evidence and incapable of accounting for international behavior in all issue areas.[6] Literatures like poverty of realism, poverty of neo-realism[7] and the dangers of real politik based policies[8] sprang up. Thus, in the existing and changing international situation, the clamour was that the real politik understood and explained on realist parlance should be reconstructed.[9] Among the many emergent problems replacing the threat of East-West ideological divide military aggression and struggle for global preponderance[10] is the global environmental crisis. It looms large in terms of global warming, acid rain, sea level rise, greenhouse effect, diminishing capacity of the agricultural system, depletion of earth's finite resources and punching holes in the ozone layer. Simply put, the global agenda has expanded since the demise of the Cold War as has the need for urgent attention to these problems for solution. It is thus seen that "welfare not warfare, will shape the rules and global threats like ozone holes and pollution will dictate the agenda".[11]

In the words of Charles W.Kegley, given the current unpredictable changing international scenario, "a prevailing paradigm can function like a badly warped piano: the players tend to hit dead keys". Any adherence to realist precepts, according to him, meant, the policy makers" will have to navigate the uncharted seas of the post-Cold War disorder with a Cold War cartography". He further stated that "blind devotion to realism could compromise their ability to prescribe paths to a more orderly and just global system".[12]

While focusing on states as unit of analysis the realist approach does not take into account the environmental issues and downplays the internal factors and the indirect transboundary effects of environmental degradation. This has led Homer Dixon to state that "realism induces scholars to squeeze environmental issues into a structure of concepts including 'state', 'sovereignty', 'territory', 'national interest' and the balance of power". This, in his opinion may "lead theorists to ignore, distort, and misunderstand important aspects of global environmental problems".[13]

The realist understanding of 'national security' as a function of the successful pursuit of interstate power competition through military means continued right through the Cold War. This version of national security sheet anchored on military, ideological and technological dimensions to understand and define social problems.[14] Security was tied closely with state secrecy, nuclear and military power, diplomacy and intelligence.' While summing up Dalby explains that "Cold War versions of security have usually been understood in spatial terms as moves of exclusion" and "protection is a spatial exercise in distancing and boundary making".[16]

During the last half century, security has been primarily a matter of concern for states and their military alliances. The legitimacy of the governments is generally understood in terms of a provision of internal security for the inhabitants residing within its territorial jurisdictions. What is secured may not be always stable or a just political order. Where stability of the regime has been held synonymous with national security, serious inroads into the realm of human rights and internal repressions have been rationalised for maintenance of status quo and national security.[17] Here, national security meant little more than securing power to those who already hold power. Where political instability has been identified as threat, national security is understood as containing and limiting political change and legitimising the status quo. The drastic changes wreaking havoc upon the world in terms of environmental degradation affecting human living and sustenance questions the very concept of national security being tied to the state which is to be maintained at any cost as a sphere of spatial exclusion and bounded places.[18]

Redefining Security

During the 1980s many moves were made to redefine national security. The Independent Commission on Disarmament and Security Issues 1987 (Palme Commission) developed ideas of finding an alternative security on the lines of common security.[19] Some European thinkers were evolving ideas on non-provocative defense or non-offensive defense (NOD) alternative to military confrontation.[20] While the peace researchers worked out the technical details of NOD proposals, the politically active intellectuals stressed on the need to dismantle old ideological and military logic of blocs. Its proponents attempted to link matters of militarization of technological development with its environmental consequences and the difficulties of democratic politics in states pre-occupied with matters of military security. Out of this logic emerged the political programme of dealignment.[21]

The Japanese suggested comprehensive security which will include more than narrow conception of security in military terms.[22] The issues of human rights were also linked to security in terms of individual security within states. Many ethnic, tribal and aboriginal groups demanded to redefine security in terms of giving protection to their cultural identity and survival. The feminist movements criticised the theorists and political scientists of international politics for having rendered them insecure by ignoring them out of their scripts and literature which gave importance only to men.[23] A new concept, 'alternative security' was developed counter to the narrow military security suggesting a 'post deterrence era of global cooperation'.[24]

In all these attempts to refashion national security is found the inadequacies of the spatially based autarkic security strategies to provide security to many communities within the boundaries of states.[25] Security couched in traditional parlance in terms of spatial strategies of distancing and boundary making is no longer the key to protection of a geographically, demarcated community. Bounded places in the words of Johnston are no longer quite as bounded as they once were.[26] For example, the threats from environmental degradation in terms of air pollution, global warming and greenhouse effects with all their disastrous consequences are transboundary and cannot be shielded against by military powers because ecological regions do not necessarily coincide with political boundaries. All of these modifications of security aim at a shift of focus from traditional concern with military by reiterating the necessity of understanding security in terms more than what the primacy of military operations convey. In the words of Barry Buzan, "the sources of threat are also diversifying away from the state. Many of the new threats seem to stem from complex systems both natural (the eco system) and the human made (the global economy)". According to him, "the operation of these systems is often poorly understood".[27]

This has resulted in many critics recognising the necessity of democratization of security.[28] They are of the view that security is broader than as seen within the confines of military security and a political order and a particular political identity.[29] The state while maintaining national security on its military matrix has rendered many individuals, populations and societies insecure.[30] The concept national security while arrogating to itself the exclusive and uncontested right to mobilisation of a high level of human and material resources for what it considers as important[31] renders not only population as insecure but also other sectors like environment and development of the people starved of proper attention and access to resources. In the traditional concerns of national security many economic and environmental problems remain beyond its purview. The most daunting challenges to the existing definition of national security comes from the problems of global environmental degradation which has appeared as a security threat to many people. As pointed out by Peter Gleick, the conventional models of national security so far developed and centering round the state "have not considered access to resources and the degradation of global environmental services a central problem of international politics and security".[32]

Environmental Security

In the light of this conceptual shift, there has been a multidisciplinary debate in recent years over whether changes to the natural environment should be considered national security concern. The term environment, just like the term security is imprecise, relatively elastic, and highly contested.

As Richard Matthew points out, both "can be given very narrow or very comprehensive definitions".[33] None the less, a persuasive definition is one that is limited to "biological or physical systems characterised either by significant ecological feedbacks or by their importance to the sustenance of human life."[34]

The mounting environmental problems and the resultant associated issues needs an attention with which the conventional outlook of national security appears to be incongruent.Furthering this argument, Jeremy Rifkin points out :

> The environmental threats facing the planet are not simply the result of scientific miscalculation. Nor are they merely the consequences of ill conceived management decisions. Ironically it is the notion of security upon which our entire modern worldview is based that has led us to the verge of ecocide..... In less than a century the practice of geopolitics has pushed the world to the brink of both nuclear Armageddon and environmental catastrophe, forcing us to reconsider the basic assumptions of security that animate the modern worldview.[35]

The study of the link between environmental degradation and national security threats has become important with many civil strifes occuring in countries such as Somalia and Rwanda often beset by environmental scarcity or degradation Policy makers seeking explanations for the subnational, ethnically motivated civil strifes which have preoccupied contemporary foreign policy debates, have been led to unearth a link between environment and national security. The environmental scarcity or degradation of renewable natural resources has become issues of conflict between and among states. Fresh water resources and fish stocks are the overt examples of renewable resources that have been the direct objective of potentially violent international conflicts. The environmental security approach offers a clear alternative to traditional, security thinking about international conflicts over renewable natural resources. The effects of environmental degradation on the economy of the society in terms of poverty and food insecurity, diseases and health hazards are quite obvious. Impoverishment may not directly lead to interstate conflict. But in case, if people being attracted by a relatively better economic prospects of a neighbouring country, starts moving in great numbers to disrupt the economic, political and social life of the receiving state, interstate conflict or conflict between various ethnic groups are likely to occur. The effects of profuse CO_2 emission and other green house gases have been predicted in terms of sea level rise and changes in precipitation patterns which will have disastrous impacts on agriculture. The sea level rise will result in flight of millions of people of the coastal countries as environmental refugees into neighbouring countries causing international instability.[36] Migration of people may be also due to natural disasters such as floods, cyclones, droughts and earthquakes caused by anthropogenic or natural factors. If environmental disasters are caused by natural phenomena not by any specific identifiable group it is said, war is not likely to result from these causes. But if it results in massive transmigration into another state an interstate conflict is most likely to happen, as between India and Bangladesh on the issue of Bangladeshi migration into Assam, Arunachal Pradesh, Tripura, other North Eastern states and other Indian States. Thus the argument that interstate conflict may not be always precipitated by environmental disasters caused by natural phenomena cannot be made a case for denouncing the link between security and environment. From a broader understanding of security, if people are made the referent rather than the state, environmental degradation is an immediate threat to numerous people in terms of deepening poverty and uprooting their way of life.[37]

A number of studies in recent years have cropped up showing a clear cut connection between environment and security.[38] Lodgaard feels that

> "the concept of environmental security challenges established frames of mind and political conflict". According to him, "It

conveyes the message that environmental problems have a legitimate claim for status as military problems have".[39]

Environmental security as a concept encompassing non-military aspects was officially mentioned for the first time in the International Conference on the Relationship between Disarmament and Development, convened by the United Nations General Assembly in New York from 24 August to 11 September 1987. In this final document adopted by consensus by the representatives from the 150 participating states, the Conference stated:

> Recently nonmilitary threats to security have moved to the forefront of global concern. Underdevelopment and the declining prospects for development as well as mismanagement and waste of resources, constitutes challenges to security. The degradation of the environment presents a threat to sustainable development...... Mass poverty, illiteracy, disease, squalor and malnutrition affecting a large proportion of the world's population often become the cause of social strain, tension and strife.[40]

Going further than this, the report by the World Commission on Environment and Development (Brundtland Report) entitled "Our Common Future" stressed the influence of environmental degradation on the relationship between states. It attempted to establish the conflictual relationship between states as :

> Environmental stress is both a cause and effect of political tension and military conflict. It states that, "nations have often fought to assert or resist control over raw materials, energy supplies, land river basin, sea passages and other key environmental resources". According to the report "such conflicts are likely to increase as these resources become scarcer and competition for them will increase".[41]

Jessica Mathews justified the reasons for encompassing resource availability questions as well as environmental issues into the framework of security.[42] American Senator Albert Gore suggested a case for strategic environmental initiative,[43] which went side by side with Springer's argument enhancing the scope of the Atlantic alliance structure to include environmental issues.[44]

Peter Gleick was of the view that food issues, water conflicts and access to Aretic minerals were likely to generate security concerns in the future.[45] Norman Myers, similarly held that :

> .... national security is not just about fighting forces and weaponry. It relates to watersheds, croplands, forests, genetic resources, climate and other factors that rarely figures in the minds of military experts and political leaders, but increasingly deserve, in their collectivity, to rank alongside military approaches as crucial to a nation's security.[46]

Westing in a similar vein suggested to incorporate environmental issues into the themes of comprehensive security in the sense of security for all citizens in a state rather than into a narrow understanding of security in military denominations.[47]

Lothar Brock defines environmental security as the avoidance of negative linkages between the environment and human activities. For him, this includes the avoidance of warfare, war over natural resources and also environmental degradation, which he defines as a form of war.[48]

Environmental Security as National Security

All these show that threats are not only military but also economic and environmental. The clearcut connection between environment and security is established beyond the realist framework. Environmental security, thus becomes a national security issue. Two distinct features of environmental security are : First the environmental causes of conflict, i.e., environmental factors behind potentially violent conflicts, second, the impact of environmental degradation on overall economy, health and life of the people. Thus, environmental degradation or deficiencies create the conditions that render conflict all the more likely or determine the source of conflict, act as multipliers that aggravate core causes of conflict[49] or act as a catalytic factor in creating conflict then environmental degradation as a security issue is fully consistent with the traditional definition of national security.[50] But the proponents of environmental security viewing the environmental degradation as the result of impersonal socio-economic forces, suggest cooperative solutions.

As stated above, environmental degradation in terms of greenhouse gases, CO_2 emission, thinning of ozone layer, land degradation, water scarcity, deforestation, desertification and other calamities like flood and cyclone etc. caused by Anthropogenic and natural reasons have been a threat to the well-being of people. Due to punching hole in the ozone layer people will be exposed to the UV-B rays and their health affected seriously. Sea level rise will submerge many low lying countries in deep sea. Changes in weather pattern will affect agricultural system. Neither the actual increased exposure to UV-B from the punching of the hole in the ozone layer nor the degree of harm it will wreak on plants, animals and humans is calculable. Neither the eventual increase in global average temperatures from a given level of greenhouse gas emissions nor the impacts on weather patterns, disease, crops or sea level rise can be gauged. Similarly the rate of land degradation on a global scale cannot be measured with accuracy and its impact on future food productivity cannot be predicted with any scientific precision. Thus, each of these environmental threats to global well being has been subject to significant empirical and scientific uncertainty and inaccuracy. That does not any way denude environmental security of its meaning and significance. Such uncertainties associated with environmental security are also found in case of military planning based on worst case contingencies which are considered most unlikely to occur. Yet military preparations are justified for such contingencies as an insurance against these unlikely threats.[51]

The very military systems of various states are held as protected polluters. They have been excluded from the purview of environmental regulation as the rationale of national security. But its activities, preparation, training, nuclear facilities, fuel consumption and demands for exotic minerals and chemicals have been disastrous to the world's environment.[52] As stated by Dalby, "Military security has been bought here at the cost of ecological devastation".[53] The number of people secured by such military establishments are numerically miniscule in comparison to the people who have been vulnerable to such ecological devastation on a vast scale. Environmental degradation, thus far outweighs the military security and stands as a greater national security issue. In the United States, for example, the potential harm that the global degradation poses to the health and livelihood of Americans is worse than those posed by its military security threats.

There are a few scholars who have declined to accept the link between environmental degradation and national security threats.[54] An early criticism led by Deudney was that " taking the term security and using it to encompass anything that threatens our well-being, might really take the term and dilute it of any significance".[55]

Such arguments suggest that traditional definition of national security was intellectually coherent or useful. But protagonists of environmental security argue that the traditional definition of national security distort, misunderstand and ignore important aspects of global environmental problems and realities.[56]

Another criticism is that defining environmental issues in terms of security threats may contribute more to the military.[57] Similarly according to L.Brock, "defining environmental issues in terms of security risks is in itself a risky operation.... We may end up contributing more to the militarization of environmental politics than to the demilitarization of security politics".[58] The resource and development nexus juxtaposed into the analysis makes it the clearest. In the Cold War parlance security issues are understood in terms of the right of access of the developed world to the resources of the South. The major problem in the current environmental crisis is the inequities in the access to resources.[59] The world economic structure and financing arrangements have been arranged in such a way as to redound to the economic bonanza of the rich North reinforcing the yawning economic discrepancies and facilitating the continued despoliation of the environments of the resource producing areas, and increased pollution. With the perpetuation of this kind of inequitous economy coupled with the debt crisis, the environment will be totally destroyed rendering many of the poorest of the planet more insecure.[60]

In the Cold War logic the concept of security is largely premised on maintaining the perpetuation of existing flows of resources from the South to the North. This is the kind of thinking found conspicuously in the American policy making, more particularly in the Gulf War, which was waged to have the American way. Conflicts or wars over access to resources are in the line of traditional understanding of security resting on state's military supremacy. But this kind of security needs refashioning in view of the fact that the ethnocentrism of western paradigms of development based on unrestricted industrialism, fossil fuel technology and extraction of non-renewable resources, has polluted and degraded the renewable resources like water, land, air, forest, and biodiversity in terms of green house gases, global warming, acid rain, desertification and deforestation. Thus, the environmental scarcity or degradation of resources, has emerged as a threat to the security of the poorest. The conflicts that may arise out of environmental causes of security threats to the poor are distinguishable from the traditional conflicts over access to resources. In the traditional realist paradigm security was understood in terms of state's military supremacy pontificating the South to allow resource flows unobstructed.

But the environmental crisis threatening the very existence and way of life of the poor people to be resolved needs reliance not on a military supremacy of a state but on an overhauling of the entire realist security metaphysics built around the state and its political-economy. Thus, the kind of threats stemming from global environmental crisis strengthen the case for linking the environment and security. Security matrixed on traditional realist framework to maintain the status quo runs counter to the changes needed to mitigate many environmental and economic problems.[61] The contradiction is apparent and crucial to understanding the question of linking the environment and security. Barry Buzan was of the view that this could be a dangerous tool for the totalitarian left who could attempt a relaunch on the basis of environmental collectivism.[62] Similarly Andre Gorz came to the conclusion that since the logic of ecology has religious potentials and holistic categories and the way the environmental issues were addressed, contained the danger of eco-fascism.[63] As has been said earlier though the focus is on environmental problems that are the causes of international conflicts the environmental security directs attention to policy priorities that are basically cooperative.

The spectre of environmental collectivism or eco-fascism could be too shortlived and counter productive to haunt the proponents of environmental security. These totalitarian regimes inclined to interpret security in terms of growing militancy of state. The parameters needed to alleviate ecological crisis in terms of economic and development rethinking, taking out the security label from the state to the local and regional, grassroot level, devolution of power and empowerment of people and the entire process of state building would run counter to their very rational of tacking security label to the state military power. When there is need for more democratization and diversification of state power and regionalisation, the appeals of eco-fascism or totalitarian left may appear demagogic to the environmentally vulnerable people. Such military regimes as the sole and ultimate arbiter of national security, may oppose and avoid many international and global environmental movements, rules and regulations, saying that these are threats to what these regimes held as national security.[64] But in the face of the deepening socio-economic crisis and poverty due to environmental scarcity or degradation of resources, these military regimes may not succeed in holding unto their positions, to counterveil the threats posed by environmental degradation which may be far greater than what these military regimes hold as security threats to their status quo.

Eco-fascism or totalitarian left in their jockeying for power in the name of environmentalism may find it futile to seek solution in state powerism. Since ecogeographical regions do not coincide with territorial units, on many issues, the priority is to be put not on state power, but on cooperation, even on a diminishment of sovereignty where there is the need for an environmental integration. This includes institutional integration, policy integration, attitudinal integration, and security integration. Institutional integration, occurs when states agree to engage in collective decision making and develop institutions to formulate and implement rules and regulations. Policy integration concerns the transfer of policy to a higher level of government or to a jointly managed or coordinated level of policy making and implementation. Attitudinal integration assesses public support for such intervention. The support of victims of environmental degradation may be a strong base for such an integration. Security integration is evident when there is a commitment and expectation among states of non-violent relation.[65]

Another criticism is that the environmental security argument is mainly a means of leveraging changes in budgetary allocations. If budgetary allocations of states are studied, there has never been a reasonable balance among components of security in the allocation of budgetary resources. One of the functions of traditional concept of national security was to ensure that sufficient resources were allocated to the military as a matter of highest national priority. To alleviate the threats of environmental crisis there is very justification for allocation of resources. The proponents of environmental security argue that military establishments consume an enormous and inproportionate amount of human and material resources. The benefits of transferring these resources to the restoration of the environment can be linked to environmental security. The critics are of the view that from a conceptual standpoint this defective and the same point could be made about health and poverty or any of the human needs that are going to be unmet because of the resources being expended on environment. But what the critics fail to notice is that the environmental scarcity of resources or degradation of the environment has led to many social effects in terms of economic decline, decreased agricultural productivity, poverty, health hazards and other human problems. The removal of the causes of the environmental degradation according to the proponents of environmental security will result in the containment of social effects. Hence, there is every justification for putting priority on environment in budgetary allocation to weed out the causes of environmental degradation.

Another objection is that in the concept of environmental security the absence of 'us vrs. them' syndrome which is a cardinal part of traditional concept of national security is "like, according to Deudney taking sex out of rock and roll". In his words, "rock and roll was originally coined as an euphemism for sex".[66]

In international conflicts over environmental scarcity of renewable resources like water and fish among nations can be seen the 'us vrs them' syndrome. The cases of intra or interstate conflicts by transmigration of people due to environmental induced social and economic disruptions, point to the very 'us vrs. them' in environmental conflicts. For example, Indo-Bangladesh conflict over Bangladeshi migration into Indian North-Eastern states strongly rebutes the charges made by critics.

A final objection is that environmental degradation coupled with population pressures are not primary causes of such conflicts. Since these are always embedded in larger socio-economic and political causes of conflict, the exponents of environmental security cannot prove that such issues are resulting in conflict. But they are of the view that the costs of responding to growing state inability and human suffering due to environmental degradation will be higher than the modest cost they demand for conservation of resources and protection of the environment.

Environmental security today stands as a national security concern. Barry Buzan, a critic who wants to see environmental security a part of the economic field, is of the view that the concept national security has been tacked on to environmental debates, because of the latter's mobilization potential. As he stated the concept of national security

> "has an enormous power as an instrument of social and political mobilization" and therefore "the obvious reason for putting environmental issues into the security agenda is the possible magnitude of the threats posed and the need to mobilize urgent and unprecedented responses to them. The security label is a useful way both of signalling danger and setting priority and for this reason alone it is likely to persist in the environmental debates".[67]

Going further than this, in a recent paper he points out that, if the predictions by scientists about climate changes in terms of global warming and green house effects come true, "then current observations such as the break up of some Antarctic ice sheets could put environmental security at the top of the global agenda very soon".[68]

Ideas of environmental security have also been incorporated into the national security framework. In 1987, the General Secretary of the Soviet Union, Mikhail Gorbachev stated:

> The world is not secure in the direct meaning of the word when currents of poison flow along river channels, when poisonous rains pour down from the sky, when an atmosphere polluted with industrial and transport waste chokes cities and whole regions, when the development of atomic engineering is justified by unacceptable risks... The relationship between man and the environment has become menacing. Problems of ecological security affect all the rich and the poor. What is required is global strategy for environmental protection and the rational use of resources.[69]

The former United States Secretary of State, James Baker has considered current environmental problems as "threats to the security of our citizens".[70] In 1994, United Nations Ambassador Madeleine K.Albright (later on US Secretary of State) stated:

> We believe that environmental degradation is not simply an irritation, but a real threat to our national security... Left unaddressed, it could become a kind of creeping Armageddon ... it could, in time, threaten our very survival.[71]

The Clinton Administration also stepped in by adopting the concept of environmental security explicitly in its 1994 National security document. A National Security Strategy of Engagement and Enlargement, which was unequivocal in its emphasis that increasing competition for dwindling renewable resources "is already a very real risk to regional stability around the world.[72] It is of the view that,

> Transnational phenomena such as terrorism, narcotics trafficking, environmental degradation, rapid population growth and refugee flows also have security implications for present and long term American policy. In addition, an emerging class of transnational environmental issues are increasingly affecting international stability and consequently will present new challenges to U.S. strategy.[73]

Environmental Causes of Conflict: Security Threats

While emphasising the obvious link between environmental degradation and conflict, Libiszewski questions the general tendency among scholars to hold this linkage as synonymous with the struggle for scarce non-renewable natural resources.[74] To him, Westing's compilation of important wars involving environmental factors from the 1st World War to the latest Falkland war should be distinguished from the environmental causes of conflict.[75] Conflicts over access to or over possession of natural resources cannot be regarded as environmental conflicts.

Environmental change or degradation does not simply mean the interaction between human beings and their environment. It implies a destabilising interference in the ecosystem's equilibrium which having negatively affected human society, expresses precisely what is meant by environmental change of conflict. Knowing the distinction between renewable and non-renewable resources helps one understand clearly the difference between conflict over natural resources and environmental conflict. The renewable resources such as fresh water, soil, air, forests, atmosphere, climate, oceans and biodiversity which are both goods and services, are renewable because they are ecologically integrated in a feed-back circle system guaranteeing their replacement or preservation of their quality. Minerals and fossil fuels on the other hand constituting the traditional targets of resource conflicts are non-renewable in the sense that they are not integrated in such an eco-system. Their exhaustion to the hilt will be termed as depletion not degradation.

Besides this, the renewable resources are not only less substituted but also in several cases are not substitutable at all. Apart from the environment being considered as a material resource bank, it also provides a space of living bringing in an existential dimension to the environment.

The concept of environmental degradation leads to another important difference concerning the concept of resource scarcity. Four distinct types of resource scarcity are underlined.[76]

1. Physical scarcity means that a resource is only available in a finite amount;
2. Geopolitical scarcity means that resources are often distributed unequally on the surface of the earth so that some countries depend on deliveries from others ;

3. Socio-economic scarcity concerns the unequal distribution of purchasing power and of property rights to provide natural resources between or within societies;
4. Environmental scarcity caused by environmental degradation means failure of human beings to sustainably manage these renewable resources which have been traditionally regarded as plentiful.

The above three scarcities are not environmental conflicts but traditional conflicts over access to resources. While defining environmental conflict in contrast to the traditional resource conflicts. Libiszewski stated :

> An environmental conflict is a conflict caused by the environmental scarcity of a resource, that means; caused by a human made disturbance of its normal regeneration rate. Environmental scarcity can result from the overuse of a renewable resource or from the overstrain of the ecosystem's sink capacity, that is pollution. Both can reach the stage of a destruction of the space of living.[77]

In a similar vein, Homer Dixon stated that environmental change referred to a human induced decline in the quantity or quality of a renewable resource which occur faster than its renewal by natural processes.[78]

According to him,

> "Environmental scarcity often encourages powerful groups to capture valuable environmental resources and encourages marginal groups to migrate to ecologically sensitive areas". In his words, "these two processes" of resource capture and resource marginalisation 'in turn reinforce environmental scarcity and raise the potential for social instability".
>
> Further he is of the view that, "Environmental scarcity can contribute to population movements, economic decline and weakened states, which in turn can cause ethnic conflicts, insurgencies, and coups d'e tat".[79]

From the above, emerges the exclusion of non-renewable resources from the environmental conflict analysis. According to Libiszewski, even the total exhaustion of non-renewable resources like fuels and minerals could not cause any destabilization of the ecosystem. The ethnocentrism of western paradigms of development based on industrialization and non-renewable fossil fuel technology, has already despoliated the planet earth and deteriorated the environment in terms of carbon dioxide emission, greenhouse effect, depletion of ozone layer, global warming, sea level rise and desertification. As a consequence, many people in the South have been vulnerable due to the mimetic western pattern of development and inordinate life styles of the North. So depletion of the non-renewable resources has been a primary factor in degrading the renewable resources of the South. The imperatives and compulsions of world economic structure dominated by the industrialised North has already been a strain on the renewable resources of the South to the latter's utter deprivation and pauperization. The Southern countries are consigned to the periphery and mercy of the world metropolis powers, which remain in the centre of their market economic structure. With structural adjustment conditionalities imposed on without taking into consideration the South's socio-economic imperatives and compulsions, these countries may experience structural, violence[80] and unending onslaughts on their already degraded and fragile environment. Population growth in the South interacting with this process of resource degradation as a requirement of the western model of development would further result in the degradation of the renewable resources causing a decline in economy and exacerbation in the already existing social and domestic differences and problems. In the face of the state's incapability to meet the growing aspirations of the people in South, the legitimacy of the government would be eroded, providing opportunities to the disgruntled in the South to disintegrate the political and social systems. If the depletion of non-renewable resources as a part of the western pattern of development being ubiquitously followed leads to the degradation of the renewable resources in terms of pollution of water, atmosphere, degradation of land, desertification, deforestation and extinction of species and biodiversity, then there will be no conceptual blundering in having a more comprehensive and broader definition than what is suggested by Libiszewski and others. Westing further buttresses this line of thinking when he concedes that

> "Environmental security has two basic sub-components. The first of these environmental protection", he says " has three parts; protection from wartime and similar vandalism: protection from medically unacceptable environmental pollution; and protection, for special areas, from all permanent human intrusions.
>
> The second subcomponent of environmental security according to Westing, "sane resource utilization, whether non-

extractive or extractive depends upon exploitation, use or harvesting at all levels and employing procedures that either maintain or restore optimal resources services or stocks". He further stated that "exploitation of renewable resources must be carried out strictly on the principle of, sustained use or sustained discard, with, exploitation of non-renewable resources strictly on the principles of frugality".[81]

Westing's concept linking environment and security is in a wider context comprising both renewable and non-renewable resources and taking into consideration the direct contribution of exploitation of non-renewable resources to the environmental degradation of the renewable resources, viz. atmosphere, climate, water, land and biodiversity etc. It always involves exploring the environmental causes of conflict which means to find out the main problems and causes of environmental degradation and map out their social effects leading to conflicts. In a complex web of social, political and economic causes and effects of conflict to explore exclusively the environmental causes of conflict is undoubtedly a very Herculean task. The Earthscan document while conceding this states:

> "Ecological pressures" have not caused any particular outbreak of hostilities given in cases where the links are obvious. It claims instead that environmental degradation is often a key cause in a complex cycle of causes and effects. It concludes that "if historians and politicians ignore the environmental component they cannot possibly understand this complex web of causality".[82]

Sources of Environmental Scarcity

According to Dixon, resource scarcity has become an omnipresent feature of human existence. Scarcity of renewable resources has become so severe that it has the potential to seriously threaten the very survival of human beings. It can arise in three ways which can be called supply induced, demand induced and structural induced.[83] Supply induced scarcity occurs and becomes worse when the resource shrinks because it has been degraded in quality and depleted in quantity.

Any human caused increase in supply induced scarcity is the product of three factors: the total human population in the region, the use per capita of each technology available to that population and the amount of resource consumption or degradation produced by each unit of use of these technologies. Use per capita of each technology in turn is influenced by available natural resources including non-renewables and renewables and by ideational factors including institutions, social relations, preferences and beliefs. Resource depletion or degradation can also influence ideational factors for example by prompting or impeding institutional reforms. Finally, the amount of consumption or degradation of a renewable resource arising from a technology's use is influenced by the sensitivity of the region's ecosystem to the use of that technology. The depletion of fisheries can be a best illustration showing how it is a function of the size of the human population consuming fish from the fishery, the type of fishing technologies used by this population, the use of per capita of these technologies and their impact on the fishery per unit use.

Apart from this, renewable resources will be depleted or degraded not by direct consumption but by technological activities that indirectly harm the resources. The western pattern of development based on industrialisation and extraction of non-renewable resources can have immense indirect effects on renewable resources in terms of degradation and pollution.

Demand induced scarcity arises, when a bourgeoning population divides the static resources into smaller slices for each individual. It is a function of population size multiplied by per capita demand for a given resource. An increase in either population or per capita demand increases total resource demand. For example, the number of people living in an arid region might go up which all other things being equal, will increase total demand for water or a constant number of inhabitants might instead demand on average more water for new agricultural technologies. In both these cases, if only a constant or limited flow of water is available, water scarcity will increase. If water is further degraded or polluted by industrial activity, the problem of water scarcity is compounded. Thus, increased population size and increased per capita demand for a given resource can both decrease supply by contributing to the resources' depletion and degradation.

Structural scarcity is caused by unequal distribution that concentrates resources in the hands of some groups and subjects the rest to greater than average scarcity.

Interactions and Social Effects

These three kinds of environmental scarcity often interact and two patterns of interaction such as resource capture and resource marginalisation are found.[84] Resource capture occurs when a deterioration in the quality and quantity of a renewable resource interacts with population growth to prompt powerful groups within a society to shift resource distribution in their favour subjecting poorer and weaker groups to dire environmental scarcity and its social effects. This happens in Bangladesh where environmental scarcity of land resources has prompted the landowners to distribute the land distribution in its favour propelling the poorer and weaker groups to migrate to urban areas or neighbouring states like India.

Ecological marginalisation occurs when unequal resource access combining with population growth causes migration to regions such as steep upland slopes, tropical rain forests, urban areas and other areas at the risk of desertification which are ecologically fragile.[85]

Environmental scarcity and its various patterns of interaction including the above terms may cause innumerable changes in the developing societies. Research has identified five main social effects that either singly or in combination may increase the probability of violence in developing societies.[86]

- Constrained agricultural productivity
- Decline in economic productivity
- Migration of affected people in search of better lives.
- Greater segmentation of society usually along existing ethnic cleavages
- Disruption of institutions especially the state.

These effects are often causally correlated, sometimes with feedback relationship. For example, the migration caused by a decline in food production can reduce the amount of labour available for work in fields further causing a fall in food production. Economic decline can lead to flight of people with education and wealth to within or outside of state which in turn eviscerates universities, courts and institution of economic management—crucial to a healthy economy.

It is very significant to note that environmental scarcity is always a sufficient cause of any of these social effects. Scarcity always interacts with other factors to produce these effects. Therefore contextual factors are important to influence the linkage between scarcity and social effects.

These contextual factors include the physical characteristics of a given environment, and ideational factors unique to the society in question including its institutions, social relations and culture. Some critics suggest that contextual factors especially failed institutions and policies explain poor harvests, large migrations and intergroup cleavages. To them, environmental scarcity is an aggravater of the already existing problems or a trigger releasing accumulated non-environmental pressures. According to Homer Dixon, "It suggests a naive, almost dichotomous view: if environmental scarcity in itself cannot be shown to be a sufficient cause of certain social hardships, then something else must be the cause. Yet a more accurate view of environmental scarcity's role is that it often acts as a deep, underlying stressor of social systems and it produces its effects by interacting with contextual factors unique to the society."[87]

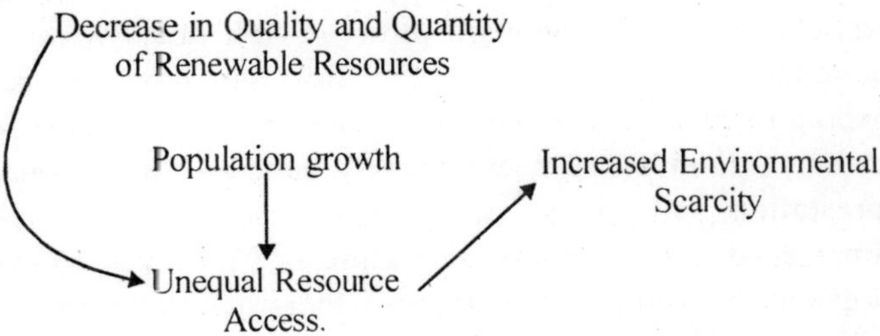

Fig. 1.1. *Resource Capture.*

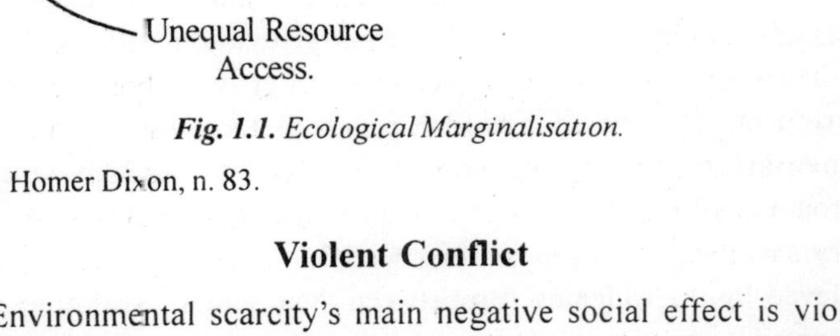

Fig. 1.1. *Ecological Marginalisation.*

Source. Homer Dixon, n. 83.

Violent Conflict

Environmental scarcity's main negative social effect is violent conflicts. Conflicts over natural resources among states are understood within traditional realist (or balance of power) paradigm of international relations theory.[88]

According to Nazli Choucri and Robert North, countries facing high resource demands and limited resource availability within their territories would seek the needed resources through trade or conquest beyond their boundaries.[89] Four environmental resources in particular would appear likely to ignite simple-scarcity conflicts over agriculturally productive land, forests, river water and fish. Simple—scarcity conflict over emanates directly from the overuse and/or pollution/destruction of a renewable natural resource.

Group identity conflicts are explained and predicted by group-identity theories. These conflicts are the result of large scale migration of people from one state to another state or within a state due to environmental scarcity of resources at home fronts. For example: "If groups of people migrate from one country to a neighbouring one, meet an indigenous population of a different ethnic origin and of different religion there, and if violent clashes between those groups occur—this would seem to be an ethno-religious conflicts at first sight ... But if it turns out that the group of people mentioned first started to move because its homeland, its hereditary grounds had been severely damaged and depleted by deforestation, soil erosion, salinization etc - then this is also an environmental conflict in a broader sense."[90] The ethnic conflict and insurgency in North-Eastern states of India due to migration from Bangladesh can be included in this category.

Violent challenges to the state - challenges that range from rebellion to guerrilla war are explained and predicted by a combination of relative - deprivation theories and structural theories of civil strife. These two theoretical perspectives suggest that insurgency is a function of both the level of grievance motivating challenger groups and the opportunities available to these groups to act violently on their grievances.[91] The likelihood of insurgency is greatest when multiple pressures at different levels in society interact to increase grievance and opportunity simultaneously. Environmental scarcity can change both variables by contributing to economic hardship and dislocation, by increasing segmentation, and by weakening institutions such as state. As environmental scarcities hinder economic progress, relative deprivation theory says that some groups will become increasingly frustrated and aggrieved by the widening gap between their actual level of economic achievement and the level they feel they deserve. At some point the disadvantaged groups may cross a critical threshold and will act violently against those groups perceived to be the agents of their economic misery.

To cause civil conflict economic crisis by the environmental scarcity of resources must be severe, persistent and pervasive enough to erode the legitimacy of the political system. If people come to this belief that the state is responsible for their plight and deprivation, the legitimacy of the state will be challenged and the possibility that they will ignite violence against the state will increase.

According to Dixon, "the extent and degree of grievance caused by environmental scarcity of resources is a function of relative deprivation but this relative deprivation must be measured at the level of specific sub-groups within a society and, it is powerfully influenced by local contextual factors such as the groups blame systems and conceptions of economic justice".[92]

The environmental degradation in Bangladesh has resulted in migration of people both intra and inter state. The Government of Bangladesh has also settled the Bengalis uprooted from cyclone, storm and flood affected coastal areas in CHT. As a result, the Chakamas, the original inhabitants of CHT were dominated by the migrant Bengalis and forced to flee to India.' This migration to Indian neighbouring states has often resulted in violent ethnic conflict and insurgency in these states.

Coupled with this is the migration of other Bangladeshis from coastal plains of Bangladesh to north-eastern states of India such as Assam, Tripura, West Bengal and other states which is due to increasing poverty, economic decline and growing incapability of Bangladesh state to meet the needs of the people—the social effects of environmental scarcity and degradation of resources in Bangladesh.

There is no dearth of literature to show that environmental scarcity and degradation of resources will produce vast numbers of environmental refugees.[93] Sea level rise, cyclone, storms and floods will drive people back from coastal and delta areas in Bangladesh to other safer regions within the state or neighbouring states. These studies imply that environmental disruption is the clear and dominant cause of refugees flow out of their homelands in vast and sudden waves. During floods, cyclones and storms, in Bangladesh environmental disruption appears to be the clear and dominant cause of refugees flow and in future sea level rise, the environmental causes of refugees flow are unmistakenly clear and dominant. During normal times in Bangladesh, it is seen that people migrate to Indian territories. This implies that environmental factors in interaction with other social, economic and physical variables produce their effects to prompt displacement of people.

Push and pull theories essentially treat migration as the outcome of the low socio-economic status or insecurity in the sending country, relative to the more affluent and politically stable systems of receiving societies. While distinguishing between refugees and migrants, Astri Suhrke argues that environmental problems are more likely to produce migrants than refugees, because such problems usually develop gradually, which means that the push effect is not sharp and sudden and that pull factors can therefore clearly enter into potential migrants' calculations.[94] According to Homer Dixon, "this push/pull distinction is not helpful, for it encourages analysts to try to determine the relative causal weights of factors in sending and receiving areas. But the real motivator of migration is the gap between the potential migrants' current level of satisfaction and the level they expect to attain in a new land. The larger the gap, the greater the incentive to migrate. This gap is not determined by an additive function of push and pull factors but by the relationship between the perceived quality of life in the home region and that in the receiving region."[95]

Anthony H. Richmond argues that there is a continuum between the rational choice behaviour of proactive migrants seeking to maximize net advantage and the reactive migration whose degrees of freedom are severely constrained :

> Under certain conditions the decision to move may be made after due consideration of all relevant information, rationally calculated to maximize net advantage, including both material and symbolic rewards. At the other extreme the decision to move may be made in a state of panic facing a crisis situation which leaves few alternatives but escape from intolerable threats.[96]

The Bangladesh-Northeast India region in South Asia is a good illustration. Over the last four decades, land scarcity and its degradation has caused millions of people to flee from Bangladesh to the Indian states of Assam, Tripura, West Bengal and other states. As studies show, migrants from Bangladesh have increased the population of neighbouring areas of India by 12 to 17 million. Scarcity of crop land—mainly demand induced scarcity brought about by burgeoning population growth appears to be the main cause of this reactive migration. Flooding, cyclone and storms sometimes act as the precipitating events causing migration, because population growth has already critically limited per capita access to land. Thus, supply induced scarcity becomes the secondary cause.

Land distribution is highly unequal and since independence in 1971 little has been done in this area to correct the structural scarcity which is another factor of migration.

Primacy to environmental determinants of migration from Bangladesh to India reflects a growing recognition that climatic change, floods, cyclone, storms and future sea level rise are not independent of predisposing or contextual factors in interaction with which the environmental factors cause migration. Contextual factors include national and community water control institutions that have sharply limited agricultural output and kept peasants from gaining full benefit from some of the most fertile land in the world.

In receiving areas of India, the politicians provide the enabling circumstances by encouraging migration to garner votes. Although such predisposing or contextual and enabling circumstances are important, they cannot obscure the fact that land scarcity coupled with population growth, and natural disasters due to climatic change and environmental degradation have been powerful forces behind large scale migration from Bangladesh to India.

These migrants coming in contact with the inhabitants of North-eastern states of India have led to group-identity conflict, insurgency and other acts of violence involving state machinaries of both India and Bangladesh. The enormous flux of migrants from Bangladesh into Assam and Tripura over these years has wrought pervasive social changes in the receiving regions. It has altered land distribution, economic relations, and the balance of political power between religious and ethnic groups, and it has triggered serious intergroup violence.

In the context of future sea level rise, many more millions will be added to the already continuing migration. This would aggravate the already volatile situation in Northeast regions of India and make the inter-group conflict more frequent and violent.

Lack of Supply of Ingenuity, and Adaptive Failure in Bangladesh to Meet the Challenges of Environmental Scarcity

The debate over the relationship between population growth, scarcity of resources and development, though has become sterile, contains some underpinnings to understand the implications of environmental scarcity of resources on development and prosperity of people. The Neo-Malthusians who are often biologists and ecologists adduce that finite natural resources put strict limits on the growth of human population and consumption. If these limits are breached, poverty and social breakdown result. A larger population increases environmental degradation, such as soil erosion, and in turn poverty. Some economists argue that a rapidly growing population causes poverty by diverting capital from savings and investment to consumption which lowers the long term productivity of the economy. According to Homer Dixon, empirical studies hold these Neo-Malthusian arguments untenable. Technological change and greater inputs of capital have dramatically increased labour productivity in agriculture. The link between population growth and low savings is unclear. Changes in agrarian structure induced by such growth can sometimes increase food output and larger populations can lower environmental degradation.[97]

Secondly, the economic optimists say that properly functioning economic institutions, especially markets provide incentives to encourage conservation, resource substitution, development of new sources of scarce resources, and technological innovation.[98] Their arguments have three important implications. The first is that natural resources are more homogenous than commonly thought, since the right institutions and technologies allow substitution among resources. Harold Barnett and Chandler Morse argue that the "reservation of particular resources for later use may contribute little to the welfare of future generations".[99] Continuing the argument they further note that "Advances in fundamental science have made it possible to take advantage of the uniformity of energy/ matter uniformity that makes it feasible, without preassignable limit, to escape the quantitative constraints imposed by the character of the earth's crust".[100]

Second, the optimists put extreme reliance in the exceptional ingenuity, creativity and adaptability of human beings which make them different from other species of life. According to them the limiting factors are knowledge and institutions not the resources.[101]

Third, resource degradation and scarcity are not problems of excessive growth of either population or consumption, but of the failure of government policy and markets.

Like economic optimists, distributionists emphasise how institutions and social arrangements within society, not the availability of natural resources are the key determinants of prosperity. James Boyce's study[102] of the factors influencing food production and prosperity in Bangladesh represents distributionists' view. Though Boyce's analysis remains valuable explanation of why Bangladeshi underdevelopment persists, it has not explained how environmental scarcity, and degradation of land and water have been determinant factors in large scale migration from Bangladesh to India.

In recent decades, the scientists have been able to focus on the thresholds, interdependence, and interactivity of complex systems of environmental resources such as climate, oceans, forests, and agricultural lands. The influence of these systems on human society is at least in part a function of the system's intrinsic character and is not, therefore, fully determined by human institutions, policies and technologies. Even if the basic features of an environmental system change only slowly and linearly, the frequency of events within the system can increase sharply. For example, although a slow two or three degree warming of mean global temperature might not seem too significant in itself, for agricultural production it could produce a large increase in frequency of crop devastating droughts.

Environmental systems—from Earth's climate to regional fisheries, soils and forests are dynamic and interdependent. Overextraction or degradation of one resource in such a system can produce ramifying effects and scarcities throughout the surrounding ecological system. For example, the loss of forests can generate much more than just a scarcity of wood for a local community, it can also create scarcities of soil, of rainfalls, of sustainable river flow and of reservoir and irrigation capacity. It can also diminish biodiversity essential for medicines and industries and boost climate change.

The dynamic and interdependent character of environmental systems also means that multiple human impacts on these systems can interact to produce synergistic outcomes. An agricultural region may, for instance, be simultaneously stressed by degraded soil and changes in precipitation caused by regional deforestation or climate change. The rich industrialised nation's emission of CO_2 to the atmosphere has been more than 3/4th of total emissions, the result of which has been the global warming and sea level rise. Bangladesh which contributes very little emission to the atmosphere is likely to be the victim of such sea level rise as predicted by scientists.

None of the above three camps—Neo-Malthusians, economic optimists and distributionists have taken full account of the recent studies and findings about the thresholds, interdependence, and interactivity of environmental systems. As said, societies must be able to supply more social and technical ingenuity to adapt to rising resource scarcity and degradation.

Can all societies meet this rising need for ingenuity ? "Rather than inspiring the wave of ingenuity predicted by economic optimists and distributionists, environmental scarcity instead, sometimes reduces the supply of ingenuity available in a society".[103]

This possibility is largely overlooked by most analysts to date. Although James Boyce does not make the point directly, it is clear from his research that worsening scarcities of land and water in Bangladesh sharply exacerbated the struggle between landlords and peasants that harnstring the innovation in water institutions. According to Homer Dixon, distributionists like Boyce are right to emphasise social imbalances in wealth and power. But they do not, in general, recognise the central reason why these imbalances matter. Highly, unequal social arrangements make it much more likely that environmental scarcity will cause severe social friction. Such arrangements in other words often interact with severe scarcity to generate destructive social competition that impedes technological and institutional adaptation"[104]

Against this backdrop, this study focuses on the following dimensions:

1. Environmental scarcity, and degradation of resources in Bangladesh.
2. Social effects of such scarcities in Bangladesh.
3. Migration of Bangladeshis to Indian states.
4. Environmental conflict due to such migration involving both Bangladesh and India.
5. Future sea level rise, migration and conflict.
6. Approaches to resolution of the conflict.

References

1. Stephen D.Krasner, "International Relations Theory and Global Environmental Issues" paper presented at the workshop, "Global Resources and Environment : Arenas for Conflict, Opportunities for Cooperation", University of California. Berkeley/Pacific Institute for Studies in Development, Environment, and Security 15-17 March, 1990.
2. Miriam R.Lowi, "Water and Conflict in the Middle East and South Asia :

Are Environmental Issues and Security Issues linked?", *The Journal of Environment and Development* Vol.8, No.4, December 1999, p. 376.

3. Charles W. Kegley, "The Neoidealist Moment in International Studies ? Realist Myths and the New International Realities". ISA Presidential Address 27 March 1993, Acapulso, see also Mexico, *International Studies Quarterly* 37 1993, p. 134.

4. O.R.Holsti, Intenational Systems, System change and Foreign Policy", *Diplomatic History* 15, 1991, p. 84.

5. R.Jervis, "A Usable Past for the Future", in M.J. Hogan, ed., *The End of the Cold War: Its Meaning and Implications* (New York: Cambridge University Press, 1992), p. 266.

6. J. A. Vasquez, *The Power of Politics* (New Brunswick, NJ. Rutgers University Press, 1983), pp. 216 ff, R.L. Rothstein, "On the Costs of Realism", Political Science Quarterly 83, 1972, pp. 347-62 and R.O.Keohane and J.S.Nye, Transnational Relations and World Politics (Cambridge, M.A.Harvard University Press, 1971).

7. C. Krauthmmer, "The Poverty of Realism,", The New Republic 194, 1986 pp. 14-22 and R.K.Ashley. The Poverty of Neo Realism", International Organisation 38, 1984, pp. 255-86.

8. C.Hitchens, "Why We are Stuck in the Sand: Real Politik in the Gulf: A Game Gone Tilt", Harper's 282, 1991, pp. 70-74, 78.

9. P. Diehl and F. Wayman ed., Reconstructing Realpolitik (AnnArbor: University of Michigan Press, 1993), T.C. Cusack and R.J. Stoll, "The Security Predicament: Assessing the Effectiveness of Realist and Idealist Principles in Interstate Politics", Berlin: International Relations Research Group, Wissehschaftszentrum Berlin fur Sozialforschung 1992),M. Griffths, "Order and International Society: The Real Realism ?" *Review of International Studies* 18, 1992, pp. 217-40.

10. Z.Brzezinski, "The Cold War and its Aftermath", *Foreign Affairs* 71, 1992, pp. 311-49.

11. J.Joffe, "Entangled Forever", in C.W. Kegley Jr. and E.R. Wittkoff, ed., *The Future of American Foreign Policy* (New York: St. Martin's Press, 1992), p. 35.

12. Charles W.Kegley, Jr. *Op. cit.*, p. 141.

13. Homer Dixon, "On the threshold: environmental changes as causes of acute conflict', *International Security* Vol.16, No. 2, Fall 1991, p. 85.

14. M. Kaldor, *The Imaginary War* (Oxford: Basil Blackwell,1990).

18. M.P.Leffler, "The American Conception of National security and the Beginning of the Cold War 1945-48", *American Historical Review* Vol. 89, 1984, pp.246-81.

16. S. Dalby, "American security discourse: the persistence of geopolitics" *Political Geography Quarterly* Vol. 9, 1990, pp. 171-88.

17. B.Job ed., *The Security dilemma: national security of third world states* (Boulder, Co: Lynne Rienner 1992).

18. R.J. Johnston, *A question of place: exploring the practice of human geography* (Oxford: Basil Blackwell, 1991).

19. Stockholm International Peace Research Institute, Policies for common Security (London: Taylor and Francis 1985).

20. B.Moller, Common Security and Non-Offensive Defense: a neorealist perspective (Boulder, Co: Lynne Rienner, 1992), see also A. Boserup and R.Neild eds., *The Foundation of Defensive Defense* (London: Macmillan, 1990).

21. M. Kaldor and R. Falk eds. *Dealignment: A New Foreign Policy Perspective* (Oxford: Basil Blackwell,1987), see also D. Smith and E.P.Thompson eds., *Prospectus for a habitable planet* (Harmondsworth: Penguin, 1987).

22. R.W.Barnett, *Beyond War: Japan's concept of comprehensive national security* (Washington: Pergamon Brassey's 1986).

23. C.Enloe, *Bananas, Beaches and Bases: Making Feminist Sense of International Politics* (London: Pandora, 1989), see also V.S. Peterson ed., *Gendered States: feminist (re) visions of international relations theory* (Boulder, Co : Lynne Rienner, 1992).

24. B.Weston, ed., Altrnative Security: Living without nuclear deterrence (Boulder Co: Westview Press, 1990) H.B. Hollis, A.L. Powers and M.Sommers eds., *The Conquest of War: Alternative Strategies for Global Security* (Boulder, Co: Lynne Rienner, 1990).

25. R.B.J.Walker and S.Mendlowitz ed., *Contending Sovereignties: Redefining* Political Community (Boulder, Co: Lynne Rienner, 1990).

26. R.J. Johnston, *op. cit.*

27. Barry Buzan, "Rethinking Security after the cold war", *Nordic Journal of International Studies* Vol. 32, No. 1, March 1997, p. 12.

28. R.C. Johansen, "Real Security is Democratic Security", *Alternatives* Vol.16, 1991, pp. 209-42.

29. See S.Dalby, *Creating the second cold war: the discourse of politics* (London: Pinter, 1990).

30. S.Dalby, "Ecopolitical discourse: environmental security and political geography", *Progress in Human Geography* Vol.16, No.4, 1992, p. 507.

31. Gareth Porter, "Environmental Security as a National Security Issue", *Current History*, May 1995, p. 218.

32. Peter H.Gleick, "Environment and Security: The clear connections". *The Bulletin of the Atomic Scientists*, April 1991, p. 18.

33. M.Levy, "Is the environment a national security issue ? *International Security* Vol. 20, No. 2, 1995, p. 35.

34. R. Matthew "Mapping contested grounds" in D. Deudney and R. Matthew ed., Contested Grounds: Security and Conflict in the new environmental politics, (Albany: State University of New York Press, 1999), pp. 1-22.

35. J. Rifkin, Biospheric Politics: A new Consciousness for a New Century (New York: Crown, 1991), p. 2.

36. J. Widgrin, "International Migration and Regional Stability", *International Affairs* Vol. 66, 1990, pp. 749-66.

37. R.H.Ullman, "Redefining Security", *International Security* Vol.8, 1983, pp. 129-53 A.H. Westing, "The Environmental Components of Comprehensive Security"', *Bulletin of Peace Proposal* Vol. 20, 1989, pp. 129-34.

38. Arthur H. Westing ed., *Global Resources and International Conflict: Environmental Factors in Strategic Policy and Action* (Oxford: New York 1986), Neville Brown "Climate, Ecology and International security", *Survival* Vol.31 No.6, Nov. Dec, 1989, pp. 519-512. Jessica Tuchman Mathews, "Redefining Security", *Foreign Affairs* Vol. 68, No. 2, June 1990, pp.121-33. Norman Myers, "Environment and Security", *Foreign Policy*, No.74, Spring 1989, pp. 23-41. Michael Renner, Pianto Mario, Franchi, Cinzia, "International Conflict and Environmental Degradation", in Vayrinen Raimo ed., *New Directions in Conflict, Resolution and Conflict Transformation* (London: Sage, 1991), pp. 108-128. Thomas F. Homer Dixon, "On the Threshold: Environmental Change and Acute Conflict", *International Security* Vol.16, No.2, 1991, pp.76-116, "Environmental Scarcities and Violent Conflict: Evidence from Cases", *International Security* Vol. 19, No. 1, Summer 1994, pp. 5-41: Elise Boulding, "States, Boundaries and Environmental security", in Dennis J.D.Sandole and Hugo Van der Merwe eds., *Conflict Resolution Theory and Practice: Integration and Application* (Manchester/New York: Manchester University Press, 1993).

39. Sverre Lodgaard, "Environmental Conflict Resolution", a paper presented at the UNEP meeting on Environmental Conflict Resolution, Nairobi, 30 March 1990, p. 18.
40. Quoted in Dietrich Fischer, Non-military Aspects of Security: A System's Approach, United Nations Institute for Disarmaments and Research (UNIDIR) (Aldershot: Dartmouth Publishing Company Ltd.,1993), p. 10.
41. *World Commission on Environment and Development, Our Common Future* (The Brundtland Report), (New York) London: Oxford University Press, 1987), p. 290.
42. Jessica Mathews, n. 38.
43. Albert Gore, Strategic Environmental Initiative (SEI), SAIS Review Vol. 10, 1990, pp. 59-71.
44. A.L. Springer, "Protecting the environment: a new focus for the Atlantic alliance", Proceedings of the Academy of Political Science Vol.38, 1991, pp. 129-39.
45. P H.Gleick, "The Implications of global climatic changes for international security", Climatic Change Vol.15, 1989, pp. 309-25.
46. Norman Myers, "The Environmental Dimension to Security Issues", *The Environmentalist* Vol. 6, No. 4, Winter 1986, p. 251.
47. Arthur H.Westing, "Environmental Security and its relation to Ethiopia and Sudan",, Ambio vol. 20, 1991, pp, 168-71 See also ——, "The Environmental Component of Comprehensive Security", *Bulletin of Peace Proposal*, *op. cit.*
48 Lothar Brock, "Peace through Parks: The Environment on the Peace Research Agenda, *Journal of Peace Research* Vol.28, (40), 1991, p. 407.
49. Norman Myer, n.46, p. 253.
50. Gareth Porter, *op. cit.*, p. 218.
51. Gareth Porter, *op. cit.*, p. 220.
52. M.Renner, "Assessing the military's war on the environment", in L.Brown, et al. *State of the World 1991*, (New York: Norton, 1991), pp. 132-52.
53. Simon Dalby, n. 30, p. 512.
54. See Daniel Deudney, "The case Against Linking Environmental Degradation and National Security" Milleniurn Vol. 19, No. 3, Winter 1990, pp. 461-476: Mathias Finger, The Military, the National State and the Environment", *The Ecologist*, Vol. 21, No. 5, 1991. Richard H.Moss, "Environmental Security? The Illogic of Centralised State Responses to Environmental

Threats", in Paul Painchaud ed., Geopolitical Perspectives on Environmental Security, Cahier du GERPE, No. 92-05 Universite Laval,Quebec, 1990.

55. Daniel Deudney, "Rethinking the Link Between Environmental and National Security Issues", Perspectives on War and Peace, Centre for International Cooperation and Security Studies University of Wisconsin, Madison Vol.7, No. 2, Spring 1990, p. 12.

56. J.T. Mathews, *op. cit.*

57. Hans Bruyninakx, "Environmental Security: An Analysis of the Conceptual Problems Defining the Relationship between the Environment and Security" Paper presented at Budapest on the Workshop on Environment and Security organized by the European Peace Research Association, 11-16, November 1993, pp. 1-16.

58. L. Brock, "Security through defending the environment: an illusion ?" in E. Boulding ed., *New Agendas for Peace Research: Conflict and Security Reexamined* (Boulder, Co: Lynne Rienner 1992), p. 98.

59. R.D. Lipschutz and J.P. Holdren, "Crossing Borders: Resource Flows, the Global Environment and International Security", *Bulletin of Peace Proposals* 21, 1990, pp. 121-33.

60. S. George, A Fate Worse than Debt (Harmondsworth: Penguin, 1988).

61. J. Sanders, "Global ecology and world economy: collision course or sustainable future", *Bulletin of Peace Proposals* 21, 1991, pp. 395-401. See also R.D.Lipschutz, "One World or Many ? Global Sustainable Economic Development in the 21st Century", *Bulletin of Peace Proposals* 22, 1991, pp. 189-93.

62. Barry Buzan, "Environment as a Security Issue" in Paul Painchaud(ed) *Geopolitical Perspectives on Environmental Security*, p. 24. quoted in Ole Waever, Securitization and Desecuritization, working paper 5, 1993, Center for Peace and Conflict Research, Copenhagen, 1993, p. 14.

63. Andre Gorz, Ecology and Freedom, 197x, quoted in Ole Waever, Securitization and Desecuritization, *Ibid.*

64. See Dalby, n. 30, p. 512.

65. Deudney, n. 55., p. 467

66. *Ibid.*

67. Barry Buzan, "Environment as a Security Issue, *op. cit.*, p. 1 and 24f, quoted in Ole Waever, *op, cit.* p. 13.

68. Barry Buzan, "Rethinking Security after the cold war", *Nordic Journal of International Studies* Vol. 32, No. 1 March 1997, p. 12.

69. M.Gorbachev, "Reality and guarantee for a secure world", *Moscow News*, No. 39, 1987, p. 3287.

70. James Baker, "Diplomacy for the Environment", address before the National Governors' Association, 26 February, 1990. Washington D.C. reprinted in Current Policy no. 1254 February 1990.

71. Quoted in Peter H.Gleick, *World's Water : The Biennial Report on Fresh Water Resources* (Washington D. C. Covels, California: Island Press, 1998), p. 106.

72. Quoted in Gareth Porter op. cit., p. 222.

73. Quoted in Thomas Homer-Dixon and Valerie Percival, Environmental Scarcity and Violent Conflict: Briefing Book (American Association for the Advancement of Science, University College, University of Toronto, 1996), p. 2.

74. See Stephan Libiszewski, What is an Environmental Conflict ? Environment and Conflict Project, Centre for Security Studies and Conflict Research, Switzerland, Bern/Zurich, Occasional Paper No. I, July 1992, pp. 1-16.

75. See Arthur H.Westing, "Environmental Factors in Strategic Policy and Action: An Overview", *Ibid*. ed., *op. cit*, pp. 3-20 and his Appendix-2 *Ibid*: Wars and Skirmishes involving Natural Resources, pp. 204-10

76. The distinction is made by Judith Rees, "Resources and the Environment, Scarcity and Sustainability" in Robert Bennett and Robert Estall (eds): Global Change and Challenge: Geography for the 1990's (London, New York, 1991), quoted in Stephan Libiszewski, *op. cit*. p. 5.

77. Stephan Libiszewski, *op. cit*., p. 6.

78. Thomas F.Homer Dixon, "Environmental Scarcities and Violent Conflict: Evidence from Cases", *International Security* Vol.19, No.1, 1994, p. 8.

79. Homer Dixon and Valerie Percival, *op. cit*, pp. 6-7.

80. Johan Galtung has introduced the concept of structural violence to denote causes of human suffering that are not the result of evil individuals but of unjust social structures. See Johan Galtung, 'Violence, Peace and Peace Research, *Journal of Peace Research* Vol. 8, No. 3, 1969, pp. 167-191.

81. Arthur H. Westing, "Comprehensive Human Security and Ecological Realities", Guest Comment, *Environmental Conservation* Vol. 16, No.4, Winter 1989, p. 295.

82. Earthscan Briefing Document, 40, *Environment and Conflict* 1984, p.9.

83. Thomas F. Homer Dixon, *Environment, Scarcity and Violence* (Princeton, New Jersey Princeton University Press, 1999), p. 48.

84. *Ibid.*

85. Paul Ehrlich and Anne Ehrlich, *The Population Explosion* (New York: Touchstone, 1991).

86. Thomas F. Homer Dixon, n. 83, p. 80.

87. *Ibid*, p. 81.

88. R.B. J.Walker, "Realism, Change, and International Political Theory, *International Studies Quarterly* 31, No. 1,1987, pp. 65-86. Robert Gilpin. *War and Change in World Politics* (Cambridge: Cambridge University Press, 1981).

89. Nazli Choucri and Robert North, *Nations in Conflict* (San Francisco: Freeman, 1975).

90. Volker Boge, "Proposal for an Analytical Framework to Grasp Environmental Conflict", ENCOP, Centre for Security Studies and Conflict Research, Swiss Federal Institute of Technology, Swiss Peace Foundation, Bern/Zurich Occasional Paper No. I, July 1992, p. 5.

91. See also Kurt Schock, "A Conjunctural Model of Political Conflict", *Journal of Conflict Research* 40, No. I (1996), pp. 98-133.

92. Homer Dixon, n. 83, p.144.

93. Astri Suhrke, "Environmental Degradation and Population Flows", *Journal of International Affairs* Vol.47, No. 2, 1994, pp. 473-524.

95. Homer Dixon, Environment, Scarcity and Violence, *op. cit*, p. 93.

96. Anthony H. Richmond, "Reactive Migration: Sociological Perspective on Refugee Movements", *Journal of Refugee Studies* Vol. 6, No. 1, 1993, p. 10.

97. Homer Dixon, *Environment, Scarcity and Violence*, *op.cit*, p.30.

98. Jesse H.Ausubel et.al., "The Liberation of the Environment", *Daedalus*, Vol. 125, No. 3. 1996; V. Kerry Smith, ed., *Scarcity and Growth Reconsidered* (Baltimore: John Hopkins Press for Resources for the Future, 1979).

99. Harold Barnett and Chandler Morse, *Scarcity and Growth : The Economics of Natural Resource Availability* (Baltimore: Johns Hopkins Press for Resources for the Future, 1963), p. 10.

100. *Ibid*, p. 11.

101. Daniel Hillel, *Out of the Earth: Civilization and the Life of the Soil* (New York: Free Press, 1991).

102. James Boyce, Agrarian Impasse in Bengal : Institutional Constraints to Technological Change (Oxford: Oxford University Press, 1987).

103. Homer Dixon, *Environment, Scarcity and Violence*, *op. cit*, p. 42.

104. *Ibid*, pp. 42-43.

2

Environmental Scarcity and Degradation of Resources

Population Explosion

Conflicting views on population and environment exist. The Malthusian concept of population as a central factor may be considered here. The left of the centre radicals stress on poverty, inequality, over consumption by the North, or technology. The right wing radicals ensconce their faith in the unlimited capacity of human ingenuity to adapt and need for free markets to enable it to do so. Despite these contrasting views, the fact remains that the demands of man on environment are multifarious. Their error lies in elevating their central concern into the universally dominant factor downgrading others as insignificant or redundant. "The real world ... is a vast system in which the immense complexity of human society interacts with the ever greater complexity of the natural world. The character of the interaction varies from one place to another and in all places it changes over time".[1]

In this light it can be said whereas population explosion has not been a central concern in the North, it has become predominantly a central concern in the South. Teitelbaum has described world demographic trends as "revolutionary", because though the human species emerged perhaps 150,000 years ago, most of its growth has been in the last forty years. The world population took tens of thousand years to reach one billion around 1800, over a century to achieve the second billion mark somewhere in the beginning of 20th century, about 33 years to the third billion around 1960 only 14 years to the fourth and 13 years to the fifth billion in the year 1987.[2]

This population explosion has been more spectacular in the developing world than in the developed one. The exorbitant consumption and life style of the North, the ethnocentrism of the dominant and mimetic westernization paradigms of development and the peripheral position of the developing South in the world economic and technological structure dominated by the North have all contributed to the elevation of population explosion to a central focus in the South. More conveniently the North has been putting the blame for what they have wrought to the environment on South's population explosion in a bid to continue the perpetration of their economic exploitation of the poor South. On the other hand it is held that the environmental problems lay more with the high consumption levels in the developed countries than with the supposed population growth in the South. The world's population is now increasing by about a quarter of a million people per day of 90-100 million people every year.[3] The population of most of the developed countries is nearly stable or declining. As the World Bank Report of 1992 states, 95 per cent of future growth will take place in developing countries of Africa, Asia and Latin America.[4]

The spawning population growth in the developing South has multiplied pressures on all renewable resources, namely, freshwater, soil, forest, air, atmosphere, climate, oceans and biodiversity. These resources are renewable because they are "ecologically integrated in a feedback circle system which guarantees their replacement or preservation of their quality".[5] Minerals and fossils fuels on the other hand, which are the traditional objects of resource conflict, are non-renewable resources because they are not integrated in such an ecosystem. The western intensive fossil fuel technology and industrialization being imitated as the universal model of development by the poor South, has resulted in depletion of the non-renewable resources to the extent of degrading the renewable resources beyond their regeneration capacity. As Alvin Weinberg and others described, this is the "age of substitutability" and there has been a considerable reduction in the growing demands on feedstocks of non-renewable resources and the need for exploration of new areas of their deposition with the increasingly advanced technology.[6] In the absence of availability of these alternative advanced technologies to the poor South, their dependence on non-renewable resources has been growing faster than what is found in the North, to the extent of degrading the renewable resources. At the same time, due to lack of economic rethinking, the poor people of the South have been proliferating, making unprecedented demands on renewable resources in their struggle for survival and economic sustenance, exacerbating further the already existing environmental problems such as land degradation, deforestation, nonavailability of pure water, air pollution and extinction of species.

As stated above, while the exploration and usage of natural resources both renewable and non-renewable have a great bearing on the environment and development debate, the demographic factors such as population growth, size, density and distribution are very significant variables in explaining their impingement on environmental security. The burgeoning population growth in Bangladesh and its increasing demands on natural resources to the point of degradation will show how these traditional perception of security threats will be replaced by the environmental security. Thus, population growth can become a direct cause of conflict as a result of the flight of refugees across national border due to environmental degradation caused by the pressures of population growth on the natural renewable resources.[7] It has also been envisaged by some that population growth can be seen as resulting in international strain, aggression and war.[8]

India

In India the population has increased from 238 m in 1901 to 860 m in 1991 and is projected to reach 1.16 bn to 2010. With its current population growth rate 2 per cent a year, India will have an estimated 480 m or 41 per cent of its total population living in urban areas by 2010. The rate of urban growth has also soared from 2.3 per cent annually in 1951-56 to over 3.9 per cent in 1990.[9]

Bangladesh

According to the 1991 census, the population of Bangladesh has reached nearly 116 m with a growth rate of 2.16 per cent from 42 m in 1951. During the period from 1951 to 1989, population has grown more than 70 million. According to a projection of the planning commission the population of Bangladesh is estimated to reach about 141 million by the year 2000. In an estimate in January 1990 of the World Resources Institute, population of Bangladesh may not stabilize before reaching 340 million despite its government being successful in implementing population control measures.[10] The density of population is 939 persons per sq km which is one of the highest in the world. With a population of this size and a land area of 144,000 sq km such a growth rate is rather alarming for a country like Bangladesh.[11] In the age structure a growth potential is also marked. Population below the age of 15 years is around 46 per cent of the total population and 48.4 per cent of the female population are within the reproduction age.[12]

Population growth rate has decreased the land-man ratio from 0.134 ha in 1981 to 0.117 ha in 1990 resulting in an increased landlessness, decreased land quality and other resources due to over and excessive exploitation and sprawling migration to urban centres.[13] According to another estimate at about 0.08 hectare per capita crop land which is already short of needs will be further slashed in half by the spawning population growth by 2025.[14] The urban population is expected to grow from 16 million at present to 99 million by 2010 at the current urban growth rate of 7 per cent.

The present rate of unemployment is around 35-40 per cent of the total labour force. It will be further aggravated by the 46 per cent population under the age 15 who are likely to attain the working age within a few years.[15]

Land Degradation and Soil Erosion

Population growth, urban migration, transport and industrialization are driving the expansion of cities over rich agricultural land. The competition between cropland and living space is not limited to city margins, but also found in the rural areas. Potential for further conflict over land use arises from the need to move towards a sustainable global energy economy. One of the most attractive options appears to be energy from processed biomass plants in view of the increasing greenhouse effects and global warming caused by the traditional combustion of fossil fuels which meets 75 per cent of the world's energy needs.[16] This would dedicate the equivalent of approximately 15 per cent of the land now in forests and 40 per cent of that in crop land to biomass energy crop production.[17]

Soil of the cropland which is a natural capital that humanity has inherited is now rapidly depleting. It is generated by ecosystems on a time scale of centimetres per millennium.[18] Because of human activities, it is eroding at rates up to centimetres per decade in many areas. Globally some 24 billion tons of soil are lost annually in excess of the natural rate of soil regeneration. As estimated, the remaining top soil on earth's crop land is being eroded at an average rate of 7 per cent per decade.[19]

Given the rate of degradation in future the current agricultural practices would be unsuitable and unsustainable.[20] Soil in itself is a complex ecosystem and its fertility is tied to the diversity of life. It contains billions of tiny organisms per gram in agricultural soil.[21] Those organisms are indispensable to maintaining soil fertility and transferring nutrients from soil to crops. Thus, crop production and healthy ecosystem are very much tied to the role that these tiny organisms play. But modern industrial agricultural system has been a threat to the life of these organisms.[22]

Soil erosion also contributes to the damages in downstream river areas through the loss of irrigation capacity, flooding and sedimentation. The other salient aspect of degradation is desertification, which is caused by the deterioration of arid and semi-arid lands as a result of human exploitation beyond the land's capacity. Desertification results from the unending capacity of human nature to exploit the land beyond its sustainability, excessive cultivation, overgrazing, lowering of water tables and plundering of vegetation.[23]

Under the heavy pressure of agricultural development, industrialization, mining, logging, firewood collection and livestock grazing, land degradation has become a serious problem in South Asian countries.

Bangladesh

The soil in Bangladesh is developed under three physiographic positions such as Northern and Eastern Hills, Madhupur and Barind Tract and Flood Plain areas. The soil variations have been determinated by their geological origin and properties. Flood plain soil constitute 80 per cent of the total area formed by the sediments deposited by three major rivers and their streams and distributaries. Out of the fourteen general types four main types of flood plains are recognized and they are piedmont alluvial plains, meander flood plains, tidal flood plains formed under the impact of tidal flooding and estuarine flood plains locally known as char Then there are terrace areas such as Northern and Estern Hills and Madhupur and Barinda Tract occupying 12.6 per cent and 8.3 per cent of country's land area respectively.[24] These two tracts appear to have been lifted as a block, 3.6 metres high from the surrounding flood plain areas. Since agriculture constituting 47 per cent of GDP in Bangladesh,[25] the soil quality of land is of immense value to its people.

In Bangladesh, factors principally contributing to soil erosion are:

1. Water erosion.
2. Wind erosion.
3. Human factor.

About 20,000 sq. km. of terrace and hilly lands are susceptible to gully erosion. The rainfall in the hilly areas is very high—2000 to 3500 m. About 75 per cent of the population practise 'Jhum' or shifting cultivation on very steep and sloppy lands. The practice of 'Jhum' cultivation makes the soil surface fully clear and 100 per cent exposed to all physical phenomena and so erosion becomes most hazardous for the exposed period when rainfall washes away the surface soil. An estimated one million hectare of depleted land in the state forest of Chittagong Hill Tracts (CHT) is completely denuded due to repeated shifting cultivation. The long time required between the cultivations to allow the forest to regenerate is no longer possible with the spawning population explosion and need for land. In some areas of hilly lands about 5 cm soils are eroded annually and as a result about 130 cm of silts are being deposited in the natural drainage systems of these areas. According to official estimates, 9.2 per cent of Bangladesh land is noted as forest but in reality the actual figure is only 6.5 per cent of which about 32 per cent is already denuded.[26] This has definitely increased the erosion of the hill and terrace soils.

In the flood plains land degradation takes place primarily due to organic matter depletion and improper use of chemical fertilizers. Bangladesh soils contain an average of meagre 1.5 to 2 per cent of organic matter. This is primarily due to intensive cropping without any organic or green manure management. This makes the soil susceptible to wind erosion as well as to sleet erosion.

Deposition of sandy material on agricultural land is a natural process of soil degradation. Deforestation and faulty cultivation practices in the piedmont areas of the hilly terrain in Sylhet and in the CHT districts have increased this phenomena.

Irrigation is one of the major reasons for degradation of soil. High Yield Varieties (HYV) Boro/Aus followed by Aman are grown in the same field by resorting to frequent irrigation. In such cases the land remains waterlogged for the entire year. Continuous submersion of land results in

1. Continued absence of oxygen in the subsoil,
2. Chemical changes of soil materials by forming compounds toxic to plants,
3. Constant loss of soil nutrients by percolation and
4. Incidence of pests or diseases associated with waterlogged environment.[27]

River bank erosion is the most important cause of land loss and degradation which have increased due to decreased river depth. Every year large areas along river banks erode during the monsoon creating environmental imbalance in terms of physical and social aspects. With the commencement of yearly monsoon rain flood and bank erosion appear as conspicuous features in about 40 of the country's major and minor rivers.

Deposits of large quantity of silt at the bottom of the rivers, continually raising their beds due to heavy rainfall and onrush of water into Bangladesh from across the border have created hindrance to the drainability of normal water channels thus causing inundations. Inundations for periods longer than necessary or expected create anaerobic situation in the soil atmosphere thus greatly shifting the ecological balance which naturally affects the whole agricultural systems.

Salinization in Bangladesh is principally caused by tidal inundations. About 2.83 million hectare of land situated in the coastal belts of the country are affected seasonally by saline intrusions. The areas include the older districts of Khulna, Barisal, Noakhali and Chittagong. Of these 2.83 million hectare about 0.95 million hectare is truly saline soil.[28] Construction of barrages in the upstream of major rivers, withholding of fresh water during the leaner periods and excessive ground water withdrawal of irrigation in certain areas of the country have caused intrusion of saline water deep into the main lands during high tides. This is contributing to salt accumulation in the soil to a substantial degree causing an ecological imbalance in many parts of the country.

Most of Bangladesh's soil is deficient in organic matter. Where an average of 5 per cent organic matter is desirable for sustained fertility and productivity the average organic matter content of Bangladesh soils is less than two per cent. As a result the soil in most of the areas have limitations in respect of low water holding capacity, low cation exchange capacity, low nutrient holding capacity and low biotic activity. As a matter of fact leaching of nutrients in well drained soils is phenomenal. Leaching of bases has contributed to the development of acidity and demand for more K.Ca. and Mg fertilizers. Excessive leaching is problematic in nitrogen fertilizer, management in upland culture. Improper use of nitrogenous fertilizers depletes soil organic matter content. The improper fertilization, high yielding crop and intensive cropping in the absence of a proper organic matter management is deteriorating the Bangladesh soils to a minimum level of soil fertility.

The rapid expansion of urban industrial development around cities and new settlements created by rapidly increasing population in villages of Bangladesh pose a serious threat to valuable agricultural land. Bangladesh really faces the challenge of conflicting land use demands bringing upon more pressures on available land and environmental degradation.

Mining of sand and shingles from agriculture land also causes the top soil to erode because after mining the depressions are abandoned and left fallow.

Unplanned human settlement in the urban areas is also a major reason for loss of land and soil degradation. At the beginning of the century 3 per cent of the total population was urban. During the 1950s Bangladesh experienced a 45 per cent increase in its urban population, 137 per cent in the 1970s and 115 per cent during the 1980s. With a present growth rate of 6. 5 per cent per annum urban population is projected to be between 30-40 million by the year 2000. Forest resources and fisheries in the vicinity of urban centres are becoming over exploited as a result of the pressure of urban requirements.

Large areas of surface soils in arable lands are being converted to brick fields which intimately are making the fertile top soil lost from the realm. Moreover with population pressure on available lands more and more agricultural lands are converted to homesteads, or are being taken for urbanization or industrialization purposes.

Over-exploitation of biomass as well as agricultural residues for fuel, fodder and thatching are causing sulphur deficiency in the soil in many places as well as the decreasing capacity of the soil to retain moisture. The areas where 'Aus' crop followed by transplanted 'Aman' are grown, are facing such critical problems. Another critical area is the Barind tract, the western part of which now shows symptoms of aridity during the dry months of April-May.[29] According to the 1989 statistics persons per hectai is calculated to be 9.6 for all cropped land including forests and plantation crops and 12.4 for land under agricultural crops only.[30]

India

Latest estimates show that nearly 53 per cent of India's area (173.6 million ha) has been subject to land degradation due to activities like excessive grazing, road construction, mining and unscientific agricultural practices, such as shifting cultivation. Out of this, 83 per cent has been affected by water and wind erosion while about 17 per cent has been subject to various types of land degradation.[31] Uncontrolled cultivation of mountain slopes without appropriate slope treatment has caused massive soil erosion. Shifting cultivation which covers an area of 4.96 m ha has not only caused soil erosion but also brought in a huge extinction of natural flora and fauna.

Faulty irrigation system and surface flooding due to natural topography and drainage congestion are estimated to have water logged a total area of 8.50 m ha against 6 m ha earlier. Use of pesticides and chemicals is another factor to have degraded the soil.

The very process of industrialization based on fossil fuel technology involves extensive extraction of minerals which are mostly found in rich forest and agricultural areas of eastern and central parts of India. In open cast mines, vegetation and soil have to be removed to reach the mineral deposits. Flora, fauna and productive soil is lost. In case of underground mining problems of debris, land subsistence and loss of land become frequent due to tunneling. Mining on hill slopes disrupting the natural drainage destroys natural vegetation and retards natural regeneration. As estimated there are 4,052 working mines excluding oil, gas and some other minerals and 478 coalmines in India most of which are open cast ones.[32]

Land degradation has considerable economic repercussions in rural economic activities like agriculture and animal husbandry. According to World Bank study, half of India's land is suffering from some form of degradation. The economic impact of land degradation has been ruinous. On-site costs associated with land degradation are reduced agricultural yields and/or economic losses resulting from the farmer being found to move towards cultivation of lower value crops. Off-site costs include siltation of drainage channels, irrigation canals and man made reservoirs, and effects of changed hydrology resulting in floods in the monsoon season and reduced water availability in the dry season. The study does not take into account any of site costs because of lack of data, yet these costs can be quite severe in certain years with heavy floods or bad droughts.

The estimated productivity losses due to land degradation are between 4.0 per cent and 6.3 per cent of total agricultural output per year. It represents an annual production loss of US $ 1.5 billion to US $ 2.4 billion. Rangeland degradation losses fall in the range of US $238 million to US $417 million per annum, based on a 20 per cent to 35 per cent over time in the carrying capacity of natural rangelands. Erosion-induced losses, accumulate over time and are not reversible in the short or medium term. Over time, the agricultural losses due to land degradation could be as much as US $30 billion to US $50 billion.[33]

Deforestation

Forests play a predominantly essential role in maintaining climate, stabilizing soil and water resources, and safeguarding biological diversity. Forests as repository of limitless resources are receding fast and becoming scarce and degraded to provide all that people need and want and all the ecological services a healthy planet is in need of. Due to industrialization, rapid expansion of cities, loss of crop land and growing population the forests have dwindled by a third over the last 10,000 years.[34] With some 17 million hectare of tropical forests being lost per year, demand for products of forests and dependence on those for wood are at an all time high and growing.[35] It is estimated that if the present deforestation continues, two-fifths of the developing world's remaining green areas will disappear by the beginning of the next century.[36] Deforestation and soil degradation are tied strongly to each other. With the clearing of the forest cover soil degradation and salinization accelerated. Deforestation often results in desertification.[37] Downstream flood is some times linked to the accelerated deforestation.

In South Asia forests play a significant role not only in the region's development process through the supply of timber and pulpwood but also in catering to people's needs through the supply of food, firewood, fodder, manure, non-edible oils and medicinal herbs. Adding to these, they provide ecological service in the form of soil and water conservation and recreational amenities.

The rapid declining forest cover and alarming rates of deforestation have already been a matter of concern among the countries of South Asia.

The magnitude of deforestation in South Asia clearly shows the impact of increase in population on environments. The indispensability of forest cover can be found in ecological, social, economic and cultural needs of living human and non-human beings. The vital ecological roles forests play can be enumerated as follows:

- Reduce air pollution and improve the environment.
- Maintain ideal atmosphere for the preservation and conservation of wild life.
- Check greenhouse effect.
- Under the coastal ecosystem mangroves are the abode and harbour of both sweet and marine fish resources.
- Conserve the soil, maintain its fertility and store water.

Apart from these ecological requirements, they provide fruits, fibre, medicine, firewood, timber and shade for human consumption as well as fodder for livestock, commercial logging, shifting cultivation, forest clearing for cropping or grazing, gathering medicinal plants, mining, flooding by reservoirs and burning.[38] The rate at which forests are destroyed has been a matter of grave concern in South Asia. Satellite imagery and remote sensing techniques reveal that only 15 per cent of the land area in South Asia is under forest cover.

Bangladesh

In Bangladesh, according to official estimates the total forested area has been reduced from over 33 per cent in the 1960's to less than 9 per cent at present which is well below the universally accepted minimum of 25 per cent. Unofficially it is estimated that only 6-7 per cent remains forested today.[39] Need for agricultural land, domestic energy consumption and raw materials for industries are responsible for such reduction. Forty per cent of the total available hill forests have been converted into plantation. 11 per cent have been kept for the resettlement of the 16,000 tribal families evacuated by the construction of the Kapatai reservoir in 1963, and the rest 48 per cent have been left to human encroachment.

Apart from the three types of forests such as hill forests, tidal forests and inland sal forests controlled direct under the jurisdiction of the forest department, there is a small area of unclassified state forest under the control of local administration which consists of 6328 sq km. These forests having been since long subjected to shifting cultivation are highly degraded. In the decade from 1976-1986 the output of firewood rose by 25 per cent while timber extraction increased by 100 per cent. About 60 per cent of the wood harvested is for fuel and 35 per cent is for timber. The sal forest has declined to 435 hectare which was over 8100 hectare in 1970.[40]

The limitless demand and need for poles, posts, fuelwood, grazing, shrimp cultivation and human settlement have already made a large part of the mangrove forest in Chakaria Sunderban denuded. Sundari and Gewa in the Khulana Sunderban have declined by 40 and 45 per cent respectively.[41] The despoliation is due to over harvesting by over 100 per cent in the case of fuel wood species. Due to upstream water withdrawal of the Ganges the increase in the salinity has caused a sharp decrease in the regeneration capability of these species of trees.[42]

In a food deficit country like Bangladesh forests play a considerable role by producing food crops of different types and fruits of various kinds under agroforestry system. Their exploitation is faster than regeneration. Like food, Bangladesh is also deficit in fodder production. There is tremendous pressure of grazing animals on forest areas. As a result, many plantations both in the coastal belt and hilly areas are subjected to heavy grazing by animals, and consequently many plantations are damaged.

Most of the fuel wood supply comes from the village homestead forests. It appears from a study carried out in 1980-81 that the total supply of firewood was 290 million cubic feet of which 13.00 million came from the government reserve forests, i.e., about 5 per cent. The average of fuel wood supply from the government managed forests from 1983-84 to 1987-88 is about 9.5 million cubic feet.[43] The dependence of the people on the forests for such a huge need for wood has degraded the forests.

Apart from meeting the domestic needs of the people for energy and timber there are many wood based industries both in the public and private sector. There are pulp and paper mills, newsprint mills, rayon mills, hard-board mills, particle board mill, veneer mill, plywood factory, match factory, tea chest factories, saw mills, furniture manufacturing plants and wood treating plants which depend on over exploitation of wood as raw material. Besides many industries under the state cooperation, there are as many as 1706 number of saw mills, 12 numbers of match factories and many other wood based industries under the private sector.[44]

Thus, the condition of both high forest and plantation have deteriorated due to population explosion and increased demands for forest produce or industry, fuel, fodder and food.

The ecological effects of such deforestation can be enumerated as follows:

- Soil erosion and silting up of river beds, lakes etc.
- Decreased river depth leading to flood, river bank erosion, shifting course.
- Deforestation in the coastal areas leading to erosion in the coastal areas.
- Soil erosion and decreasing soil fertility leading to desertification.
- Decreased evapotranspiration and decreased cooling effect of the atmosphere, decreased rain fall.
- Increased intensity of cyclones and storm surges in the coastal areas.

- Loosening of the soil in the coastal areas and easy intrusion of saline water in the mangrove forest which further destroys the rest of the forest and aquatic habitats.

India

Of the total geographical area 22.8 per cent, i.e., 75.18 million ha happens to be the estimated forest cover in India. But the land sat imagery for the period 1982-84 recorded that 64.20 mha or 19.5 per cent contained actual forest cover.[45]

The major causes of deforestation in India are encroachment of forest lands for cultivation, shifting cultivation, diversion of forest land to non-forest uses, grazing and forests, unauthorized and commercial fellings and industrial use. As estimated from 1951 to 1980, 4,238 mha of forest land was diverted for non-forest use, for agriculture 2,623 mha, river valley projects 0.502 mha, industries, township and urbanization 0.134 mha, roads 0.061 mha and others 1,008 mha, coupled with these are the spawning population growth and migration of refugees from neighbouring countries. During 1980-85 fires which are deliberately caused to collect charcoal, forest produce and to get new shoots of grasses and leaves destroyed 0.57 mha of forest in India.[46]

The state of forest report 1995 produced by the Ministry of Environment and Forests, Government of India, has repeatedly claimed that forest land in India is more or less constant or slightly increasing. But the WB study quoting the FAO Tropical Forests Resource Assessment Report point out that between 1981 and 1990, India suffered a rate of deforestation to the tune of 0.6 per cent per year, which is equivalent to about 3.37 million ha or about one third of a mha a year. Of this, 15 per cent tropical rain forest, 11 per cent moist deciduous forest, 64 per cent dry deciduous forest and 11 per cent hill and mountain areas have been lost during the 1980s.

So while commercial plantation may be increasing, compensating for this loss to some extent, valuable and unique natural forests of the country are being steadily destroyed. According to the WB study, the trend shows that forest resources rich in flora and fauna are decreasing.

According to the study, since deforestation related losses cannot be reversed in most cases within 10 years, the economic losses would range from U.S.$ 1.4 - 1.9 billion. These losses will grow with time because of continued deforestation and absence of adequate maintenance of existing forest areas.[47] According to Anil Agarwal, the WB study due to methodological shortcomings has underestimated the total costs resulting from deforestation. "The costs accrue to the nation as a whole and to local communities which have complex economic and survival relationships with forests.[48] As a result of deforestation, according to him, "The impacts are in terms of increased work burden, foregone opportunities for female literacy, serious health impacts on women, male migration, increased chances of spread of diseases like AIDS, etc.

Freshwater Scarcity

Since time immemorial water has been accepted as one of the five organic elements constituting this universe and creation. Water is essential not only for human survival, but also for other activities like urban and industrial development, energy production, plant and fish production, navigation and recreation. It becomes a disaster only when it is "too much" or "too little". So water is closely related to the socio-economic development of mankind. With the growing pace of development, the demand for water increases manifold.[49] Problems become crucial when the allocation of fixed supply of water to support the demands of growing population and for an improved quality of life arises, and water related natural hazards like flood and drought, health hazards like water borne diseases and aquatic hazards like pollutants, industrial and agricultural affect the humanity.[50] So water management has been very much difficult to maintain balance between supply and demand. As water demands increase in size and number, water management proceeds from being supply oriented to being resource oriented and then to being demand oriented.[51]

In case of major bodies of water—rivers, lakes and aquifers, being shared by two or more countries, the competition for limited supplies of water between such neighbouring countries leads to severe political tension and even to war.[52]

In South Asia, the increasing needs of industrialization and development, urbanization and agricultural development for water with the ever increasing population, have posed serious problems for the availability of fresh water in its plentitude and purity in various forms like degradation in water quality, intrusion of saline sea water into coastal fresh water aquifers, waterlogging and water pollution from industrial and modernized agricultural sector. This has already led to tension between the neighbouring states of surplus and scarcity. While water scarcity and its degraded effects have become an issue between India and Bangladesh, 'water surplus', its management, accretion of benefits and sharing of resources have become a problem between India and Nepal, and India and Bhutan.

Bangladesh

Bangladesh has been called a land of rivers. There are about 250 rivers of varying sizes forming a network along with the three major rivers, viz. the Padma, the Bramhaputra-Jamuna and the Meghna. Bangladesh water resources consist of three general components such as rainfall, surface water and ground water storage.

Rainfall is an important element of surface water. Looking at the history of rainfall records in various part of the country. Bangladesh can ironically be called a land of plenty as well as paucity of rainfall. But the fact is that the distribution of rainfall both in time and space is very uneven. During the monsoon period which is limited to four months from June to September 90 per cent of the rainfall occurs. Dry season which starts from October to March gets very scanty rain.

Main components of surface water are stream flow, static water and in stream storage. As regards surface water approximately 2.98 billion m^3 of stream flow are discharged in the Bay of Bengal everyday. The 1990 water usage conditions neglect the disparity as total stream flows varies sharply from about 89,000 m^3/s in August to only 5714 m^3 /s in February.[53] With a gross areas of 1,44,000 km^2 the country receives about 914 m^3 of water per hectare per year. The average annual evaporation is about 144 cm or 16, 264 km^3 over the gross area.[54] Only a little more than 12 per cent of the total volume of water entering Bangladesh used for agriculture and the rest flows into the sea.

In addition to the rivers, there are a good number of static water bodies known as beels, haors and baors. They are also a source of water for the general habitat and many usual purposes. The potential output has been estimated as 79 m^3 /sec or about 612 million cubic metres under 1983 water use conditions.

Creation of surface storage by constructing barriers across channel is the traditional practice in Bangladesh. Based on available topographic maps and aerial photographs instream storage was estimated to be about 500 million cubic metre. Multifarious demands of agriculture, navigation, fisheries, industries and the need to delimit inland penetration of sea water on the water which is on average 7-11 mm and at a very low flow in the rivers during November-March have deleterious effects on water availability and ecology of the coastal areas.[55]

The study of ground water availability shows that excepting the central high land and western Barind tract, most of the area of Bangladesh has ground water with water table depth ranging from zero to 9 metre depending on location and season. In many areas of Bangladesh where irrigation from surface water is very difficult and water demand is very high, dependence on ground water is essential. The safe seasonal volume of ground water available for use is highly variable from place to place because the recharge of the ground water depends on the surface flow and rain water. Ground water levels are highest from August to October and lowest in April and May. The ground water potential of the Barind tract is limited. On the other hand the ground water potential of the southern and south-western districts is constrained due to hazard of salt water intrusion which is allegedly caused by Ganges water withdrawal by India.

Reduced Ganges' water flow at Farakka during the dry season has affected the ground water in the region in terms of sharp fall in the river stage causing steep ground water gradient towards the river. This results in fast lowering of the ground water table, leading to a continuous depletion in the ground water reserves in the region.

Further, degraded quality of ground water due to increased concentration of total dissolved solids (TDS) affects the agriculture, industry domestic and municipal water supply and the soil itself over a large area. A survey conducted on the status of ground water level in 1992 in 3300 unions of Bangladesh shows that the water table dropped down below 9 metre from the pre-division levels by 100 per cent in Rajshahi, 80 per cent in Pabna and 64 per cent in Faridpur.[56]

The Sylhet, Chittagong and Chittagong Hill Tracts areas are constrained due to complex geological conditions. As studies show, for generations about 0.49 million hectare is irrigated by traditional devices like dons, swing baskets, dug wells and earthen jugs.[57] Due to limited availability of surface water particularly in the north-west, the exclusive dependence has been on ground water for irrigation. In 1985, 6,20,000 hectare was irrigated by tube wells. Both shallow and deep tube wells are used to tap the ground water for irrigation.

The use, planning and management of ground water has reached a critical stage in Bangladesh. It is estimated that since 1972 the period of rapid exploitation, the number of irrigation wells has increased from 1800 to 3,99,00 at a compound rate in excess of 40 per cent annually.[58] The consequences are disastrous for the environment. Use of ground water as a source of irrigation has tremendously increased so much so that unplanned sinking of shallow tube wells has rendered domestic dug wells and hand tube wells inoperative due to lowering of ground water table below suction lift.[59] Due to increased seasonal decline of ground water levels in many regions like Rajshahi and Bogra district, suction lift pumps and hand tube wells were found to be incapable of pumping as a result, the agricultural credit of STWS under IDA Agricultural credit 7-project was stopped during 1983.[60]

Extraction of ground water beyond its threshold has caused a series of ecological effects in Bangladesh. The roots of vegetation are always adapted to a particular level of ground water. Because of the lowering down of the depth of the water level the vegetation fails to adapt to the new lower level. The result is the dying of the top natural vegetation.

As a result of the lowering down of the ground water level, the saline water enters inland in the coastal areas whereby the salinity intrudes into the mainland. Besides reduction in the ground water level, the reduction of surface water also contributes to the increased salinity.

It is alleged that salinization within the south western region of Bangladesh is due to the diversion of water through various flood control and irrigation projects for the drought prone areas of Bihar and Uttar Pradesh undertaken by the upper riparian state India.[61]

The agreement over the sharing of Ganges water between India and Bangladesh (Farakka) which allowed Bangladesh 34,500 m^3/s expired in 1986. In the absence of any new agreement or extension of the earlier one, India was free to withdraw any amount of water it wants through this barrage. Due to upstream withdrawal in the dry season flow of the Ganges, Gorai-Madhumati, the tributaries of the Ganges receive very little amount of water to check salinity. Salinity observed at Khulana topped all past records reaching 17,100 micro mhos in April 1983.[62] As alleged by the Bangladesh Government, the most devastating effect of the upstream diversion of the Ganges waters by India has led to a higher soil salinity in the south western region of Bangladesh. The reduction in the dry season Ganges flow has increased the salinity of Khulana area from 380 micro-mhos/cm in the prediversion period (1974) to about 29,500 micro mhos/cm in April 1992. The salinity of 500 micro-mhoms/cm moved through the

Passur Estuary from 146 km. to about 220 km inland after the diversion. The salinity affecting the greater districts of Kushtia, Jessore, Khulna, Faridpur and Barisal has at present enveloped more than 25,900 sq km.[63] In the recent years the diversion of water has increased to the extent of reducing the surface water level at the Hardings to only 4 to 25 m compared to the historical height of 6.7 m. At present about 38 per cent of the country's territory and 33 per cent of the population are seriously affected by salinity in the water supply.[64] Notwithstanding the contribution made by the upper riparian states' control of water flow to salinization, various flood control, drainage and irrigation projects undertaken by the Bangladesh Government have contributed to salinization of 20 per cent of net cultivable area.

Seasonal fluctuation and withdrawal of water through numerous project and dams by the upper riparian state, India, have resulted in a significant reduction of water in Bangladesh. The water level registered at Hardings Bridge fell below the minimum ever recorded, i.e., 23,000 m^3 /s compared to a historical average of 64,430 m^3/s.[65] Due to this upper riparian withdrawal, the water level at Hardings which was 6.7 m came down to 5.2 m in the mid eighties while in the 1992 dry season it came down to about 4.3 m. The Ganges Kobadak irrigation project would be inoperative, as experts sound warnings, if water level came down below 4.3 m.[66]

Besides the Ganges water, India is withdrawing water from Brahmaputra, Teesta and other small rivers. As a part of its flood control and irrigation measures, India has made 3830 km of embankments along the main river tributaries, 770 km of drainage channels and 44 town protection projects. Along with this, another scheme for massive irrigation involves near about 1.7 million hectare out of 3.1 million hectare of cultivable areas in the Brahmaputra basin in India. It is estimated that the total water use for these schemes will require withdrawal of 50,000 to 60,000 m^3 /s.[67] It is also alleged by the Bangladesh Government that the Teesta Barrage Project completed by it in 1990 to irrigate, 5,66,000 hectare of land and to protect 7,60,000 hectare from flood and other natural disasters would not be accomplished due to Gajaldopa Project undertaken by India.

As a result of the reduced water flow the south-west region of Bangladesh mostly dependent on the Ganges water is facing serious environmental problems. Deforestation in the Himalayan region by India and Nepal, melting of Himalayan ice cap and other obstructions created within Bangladesh are considered as sole reasons for flooding the Farakka as well as other barrages. Dams in India contribute to their intensity and frequency. The silt free water diverted into the upper stream pushes a large amount of silt into the downstream river causing a considerable decrease in the carrying capacity of the rivers. As studies show 30 per cent of the country is subjected to flood due to the spill over from major rivers while the flood from small rivers cover about 43 per cent area of the country.[68] More than 80 per cent of the flood run off is brought from outside the country of which 90 per cent is contributed by the major rivers.[69]

Reduction in the ground water level is due to reduced water flow and exorbitant extraction of ground water beyond its limit for irrigation. This is responsible for salinity and desertification in coastal areas of Bangladesh. Due to reduced water flow and salinization, the mangrove forests in the coastal areas face the problems of regeneration along with the possible extinction of wild life, aquatic habitats and various species of plants and trees.

Decreasing river depth and absence of strong water flow not pushing the sediment far away in the sea from the coast have led to the land formation in the coastal areas. The dispute over New Moore/Talpatty island is an illustrations of this.

Apart from problems of flood and drought, the rivers due to erosion in Bangladesh side and land formation on Indian side tend to change their course causing a major shift of mid-channel considered as the international boundary line between India and Bangladesh.

The fluctuation in the hydrological cycle, reduced water flow, shifting river courses, reduced forest cover in the Himalayas and frequent tectonic movements have led to the increasing rise of sittation in the country affecting major rivers like Padma, Jamuna, Teesta, Mahananda and Punarbhaba. An amount of 2.4 billion tons of silt load is being carried by the major rivers and deposited on the beds of shallow deltaic rivers.

The link between deforestation in the Himalayas and intensity and frequency of flood in Bangladesh is thus challenged.[70] It is also considered to be a result of human being's considerable interference with the ecological system of the subcontinent.

Prior to the 1962 China war, the Indian Himalayas were for the most part, accessible only on foot along trails. The very Chinese military presence on the Himalayas frontier prompted a massive road construction after 1962 overlooking environmental concerns. According to one authority, post 1962 road construction had produced more than 10,000 km. of highways in the Indian Himalayas resulting in a total soil loss of 1.99 million tonnes annually. This is equated to slope improvement of 1.99 million tonnes of sediment per linear metre of road per annum.[71] Another study establishes this figure at 44,000 km and estimated that during the construction an average km of road required the removal of 40,000-80,000 m^3 debris which found their ways into the Ganges.[72] This discrepancy in data reflecting the uncertainty of effects of mass wasting and debris on flooding and sedimentation in the Ganges plain due to road construction in the Himalayas cannot be down played.[73] The peculiar hydrological cycles, geomorphological and physiological setting of Bangladesh have much to do with flooding in Bangladesh. In recent years, floods have become not only a regular phenomenon, but also increased in intensity and severity. Each year about 26,000 sq km or 18 per cent of the total land area of Bangladesh is flooded and during severe floods the affected area can be twice as much and nearly 60 per cent of the net cultivable area.[74] The affected area in the 1988 floods was 82,000 sq. km.

Apart from damage to human life and various sectors of economy, ecological degradation mounts high. It includes destruction of fertile agricultural land by deposition of new flood alluvium to the detriment of human and aquatic health.

Industrial pollution destroys the ecology. An example is the magnitude of chemical pollution in 1988 floods where the three distillery units producing rectified spirit at Rangpur, Panchagarh and Darshana used over 3,15,000 litres of toxic chemicals per day and effluents from one such distillery unit was enough to pollute the entire region.[75] After the flood the Ghorashal and Palash Fertilizer Plants released ammonia and chromium effluents to the water of Lakhya river which is already known not to have any fish habitat. Poor drainage system and lack of sanitation in rural areas and urban slums have accelerated the water borne diseases more acute.

The soil of Bangladesh with sandy silt and sand in the deeper layer and silt and silty clays on the top layer is very much vulnerable to erosion. As said above, man made activities like deforestation with soil erosion, siltation, flood, the meandering river courses and water withdrawal by the upper riparian state India causing siltation and reduction in the river depth and deforestation in the Himalayas causing flood by reducing sponge effects of soil, have all contributed to river bank erosion, when heavy rainfall enters into the river. The Brahmaputra right bank embakment (BRE) and other embankments along most of the eastern rivers have been breached several times allowing serious flooding to occur periodically on adjoining projected land. More than half the 217 km length of the BRE has been retired since it was completed in 1968 some sections several times.[76] The river Ganges eroded about 5.5 km of its right bank south-east of Sujanagar between 1965 and 1975.[77]

Of the 24,000 km of total length, 1200 km of river bank are subjected to erosion of which more than 380 km face severe erosion problems.[78] Ecological effect of such erosion is wide ranging which included destruction of agricultural land, forests, and fishing grounds, changes in river course and morphological characteristics. Most of the industries situated on the bank of rivers in Bangladesh used to discharge their waters in the form of mercury,lead chromium, arsenic and iron into the water causing serious health hazards. It is reported that the industries along the Karnaphuli, Sitalakhya and Bhirab rivers by releasing hazardous toxic wastes into the water have caused serious damage to the health and life of habitats. As studies show, Karnaphuli Paper Mill and Rayon Complex discharge about 45-55 million litres of untreated waste almost daily in the river Karnaphuli. This has resulted in mortality of fish in a stretch of 8 km downstream and 1.5 km upstream from the mill.[79] In the waste discharge of Urea Fertilizer Factory of Ghorashal situated by the side of the river Shitalakhya, was found about 22 ppm (parts per million) of ammonia concentration by the Environmental Pollution Control technicians.[80]

Monitorings by the Department of Environment have noted significant degradation of stream water quality by the industrial effluent discharges at a number of situations.[81] Examples would be (i) the raising of Buri Ganga Stream BOD by 1-1.5 mg/1 by tannery discharges at Hazaribagh, (ii) raising of EC, TDC, and BOD of river Jamuna by effluents of Paksey Paper Mills by 100/u/mho/cm. 60 mg/1 and 1-2 mg/1 respectively, (iii) raising of BOD of river Sitalakhya by ICI effluents at Godnail by 0.5-1.0 mg/1.(iv) causing NH concentrations of upto 2 mg/1 in Sitalakhya by Ghorasal fertilizer factory effluents. Moreover, in the upper riparian country there are big cities by the river side and there is a possibility of disposal of sewage and industrial wastes in the rivers. According to a study, arsenic pollution of ground water in West Bengal of India is threatening thirteen border districts in Bangladesh. Bangladesh scientists have found arsenic content in water samples collected from the bordering districts.[82]

The use of agricultural chemicals including various types of fertilizers, insecticides, fungicides and weedicides to produce more high yielding varieties of rice replacing the traditionally adopted resistant varieties, due to increased man-land ratio, has resulted in pollution of water through irrigation, rain, ground water aquifer.

The large number of mini lakes, beels, haors/ponds and khals that together cover over 10 per cent of total land area and grow much larger during rains play an important part in the living style, culture and ecology of Bangladesh. It is these water bodies that have suffered most from the pressures of growing pollution and consumerism. Not only larger quantities of sullage but effluents of cottage and small scale industries flow into them and solid wastes are dumped on the banks. Residuals of agricultural chemicals are also located in these much more often than in rivers. These pose a threat to the living human and non-human beings.

India

The pollution of water is increasing in India, more than 80 per cent of the total pollution load comes from the municipal sewage. The total discharge of domestic wastes in India which accounts for 33 million m^3 annually enters into the river system. The extent of pollution from industries is also increasing. Tanneries in Madras, Kanpur, Agra and Calcutta and dyeing units in Gujurat, Madhya Pradesh and Madras create heavy pollution loads without having effective treatment facilities.

India also uses about 5 million tonnes of chemical fertilizers and 77,000 tonnes of pesticides and insecticides, which usually find their way into rivers or into ground water. About 25 per cent reach the sea, pollute coastal waters affecting marine life. Profuse use of organo/chlorine pesticides in India, though banned in developing countries has wrought damage on the marine life.[83]

Most of the rivers such as the Ganges, Jamuna, Cauvery, etc. in India are unfit for drinking, or even bathing. Wastes discharged from pulp and paper units have proved detrimental to fish. The Kalu river on the outskirts of Bombay receives effluents including mercury, lead, copper, cadmium and chloride from over 150 industrial units.[84]

Water Pollution—Ocean and Sea

Bangladesh

Bangladesh has two seaports. Ocean going vessels call on these ports. Coastal and lighter vessels ply between the ports and inland river ports. Leakage of oil from carriers, engine blasts of ships and ship break industry is polluting the waters in and around the ports. The problem has become more serious with increased activity going on along the coast due to population growth and industrial development.

The agro-chemical, industrial as well as the soil wastes and sewage pollutants are all disposed off in the water bodies in an untreated form which through various rivers and their tributaries and distributaries reach the ocean. This destroys the balance of the marine environment to the grave detriment of aquatic resources. The pollution depleted the fish production much more than overuse or over-exploitation. Deep sea fishing is not carried out, besides saline water fish is not eaten. Within the territorial water of Bangladesh many foreign trawlers fish illegally in the absence of police patrolling. Industrialized countries have been dumping toxic wastes in the Bay of Bengal and adjacent Indian Ocean to the detriment of marine environment of Bangladesh.[85]

India

The Indian marine environment is seriously affected by land based sources of pollution and offshore activities. The chemical fertilizers and pesticides reaching the sea increase the nutrient pool, particularly of phosphates, ammonia and urea. Since 1970, the phosphate concentration in the water around Bombay has registered a 33 per cent increase. The coastline along Madras city marks an unusually high level of phosphates in the upper 10 metres of water.[86] Frequent and periodic mortality of marine fauna caused by an excess of ammonia, has been found near the discharge points of fertilizer factories. Concentration of organochlorine and organophosphorus pesticides in some of the fish catch from India's exclusive economic zone in plankton feeders has been found to be detrimental to fish catch.

One of the principal routes of oil tankers from the Gulf countries to the Far East and Japan goes through India's exclusive economic zone polluting the marine environment and water. The rate of appearance of tar balls which is currently estimated at 3,700 tonnes per year in the Arabian sea compared to 1,100 tonnes per year in the Bay of Bengal has been constantly rising.[87]

Heavy metal pollution in the sea around India is caused mostly by the discharge of municipal sewage and industrial effluents. The surface water of the Bay of Bengal shows a higher presence of almost all metals as compared to the Arabian sea as the former receives the large river run off.

Polluted waters lead to various gastrointestinal problems, liver infections, tropical diseases and terminal diseases like cancer. Children are often worst affected, dying in large numbers because of diarrhoea.

A World Bank study estimates that some 30.5 million Dalys (Disability Adjusted Life Years) are lost each year in India due to poor water quality, sanitation and hygiene. Dalys is a continuation of discounted and weighted years of life lost as a result of death at a given age and disability as a result of sickness, adjusted by severity.[88]

Inland fisheries are in a state of crisis in India both because of wetland destruction and because of engineered changes in riverine ecology. with the construction of dams, the hilsa has disappeared in the upstream region of the Ganga. Construction of the embankments along the Brahmaputra and its tributaries in Assam has led to the death of fisheries in the local wetlands called bheels to a point that this poverty stricken state today imports hundred of rupees worth of fish from Andhra Pradesh.

Air Pollution

One of the constituent fundamental elements of the universe is air on which both human beings and living nonhuman beings depend for their sustenance and well being. But the ethnocentrism of western paradigms of development based on industrialization and fossil fuel technology has contributed to a greater extent to the pollution of the atmosphere in terms of carbon dioxide emission, greenhouse effect, punching hole in the ozone layer and global warming. Apart from this, the inordinate and exorbitant consumption style of the industrialized and rich people of North who are merely a narrow minority of the world's population has been responsible for subjecting over a billion people steeped in absolute poverty to the threats posed by the disastrous effects of pollution of the atmosphere.

South Asia accounts for a slowly rising proportion of global greenhouse gas emissions. In terms of per capita emission, each South Asian contributed 0.18 tonnes of carbon compared to the 5.34 tonnes produced by US consumers and the global average by 1.12 tonnes.[89] But, however insignificant may be the contribution made by the South Asian countries, its people, ecology, economy and agricultural system would be seriously affected by global warming and sea level rise because of its geophysical location. According to a report of the World Resources Institute 1990-91. Bangladesh's contribution to the net carbon dioxide emission to the atmosphere among the South Asian states is only 1.61 per cent compared to 90.72 per cent by India. While South Asia's contribution to the global total greenhouse gas is 4.7 per cent, Bangladesh's is 0.4 per cent only.[90] But the worst victims of such environmental degradation which will be in the form of changed weather patterns, sea level rise, destruction of fisheries, agriculture, displacement of millions of people will be Bangladesh, Maldives, India, Sri Lanka and Pakistan.[91] Methane is the second largest contributor to the greenhouse effect, accounting for 18 per cent of greenhouse warming. Although the amount of methane entering the atmosphere is very small in comparison to the emissions of carbon dioxide, methane is a much more potent greenhouse gas. Methane traps 25 times as much heat in the atmosphere as carbon dioxide. Since 1950, the concentration of methane has been increasing by 1 per cent a year. Asia has been targeted as the main source of methane, as 90 per cent of the world's rice grows there. India's rice fields cover some 42 million hectares mounting to 60 per cent of Asia's total. Methane emissions from India's rice fields found an average annual output of 4.3 million tonnes, while the US Environmental Protection Agency put the figure almost ten times as high at 37.8 million tones.[92] The exaggerated data while highlighting the deficiencies of estimates extrapolated from small anounts of data indicate the industrialized nations' scuttling of responsibilities for their own carbon dioxide emissions.[93] But the growing population and the need for more rice to feed the people are likely to increase the emissions of methane in South Asia.

South Asia has hitherto contributed little to global emissions of greenhouse gases, despite being the most populous region. That does not deter one from detecting the future trends that would show a significant rise in emissions from this region. South Asia shows signs of transformation into a complex pattern of agricultural modernization, industrialization and urbanization accompanied by a large increase in energy demand.

Between 1980-89 energy consumption of liquid fuel and solid fuels, gas and even fuelwood and charcoal grew at a rate faster than any other region and country groups. Looking at the period (1979-1989) absolute consumption of commercial energy increased manifold in almost all countries of South Asia by 125 per cent in Bangladesh by 155 per cent in Bhutan, by 94 per cent in India, by 80 per cent in Nepal and 119 per cent in Pakistan, compared to a global increase of only 18 per cent.[94] Similar trends can be noticed in per capita terms. From 1971-1993 per capita (kg) energy use (equivalent oil) Nepal has shown an increase from 6 to 22, almost 4 times Bangladesh 18 to 59, almost 3 times, Pakistan from 103 to 339, almost two times, India from 111 to 242, more than two times, and Sri Lanka from 80 to 110[95]. This marks the declining share of traditional fuels in meeting the energy requirements. In the absence of improved know-how, clearer and more efficient technologies and a different fuel mix, the industrial growth in South Asia will mark a phenomenal increase in energy consumption and greenhouse gas emissions.

In most of the twenty-three Indian cities air pollution level exceed WHO recommended health standard. Six of India's largest cities—Mumbai, Delhi, Kolkata, Kanpur, Nagpur, Ahmedabad – face severe air pollution problems with the annual average levels of total suspended particulates (TSP) at least three times as high as the WHO standard.

As far as exposure to pollutants is concerned the study revealed that some 40,000 premature deaths in 36 cities of India, with Delhi alone accounting for about one-fifth of them. The monetary estimate of the loss resulting from these premature deaths came to between US $ 170 million and US $ 1615 million.

Similarly, estimates of the increased sickness because of high particulate levels were put at US $ 350-490 million per annum. Of the total health cost resulting from pollutant levels exceeding WHO guidelines which were estimated at US $ 517-2102 million per annum. P.M. 10 and sulphur dioxide accounted for 95 per cent and lead for another five per cent.[96]

Sea Level Rise

Bangladesh

Just how severely sea level rise will affect Bangladesh depends in part on the pace at which damming and channeling of rivers proceed and the rate of ground water withdrawal. On the basis of data available, the Woods Hole researchers have concluded that the increasing withdrawal of ground water in Bangladesh is affecting subsidence rates. Between 1978 and 1985 there was at least a six-fold increase in the number of wells drilled in the country, more than 1,00,000 shallow tube wells and 20,000 deeper ones were counted. Sediment samples suggest that ground water withdrawal may have raised subsidence to at least twice the natural rate. Taking these factors into account Milliman and his colleagues estimate that the sea level will rise as much as 239 centimetres along the Bangladesh coast by 2050. Half the country lies at elevations of less than 5 metres.[97] Loss of land under the 13 centimetre rise in the best case scenario is minimal, less than one per cent of the country's total. In the 144 centimetre rise in the worst case, however 16 per cent of the nation's land would be lost. In the worst case scenario local sea level rise would be 239 centimetres and 18 per cent of the habitable land would be under water. As a result, more than 17 million people would become environmental refugees. By the year 2100, the really worst scenario shows that 35 per cent of the nation's population—some 38 million people will be forced to relocate. Table 2.1 shows the areas likely to be affected due to expected sea level change of 1 metre.

The extensive river diversions will markedly decrease the amount of fresh water discharge into this coastal environment while higher sea levels will increase salt water thus reducing mangrove forest cover and disrupting major fisheries within this fragile ecosystem. One metre rise in sea level would destroy the entire 4,01,600 hectare of mangrove forest in the Sunderbans as well as 36,000 ha of mangrove forest along the coast.[98] Reduction in river out flow may also accelerate the intrusion of brackish water into aquifers, a problem that already extends 240 km. in land.[99]

Table 2.1. Area Likely to be Affected due to Expected Sea-change of 1 metre

Greater District	Existing New District	No. of Upzilas to be affected			Area to be affected (acres).	Remarks
		Part	Full	Total		
Khulan	Khulna	2	2	4	807072	Part
	Satkhira	32	–	3	527185	Part
	Bagerhat	7	5	7	567281	Almost Whole
	Sub-Total	41	7	14	1901538	64.7% of Dist.

Greater District	Existing New District	No. of Upzilas to be affected			Area to be affected (acres).	Remarks
		Part	Full	Total		
Barisal	Barisal	4	3	7	444366	Part
	Bhola	–	7	7	768969	Whole
	Jhalokati	–	4	4	187323	Whole
	Pirojppur	–	8	8	355179	Whole
	Sub-Total	4	22	26	1755837	99.1% of Dist.
Patuakhali	Patuakhali	–	6	6	741723	Whole
	Barguna	–	5	5	434657	Whole
	Sub-total	–	11	11	1176380	Whole Dist.
Faridpur	Madaripur	1	–	1	11332	Part
	Gopalganj	4	1	5	198974	Part
	Sub-Total	5	1	6	210306	12.4% of Dist.
Noakhali	Noakhali	1	1	2	340597	Part
	Lakshmipur	2	1	4	223218	Part
	Sub-Total	3	2	5	563815	44.2% of Dist.
Total		19	42	6	5607876	15.8% of the Country

Source : SAARC, Regional Study on Greenhouse Effect and its Impact on the Region (Kathmandu : SAARC Secretariat, 1992), p. 54.

The combined effect of warmer climates and higher seas will make tropical storms more frequent and destructive. Storm surges as much as 6 metres higher than normal can reach as far as 200 km in land. But the height of the surge was 15 to 20 metre in the 1991 cyclone.[100] A comparative study of monthly frequency of tropical cyclones in the Bay of Bengal for the period 1991 to 1960 against subsequent 14 year period 1961-1974 clearly indicates a significant increase in the latter.[101] The reason behind the 1991 cyclone's catastrophic turn has been indicated as the rising sea and warmer climate.[102]

Another important effect of climate change would be change in spatial and temporal distribution of temperature and precipitation. The analysis of rainfall variation made by a study in 1989 taking into account 85 years rainfall data of six different stations including the driest area, indicates that the coefficient of variation is more in the drier areas as well as during pre and post monsoon period. On the magnitude and frequency of heavy rainfall, the study shows that the annual frequency of heavy rainfall depict an increasing trend in rainfall areas and decreasing trend in relatively drier areas.[103]

The local rate of subsidence, increased rainfall, rising sea as well as the vast volume of Himalayan water (due to increasing temperature of the earth, the Himalaya ice cap will melt) would result in massive flooding of the entire country, The area affected by the major floods during the last 33 years increased from 50,500 sq km. in 1955 to 90,000 sq km in 1988.[104] Since this mid-century the number and severity of large scale floods have increased significantly. In the 1988 floods 80 per cent of the country was submerged.[105] Rise in sea level will increase the process of shore line erosion. Per Braun of Technical University of Norway in a study shows that shoreline erosion was of the order of 0.3 metre per year. If sea level rises 1. 5 metre by 2,000, shoreline recession will be about 150 metres.[106] Vast areas of coast of Bangladesh will be flooded.

India

The levels of sulphur dioxide has shown an increasing trend in Delhi and Nagpur. No significant change in the levels of suspended particulate matter in the cities of Delhi, Mumbai, Kanpur, Hyderabad, Jaipur and Cochin has been observed.

India does not face the immediate threat of acid rain due to the low sulphur content of coal and oil, which is less than 0.5 per cent. But the ash content of Indian coal is high which is 30 to 45 per cent. Coal burning in power plants has been causing considerable fly ash emissions.[107]

Unlike development countries, India consumes very small quantities of CFCs. India produced 6500 tonnes of CFCs in 1986. The per capita consumption of CFCs per annum is hardly 0.005 kg in India whereas the comparable figure is more than 100 times in certain developed countries such as USA and Japan.[108]

Position of South Asia in World Economic Structure

The South Asian countries, like other countries in South are dependent on the industrialized North for their economic development. The ethnocentrism of western paradigms of development has been the ideal for the South. In the world economic structure dominated by the

North, the South has been extorted to remain at the periphery. The working nuances of the world economic structure leads to what Andre Gunder Frank once opined: "The development of the under development". The periphery is the source of the wealth of the core; the latter exploits and siphons off the resources of the former. To quote him :

> ... the metropolis expropriated economic surplus from its satellites and appropriates it for its own economic development. The satellite remains underdeveloped for lack of access to their own surplus and as a consequence of the same polarization and exploitative contradictions which the metropolis introduces and maintains in the satellite's domestic economic structure.[109]

The result of this economic system is that while the industrialized countries continue to grow economically, developing countries continue to decline, their natural resources get over–exploited, poverty and indebtedness increase, the future gets discounted, pollution gets worse and quality of life declines. The overwhelming dependence of South Asian countries on the North dominated economic institutions such as the IMF and World Bank for aids and loans for industrial development, projects and plants has introduced many conditionalities like structural adjustment programmes, devaluation of currency, and export oriented economy into their economy thereby inflating their debt service bills, increasing their poverty and deteriorating their environment. Environmental degradation has been strongly related to the global processes of trade and economic relations. Instead of managing their resource base, they have been pontificated to mine their already degraded natural resource base.[110]

In 1990, half of the world's poor lived in South Asia. Not only do South Asian countries have low per capita income, but these incomes are unevenly distributed, leading to extreme poverty on massive scale. Given the limited availability of sufficient job creation and income generation opportunities in the agricultural sector in South Asia, industrial growth has been looked upon as the anodyne. Introduction of market economy, privatization and penetration of multinationals into South Asian economy, has been done keeping in view the target of maximizing industrial growth. But the pressures of debt servicing, interest payment, foreign exchange, technology transfer and poverty alleviation will keep South Asia more dependent on foreign aids and loans with many conditionalities and strings. South Asia will not only be walletted in debt trap, but continue to deteriorate its environment and natural resource base due to its finding in western industrialization an alchemy. Deepening poverty, increasing environmental degradation and mounting indebtedness to the industrialized North, have been the pathological consequences of South Asia being exhorted to remain at the periphery of the world economic structure.

References

1. Paul Harrison, *The Third Revolution : Environment, Population and a Sustainable World* (London/New York : I.B. Tarris and Co. 1992) p. 236.
2. Michael S Teitelbaum "The population threat", *Foreign Affairs* Vol. 71, No. 5, Winter 1992/1993, p. 64.
3. N. Sadik, *The State of the World Population 1990* (New York : World Population Fund, 1990).
4. World Bank, *World Development Report 1992 : Development and the Environment* (London : Oxford University Press, 1992), p. 26.
5. Stephan Libiszewski, *What is an Environmental Conflict?* Environment and Conflict Project (ENCOP) Occasional Paper No. 1, Zurich and Bern, July 1992, p. 4.
6. See Daniel Deudney, "Rethinking the link between environmental and national security issues" *Perspectives on War and Peace* Vol. 7, n. 2. Spring 1990, p. 15. Also The United Nations Populations Fund, *The State of World Population 1992* (New York : 1992), pp. 23-25.
7. See Marcel Leroy, "Human population as a factor in strategic policy and action", in Arthur H. Westing, ed., *Global Resources and International Conflict : Environmental Factor for Strategic Policy and Action* (Oxford : Oxford University Press, 1986), pp. 159-181. Essam EL-Hinnawi, *Environmental Refugees* (New York : United Nations Development Programme, 1985).
8. J. Huxley, *Human Crisis* (Seattle : University of Washington Press, 1963) p. 78; H. Khan, *On Thermonuclear War* (Princeton, New Jersey : Princeton University Press 1961) edn., 2, p. 570 : J.D. Nef, *War and Human Progress An Essay on the Rise of Industrial Civilization* (Cambridge, Mass : Harvard University Press, 1950), p. 340.
9. *The State of India's Environment: The First Citizens Report* (New Delhi, Centre for Science and Environment (CSE), 1987, 1991; World Population Data Sheet (Washington, D.C. : Population Reference Bureau, April 1991).
10. Quoted in *Towards Sustainable Development: The National Conservation Strategy of Bangladesh*, First Draft, Ministry of Environment and Forest

(Government of Bangladesh) and International Union for Conservation of Nature and Natural Resources 1991, p. 65.

11. *Environmental Policy, Report of the Task Force on Bangladesh Development Strategies for the 1990's* Vol. 4, Dhaka 1991, p. 15.
12. *Ibid.*
13. *Ibid*, p. 16.
14. Thomas Homer Dixon, Jeffrey Boutwell and George Rathjens, "Environmental change and violent conflict", *Scientific American*, February 1993, p. 40.
15. Environmental Policy, *op. cit.*
16. D. Hall et. al., "Biomass for energy : supply prospects" in T.B. Johanson et.al., ed., *Renewable Energy: Sources for Fuels and Electricity* (Washington D.C.: Island Press 1992), pp. 593-662.
17. D. Hall, H. Mynick and R. Williams, "Alternative roles for biomass in coping with greenhouse warming", *Science and Global Security* 2, 1991, pp. 1-39.
18. D. Hillel, *Out of the Earth: Civilization and the Life of the Soil* (New York : The Free Press, 1991).
19. L. Brown and E. Wolfe, "Soil Erosion: Quiet Crisis in the World Watch Economy", *World Watch Paper* 60, 1991, World Watch Institute Washington D.C.
20. G. Daily and P. Ehrlich, "Population, sustainability, and earth's carrying capacity", *Bioscience* Vol. 42, No. 10, 1992, pp. 761-771.
21. C. Overgaard Nielsen, "Studies on enchyfreidaez field studies", *Nature Jutlandica*, 4, 1955, pp. 5-58.
22. D. Pimentel et.al., "Environmental and social costs of biomass energy", *Bioscience*, 34, No. 2, 1992, pp. 354-362.
23. F. Kenneth Hare, "Climate, drought and desertification", *Nature and Resources* Vol. 20, No. 1, January-March 1984, pp. 2-8.
24. Government of the People's Republic of Bangladesh, *Study on the Causes and Consequences of Natural Disasters and Protection and Preservation of the Environment* (Dhaka, December, 1989), Chapter 3.
25. World Bank, *World Development Report 1988* (New York : Oxford University Press, 1988).
26. Government of People's Republic of Bangladesh, *op.cit.*
27. *Towards Sustainable Development*, *op.cit.*, p.73.

28. Government of People's Republic of Bangladesh Report, *op.cit.* Chapter 3, p. 12.
29. *Towards Substainable Development, op.cit.*
30. *Ibid.*, p. 68.
31. SAARC, *Regional Study on the Causes and Consequences of Natural Disasters and the Protection and Preservation of the Environment* (Kathmandu, SAARC Secretariat, 1992) p. 27.
32. *Ibid.*
33. Carter Brandon and Kisten Hommann, "The cost of inaction: valuing the economy-wide cost of environmental degradation in India", quoted in A. Agarwal, "Pay-offs to Progress", *Down to Earth* Vol. 5, No. 10, 15 October 1996, p. 35.
34. Sandra Postel and John C. Ryan, "Reforming forestry" in *State of the World 1991*, A World Watch Institute Report on Progress Towards a Sustainable Society (New York, W.W. Norton and Co. Inc. 1991), p. 74.
35. *Ibid.*
36. United Nations Environment Programme (UNEP), *Profile* (Nairobi, 1990), p. 17.
37. P.S. Ramakrishna, "Tropical forests: Exploitation, conservation and management", *Environment and Development* No. 166, 1993, pp. 145-162.
38. For details on deforestation, see Lawrence S. Hamilton "What are the impacts of Himalayan Deforestation on the Ganges-Brahmaputra low lands and deltas? Assumption and facts", *Mountain Research and Development* (Kathmandu) Vol. 7, No. 3, 1987, p. 256.
39. Quoted in M. Abdul Hafiz and Nahid Islam, *Environmental Degradation and Intra-inter State Conflicts in Bangladesh, Environmental Conflict Project* (ENCOP), Zurich and Bern, Occasional Paper No. 6, May 1993, p. 23.
40. *Bangladesh Bureau of Statistics*, Year Book 1987.
41. *The Environment and Development in Bangladesh: An Overview and Strategy for the Future*, prepared by the Canadian International Development Agency for Bangladesh Programme, Asia Branch, October 1989, p. 17.
42. ESCAP, ST/ESCAP/618 cited in, The Environment and Development in Bangladesh: An Overview of Strategy for the Future, *Ibid.*
43. Government of the People's Republic of Bangladesh Report, *op.cit.*, Chapter 4, p. 4.
44. *Ibid.*, p. 4.

45. SAARC, Regional Study on the Causes and Consequence of Natural Disasters and the Protection and Preservation of the Environment, *op.cit.*, p. 43.

46. *Ibid.*

47. Carter Brandon and Kisten Hommanna, *op.cit.*

48. *Ibid.*

49. S. Postel, "Water: Rethinking management in an age of scarcity", Washington, World Watch Institute, Paper No. 62, 1984, pp. 66.

50. M. Falkenmark, "Water: the silent messenger between cause and effect in environmental problems", *Water International* (Lausannel, 9(2)), 1984, pp. 62-65.

51. L. David, *River Basin Development for Socio-economic Growth*, General Report in UN Development Programme, ed., River : UNDP, 1976 Vol. 1, pp. 25-37.

52. Malin Falkenmark, "Fresh Water as a factor in strategic policy and action" in Arthur H. Westing, ed., *Global Resources and International Conflict: Environmental Factors in Strategic Policy and Action* (New York: Oxford University Press, 1986), Chapter V., pp. 85-113.

53. Environmental Policy, Report of the Task Force on Bangladesh Development Strategies for the 1990's Vol. 4, Dhaka 1991, p. 45.

54. *Ibid.*

55. M. Abdul Hafiz and Nahid Islam, *op.cit.*, p. 29.

56. Impact on Bangladesh due to withdrawals at Farakka of dry season Ganges flows, a report received from Farroq Shobhan, Foreign Secretary of the People's Republic of Bangladesh, 30 October, 1995.

57. Hamidur Rahman Khan "Water Resources Development in Bangladesh : Problems and Prospects" Paper presented at a Regional Seminar on Water Resources Policy in Agro Socio-Economic Development, 4-8 August 1985, Dhaka.

58. Master Plan Organization, Second Interim Report, June 1964, p. 3. quoted in M. Abdul Hafiz and Nahid Islam, *op.cit.*, p. 11.

59. Census of Minor Irrigation Equipment, June, 1989, prepared by Bangladesh-Canada Agricultural Sector Team.

60. Master Plan Organization, *op.cit.*, p. 58.

61. Government of People's Republic of Bangladesh Report, *op.cit.*, chapter 6 p. 6.

62. Ainun Nishat and Shahjahan Kabir Chowdhury, *Water Quality: Problem and Needs for Integrated Control in Bangladesh*, paper presented in a Regional Seminar on Development, 4-8 August 1985, Dhaka.
63. Impact on Bangladesh due to withdrawal at Farakka of dry season Ganges flow, *op.cit.*
64. ESCAP, ECU/M CEA/PM/4 quoted in Hafiz and Islam, *op.cit.*, p. 13.
65. Khurshida Bagum, *Tension over the Farakka Barrage : A Technopolitical Tangle in South Asia* (Dhaka, University Publishers Ltd, 1987), p. 137.
66. M. Abdul Hafiz and Nahid Islam, *op.cit.*, p. 14.
67. Amjad H. Khan and Shahajahan Miah, The Brahmaputra River Basin Development, Dublin 1983, p. 94, quoted in Hafiz and Islam, *Ibid.*
68. Md. N. Huda and J.U. Chowdhury, Floods and Erosion, paper presented in a Regional Conference on Flood and Erosion, Dhaka 7-10 September 1989, p. 9.
69. Amjad H. Khan, Flood Problems and Prospects: A Regional Overview, Keynote address on Regional Conference on Flood and Erosion, Dhaka, 7-10 September 1989. See also Bryan Johnson, "Bangladesh floods may be harnessed", *Globe and Mall*, 14 September 1988.
70. Lawrence S. Hamitan, "What are the Impacts of Himalayan Deforestation on the Ganges-Brahmaputra Low Lands and Delta? Assumption and Facts", *Mountain Research and Development*. Vol. 7, No. 3, August 1987. See *State of India's Environment*. A Citizen's Report : Floods, Flood Plains and Environmental Myths (Centre for Science and Environment, New Delhi, 1991), pp. 59-62, D.A. Gilmour, M. Bonnell and D.S. Cassells, "The Effects of Forestation on Soil Hydraulic Properties in the Middle Hills of Nepal : A Preliminary Assessment", *Mountain Research and Development* Vol. 7, No. 3, Aug. 1987. Other Environmentalists have reacted strongly against Anil Agarwal's assertions accusing him of shallow analysis and poor judgement. His report and conclusions are misleading. See *International Herald Tribune* (Paris), 10 December 1991.
71. K.G. Tejwani, "Sedimentation of Reservoirs, in the Himalayan region", *Mountain Research and Development* 7 (3) 1987, pp. 323-327.
72. K.S. Vilidya, "Accelerated erosion and landslide prone zones in the Himalayan region", in J.S. Singh, ed., *Environmental Regeneration in Himalaya: Concepts and Strategies* (Nainital: Central Himalayan Environment Association, 1985).
73. D.V.V. Narayan, "Downstream impacts of soil conservation in the Himalayan region", *Mountain Research and Development*, 7(3) 1987, pp. 287-298.

M.J. Haiqh, "Road development and rural stresses in the Indian Himalaya", *Nordia*, Vol. 16, 1982, pp. 135-40. M.J. Haigh, "A comparison of sediment accumulations beneath forested and deforested microcatchments, Garhwal Himalaya", *Himalayan Research and Development* Vol. 1, Vol. II, 1982, pp. 118-120.

74. Shaukat Hassan, "Environmental issues and security in South Asia", Adelphi Papers No. 262, 1991, *op.cit*, p. 18.
75. Mustafa Kamal Majumar, *Holiday*, 30 September 1988.
76. Asian Development Bank Report, *Disaster Mitigation in Asia and the Pacific*, Manila, 1991, p. 84.
77. Md. Huda and J.U. Chowdhury, *op.cit.*, p. 16.
78. *Ibid.*
79. Ainun Nishat and Shahajahan Kabir Chowdhury, *op.cit.*
80. *Ibid.*
81. Government of People's Republic of Bangladesh Report, *op.cit.* Chapter 6, p. 9.
82. Panos Report, quoted in *Down to Earth* Vol. 2, No. 13, 30, November 1993, p. 19.
83. SAARC, Regional Study, op.cit., pp. 77-78.
84. *Ibid.*
85. M. Abdul Hafiz and Nahid Islam, *op.cit.*, p. 28. See also Haroon Habib, "US ship dumped toxic wastes in Bay of Bengal?" *The Hindu* (Madras), 20 March 1989.
86. SAARC, Regional Study, *op.cit.*, pp. 77-78
87. *Ibid.* See for details, R. Sen Gupta et.al., State of the Marine Environment in the South Asia Seas Region, UNEP Regional Seas Reports and Studies, No. 123, UNEP 1990: and K. P. Pratapchandra Nair, "Are they oceans or dumping grounds?" *The Hindu*, 10 May 1991.
88. World Bank Development Report 1992 (Oxford: Oxford University Press, 1992), p. 104.
89. Regional Study on Green House Effect and its Impact on the Region, Kathmandu, SAARC Secretariat, 1992.
90. M. Abdul Hafiz and Nahid Islam, *op.cit.*, p. 25.
91. See Climate Report 1994, Climate Institute (Washington) funded by Asian Development Bank (Manila) Quoted in Kurt Kleiner "Climate change threatens South Asia", *New Scientist*, 143 (1990), 27 August 1994, p. 6.

92. Subhadra Menon, "Wrong paddy fields measured by methane", *New Scientist*, *Ibid.*

93. *Ibid.*

94. World Bank, *World Development Report 1992* (Oxford: Oxford University Press, 1992), p. 205.

95. World Bank, *World Development Report 1995* (Oxford: Oxford University Press, 1995). Table 5, p. 170.

96. Carter Brandon and Kistan Hommann, *op.cit.*

97. John D. Milliman, Environmental and Economic Impact cited in Jodi L. Jacobson, *Environmental Refugees: A Yardstick of Habitability,* World Watch Paper No. 86, 1988, p. 35.

98. Environmental Policy, *op.cit.*, p. 179.

99. John D. Milliman, *op.cit.*

100. M. Abdul Hafiz et.at., *op.cit.*, p.28.

101. Environmental Policy, *op.cit.*, p. 183.

102. Mahtab, quoted in Environmental Policy, *op.cit.*

103. *Ibid.*

104. Environmental Policy, *op.cit.*, p. 183.

105. Jodi L. Jacobson, "An unnatural disaster, Bangladesh", *Observer*, 8 December 1990.

106. Quoted in Mohiuddin Ahmed, *Holiday*, 31 May 1991, p. 5

107. SAARC, Regional Study, *op. cit.*

108. *Ibid.*

109. Andre Gunder Frank, quoted in Robert Gilpin, *The Political Economy of International Relations* (Princeton New Jersy: Princeton University Press, 1987), p. 69.

110. See David Pearce, Anil Markandya and Edward B. Barbier, *Blue Print for a Green Economy* (London : Earthscan Publications 1989) November 1993, p. 19.

3

Social Effects

Environmental scarcity of resources and their degradation may cause innumerable social effects in the countries of South Asia, which will ultimately affect their security. If a disaster or environmental degradation due to human activities or nature can be defined as a crisis event which outstrips the capacity of a society to manage or cope with it at least for a time[1], it is the poorer countries "which are most vulnerable to the effects of environmental degradation". It also "tends to be the poorest people in those countries who suffer most from environmental degradation".[2] Here Bangladesh in South Asia can be seen as most vulnerable to the effects of environmental degradation.

Economic Decline

If we are interested in environment conflict linkages, perhaps environmental scarcity's most important negative social effect is the constraint it sometimes imposes on economic development. We should note, however, that because of resource capture and ecological marginalization, the main result of demographic and ecological stress is not so much generalized economic hardship as an increase in the wealth gap between those elites that take advantage of the opportunities scarcity offers and those marginal groups that suffer the brunt of scarcity.

Figure 3.1 shows some ways that scarcity might negatively affect economic wellbeing, especially of less advantaged groups. Again the future focuses solely on the effects of supply induced scarcities. It shows that environmental degradation or depletion might influence economic productivity directly or indirectly via other social effects, such as changes in agricultural productivity.

A great variety of environmental stresses could affect wealth production. Hypothetically, for example, increased ultraviolet radiation caused by ozone depletion could eventually raise the rate of disease in

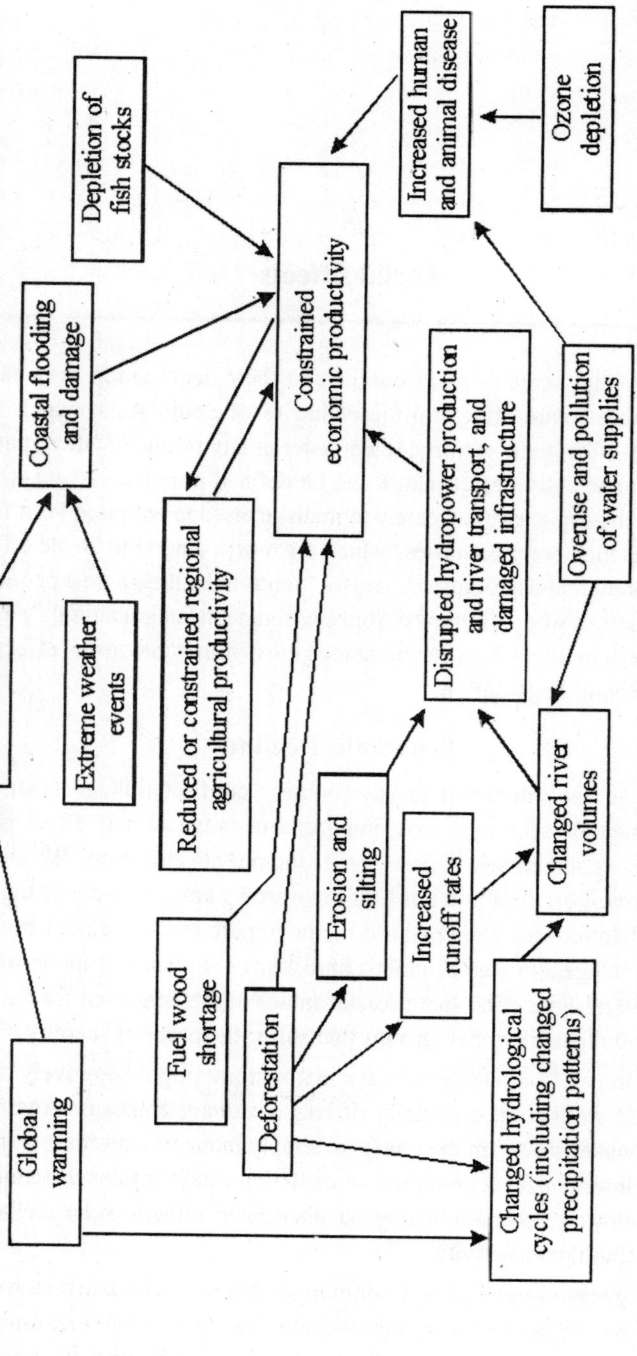

Fig. 3.1. Possible Effects of Environmental Change on Economic Productivity.

Source : Thomas F. Homer Dixon, Environment, Scarcity and Conflict, op.cit., p. 89.

humans, with serious economic results over the long term.[3] Although we have yet to see clear evidence of this particular effect, there is nonetheless abundant evidence of a strong link between other kinds of environmental scarcity and economic productivity. For instance, logging for export markets often creates short-term economic gain for the exporting country's elite, but the resulting deforestation can depress the economy's longer-term productivity. Increased run off damages roads, bridges, and other valuable infrastructure, while the extra siltation reduces the transport and hydroelectric capacity of rivers. As forests are destroyed, "wood becomes scarcer and more expensive, and it absorbs an increasing share of the household budget for the poor families that use it for fuel.

Agriculture is the source of a large share of the wealth generated in developing societies. Per Pinstrup Andersen notes that " in most low-income developing countries, growth in the agricultural sector, whether through food or non-food agricultural commodities, is the most effective and often the only viable lead approach to sustainable economic growth and poverty alleviation."[4] Consequently, if environmental scarcity constrains agricultural production, as suggested above, it may have a large effect on a country's overall economic development. Some experts believe that the economic relief brought by the green revolution within many poor countries will be shortlived. Jeffrey Leonard writes: "Millions of previously very poor families that have experienced less than one generation of increasing wealth due to rising agricultural productivity could see that trend reversed if environmental degradation is not checked.[5] Reduced or constrained agricultural productivity is often mentioned as potentially the most worried consequences of environmental change. Fig. 3. 2 present some of the causal connections between environmental change and agricultural output. It focuses on the consequences for agriculture of supply induced environmental scarcities, i.e., the depletion and degradation of environmental resources It also identifies the effects of global warming on coastal cropland of Bangladesh.

Many plants grow faster and larger in a warm environment rich in carbon dioxide and they often use water more efficiently. But optimistic estimates of greatly increased crop yields in a warmer, carbon-rich world have usually been based on laboratory experiments under ideal growing conditions. In addition, these estimates have generally ignored the influence on yields of more frequent extreme climate events caused by

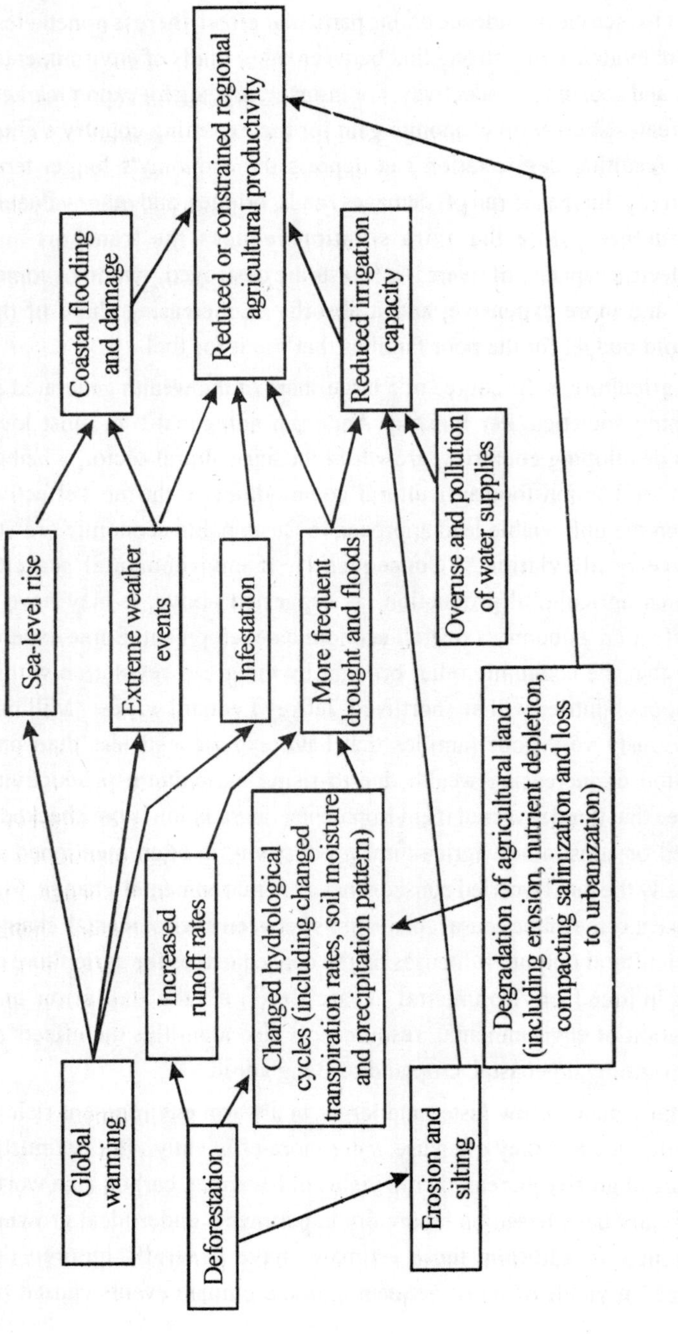

Fig. 3.2. Possible Effects of Environmental Change on Agricultural Productivity.

Source : Thomas F. Homer Dixon, Environment, Scarcity and Violence, *op.cit.* p. 82.

global warming (especially droughts and heat waves), increased pest infestation, and the decreased nutritional quality of crops grown in a carbon-enriched atmosphere.[6]

An important recent study of the impact of greenhouse warming on agriculture by Cynthia Rosenzweig and Martin Party takes many of the above factors into account. It suggests that a doubling of atmospheric carbon dioxide concentration and the resulting climate changes, will cause only a small drop to the world's total crop output. However, the differential impacts will be large the researchers conclude that "developing countries are likely to bear the brunt of the problem.[7]

Fig. 3.2 also identifies some of deforestation's possible effects on food output. Logging and land-clearing can accelerate erosion, change regional hydrological cycles and precipitation patterns, and decrease the land's ability to retain water during rainy periods. The resulting flash floods damage irrigation works while plugging reservoirs and irrigation channels with silt. These changes can seriously affect crop production.

Decreased Agricultural Production

Agriculture which is one of the prime sectors of Bangladesh's economy constitutes about 50 per cent of its GDP and provides employment to 60.3 per cent of the total labour force.[8] In recent years there has persistently been a continuing decline in the growth rates of agriculture due to environmental scarcity of various renewable resources like fresh water, soil, forest and atmosphere. The 3 per cent food grain, output per annum in the mid – 1970's lowered down to 2.2 per cent in the 1980's. Land degradation being accentuated by the growing population can bring out shortfalls in agricultural productivity. "If population increases, while the soil deteriorates food production per capita can be expected to decline.[9] As seen above, due to reduced water flow for various reasons like upper riparian excessive water withdrawal from the Ganges over Farakka, unlimited general water withdrawal and reduced rainfall accompanied by other factors and consequences like deforestation, salinization, siltation, soil erosion, periodic flood and cyclone, a vast sum of agricultural land is being degraded every year. This amounts to 22.92 per cent of the net cropped area.[10] Bangladesh blames India for food shortages.

As alleged, "more than 9,000 hectares of land in the Ganges-Kobadak Project could not be brought under irrigation during the dry season in the fiscal year 1991-92 because of adverse effects of the Farakka barrage. This has deprived Bangladesh at least 40,000 tonnes of foodgrains as revealed by Bangladesh's Agriculture Minister Majedual Huq to the Parliament."

The area degraded by the water shortage during the year 1988-89 was estimated to be 38,449 hectares against 11,215 hectares damaged during the year 1987-88.[12] Salinity affected in the year 1988-89 was nearly 43,254 ha against 8218 ha of the previous year. According to another estimate, the net loss of the area solely dependent on the Ganges water stands at US $ 85 million during the year 1988-89.[13]

Drought in varying intensity seems to have affected the entire country, though the most hit is the north-west and south-west region. During the perennial dry season about 0.574 mha of T.Aman crops are damaged and more than 1.748 mha of T.Aman crops are severely affected by drought.[14]

Flood has always been a severe constraint on agricultural production in Bangladesh. Normally each year 18 per cent of the country is used to be flooded. But in 1987, 35 per cent of the total land area was submerged against the more disastrous inundation of 84 per cent of the country, i.e., 1,22,000 km^2 in 1988.[15] Whereas rice production lost in 1987 flood was estimated at 3.5 million tonnes, in 1988 it was 2 million tonnes.[16] According to an official estimate livestock lost in 1987 was 270,700 against 582,000 lost in 1988.[17] Direct losses to capital stock by the 1987 and 1988 floods were estimated at US $456 million and $1300 million respectively.[18] Tables 3.1 and 3.2 show the magnitude of losses due to flood in 1987 and 1988.

It is noticed that there has already been a tough competition between crop land and living space in rural Bangladesh. People used to live on bulwarks raised above the water level of the countryside flooded annually by rainfall and run off. During the dry season, soil for the bulwarks is dug from the centres of the paddies at the expense of the paddy area. With population growing the area of the bulwark thus increases and the water in the excavated paddies deepens to the point where the highest yielding rice stains can no longer be planted, leading to a decline in rice production.[19]

Due to various flood control measures, water withdrawal and salinity, forest and fisheries declined to a greater extent. As an economic activity the inland fisheries rank only next to agriculture contributing more than 90 per cent of the total fish landings. The total fish production though has gone up slightly from 0.81 million tonnes in 1968-69 to 0.85 million tonnes in 1989-90 and has not been keeping pace with the spawning population.[20]

Table-3.1. Offical Estimates of Losses and Damage by Flood in 1987 and 1988

Loss in	1987	1988
Area flooded (km^2)	57,000	82,000
House totally/partially damaged (million)	2.5	7.2
Human lives lost	1,657	2,379
Livestock lost		
Cattle, goats, etc.	64,700	172,0000
Poultry	206,000	410,000
Rice production lost (million tonnes)	3.5	2
Roads : trunk (km)	1,523	3,000
	15,107	10,000
bridges, culverts	1,102	898
Railways: embankments (km)	698	1,300
bridges	166	270
Flood embankments (km)	1,279	1,990
Irrigation/drainage canals (km)	222	283
Irrigation/drainage canals structures.	541	1,465
Electricty Power Substations floods	n/a	18
11 KV power lines de-energized (km)	n/a	2,000
Industrial units floods	n/a	1,000
Hospital floods	n/a	45
Health Centres floods	1,305	1,400
Schools floods	6,689	19,000
Rural hand tubewells floods	n/a	240,000

Source: BWDB, 1987 and MOI 1988.

Table-3.2. Estimates for Cost of Repair and Reconstruction by Sector, 1998 (in US $ millon)

Sector	Immediate	Long Term	Total
Agriculture	34.6	133.4	168.0
Agriculture	34.6	133.4	168.0
Crops	24.4	91.2	115.6
Livestock	2.0	11.9	13.9
Fisheries	2.8	0.0	2.8
Forestry	0.7	3.1	3.8
Flood	4.7	27.2	31.9
Flood control/irrigation	53.8	72.8	126.6
Roads and highways	39.8	125.0	164.8
Roads and highways Department	25.5	97.6	123.1
Local government	11.8	22.7	34.5
Technical assistance	2.5	4.7	7.2
Rail roads	28.9	52.3	81.2
Inland waterways and ports	4.6	16.3	20.4
Civil aviation	7.0	36.0	43.0
Post and telecommunication	23.2	78.2	101.2
Power and electricity	8.8	46.6	55.2
Bangladesh Power Development Board	6.7	35.3	41.8
Rurul Electrification Board	2.1	11.3	13.45
Industry	124.4	100.8	225.2
Pubic infrastructure	1.2	2.3	3.5
Small and cottage industries	75.5	70.7	146.2
Medium and Large industries	47.7	27.8	75.8
Health	16.7	21.0	37.7
Education	58.0	0.0	58.0
Rural Water and sanitation	3.2	0.0	3.2
Urban infrastructure	21.5	30.4	51.9
Local Government	20.3	28.6	48.9
Technical assistance	1.2	1.8	3.0
Grand Total	424.5	718.6	1,137.1

Source : Report of the Task Force of the Government of the People's Republic of Bangladesh and United Nations on the 1988 Flood, 1 November 1988 (updated February 1989).

It is projected by a study that the total production of inland capture fisheries has come down from 0.47 million tonnes in 1983-84 to 0.42 million tonnes in 1988-89. If this trend persists by the year 2000, the total fish production will decline by 0.25 million tonnes.[21]

It is alleged that due to upstream water withdrawal fish landing in the upstream has declined by more than 90 per cent. Moreover, embankments, road construction and drainage channel have registered the direct loss of fish production at 37 kg/ha.[22]

Water withdrawal by India at Farakka has brought about drastic changes in hydrological and hydrobiological conditions in the lower reaches of the Ganges and its distributors causing an alarming reduction in fish production during the post Farakka era. Hilsa and other species of fish like Ruhi, Katla, Mrigel etc. are the worst affected.[23] Various flood control measures taken up in 1990 making 336 million hectares of inundable flood plains flood free, have marked a 11.4 per cent decline in fish production.[24] Owing to the growing needs of the people low lying lands are also being brought under cultivation. Once a depression abounding in fish, the site has been reclaimed in favour of agriculture causing further a decline in fish production.[25]

As seen in the former chapter, greenhouse warming and climate change have downward effects on agricultural production. Coastal crop lands in Bangladesh are seriously affected. Sea level rise, as projected, will further hasten the frequency and intensity of storms destroying crop land, livestock and fisheries. A rise in sea level by the middle of the next century will cause inundation of 2,915 million acres of net cropped land resulting in production losses of more than 2 million tonnes of rice, 13000 tonnes of wheat, 214,000 tonnes of sugarcane, 405,000 tonnes of vegetables, 10,000 tonnes of jute, 97,000 tonnes of pulses, 37,000 tonnes of oilseeds and 97,000 tonnes of spices. This amounts to a loss of nearly Tk 29.71 billion worth of agricultural crops. Adding to these 2.73 million of cattle and buffaloes, 986,000 of goats and sheep and 9.83 million of poultry will be affected. In addition to the inundation of the coastal area some of the low lying areas within the mainland will be also inundated due to the backwater effect. As estimated, due to the backwater effect of sea level change, considerable amount of cropland suitable for transported Aman will be damaged and different land categories based on seasonal depth of flooding in the mainland will increase due to sea level change.[26] Even more critical, coastal wetlands and estuaries being rapidly destroyed, and many would be balked in their efforts to migrate inland because of human imposed barriers. Their disruption would further damage oceanic fisheries that find nurseries or food sources in such areas.[27] In the cyclone of 1970, the loss of crops stood at US $ 63 million, the loss of cattle was 280,000 and poultry 500,000.[28] In the 1991 cyclone 100 per cent of the standing crops were totally destroyed, loss of cattle was 110,000. Table 3.3 depicts the economic losses due to 1 metre sea rise.

In sum, it can be said that, agriculture basic to the economy of Bangladesh, is much constrained by adverse environmental condition. Land use and development potentials are primarily determined by hydrological conditions. But for at least half of the year soil moisture deficiency results in insufficient water for crop production, and for the other half of the year excessive water hampers cultivation of any other crop excepting Aman paddy. Not only is the seasonal variation of water surplus or water deficit a problem to agricultural development but also the problem is aggravated by the excessive variability of Nor' wester and monsoon rainfall. The natural hazards, such as flood, cyclone, drought and salinity further compounded by environmental degradation affect very much the efficiency as well as productivity of crops grown - at times crops were totally destroyed.

Environmental Scarcity of Drinking Water

Drinking water is one of the essential requirements for the population which includes items like food, water, shelter, clothing, energy, sanitation, health and education.

In the urban areas of Bangladesh, 38 per cent of the people find access to water of reasonably reliable quality and the rest 62 per cent depend entirely on the polluted sources such as ponds and surface water for drinking and cooking purposes.[30] In Dhaka which is populated by nearly 8 million, the domestic demand of water is 431 million litres per day against the actual supply of 281 million litres.[31] In Chittagong the demand is also much higher than the supply. In rural areas the supply of drinking water from tube wells is 53 per cent and the rest is left to water derived solely from ponds, rivers and canals where the water quality is far below the drinking standard.[32]

Table-3.3 Physical Assets, Infrastructure, etc. Likely to be Affected by 1 metre Sea Level Rise.

Physical assets/ infrastruture, etc.		No. (if not otherwise mentioned).	Value (in million Tk).
1.	Land area (,000 acre)	5.6079	
	a. Not available for cultivation	87.9	8,744.92
	b. Current fallow	77.4	3,877.00
	c. Single cropped area	202.8	1,21,248.00
	d. Double cropped area	744.9	55,867.50
	e. Tripal cropped area	149.6	11,968.00
	f. Forest	1,304.1	–
	g. Others	1,223.7	61,185.00
2.	Dwelling Units.	1,867,308	1,23,274.50
4.	Business/Industry House hold	20,154	4,227.45
4.	Institutional House Hold	7,602	1,900.50
5.	Educational Institutions	8,273	1,902.50
	a. Primary school	4,900	1,078.00
	b. Secondary school	1,200	552.00
	c. College	111	71.04
	d. Madrash	2,062	206.00
6.	Rural Electrification (village)	543	497.75
7.	Communication		
	a. Railway tract (km)	1,466	—
	b. Metalled road (km)	706	3,838.91
	c. Unmetalled road (km)	19,772	26,199.52
	d. Bridges/culverts	10,383	10,383.00
	e. T & T offices	148	—
8.	Godown of		
	a. Food	281	196.70
	b. Fertilizer	94	66.45
9.	Hats and Bazaars (Market centres)	1,757	—
10.	Industries		
	a. Cottage Industries (Household)	97,777	988.32*
	b. Small Industries	1,911	89.39*
11.	Health Centres		
	a. Health Complex	49	490.00
	b. Health and FP Centre	133	399.00

Physical assets/ infrastruture, etc.	No. (if not otherwise mentioned).		Value (in million Tk).
11. Health Centres			
a. Health Complex		49	490.00
b. Health and FP Centre		133	399.00
12. Livestock and Pollutry ('000)			
a. Cattle and Buffalo		2,734	4,217.92
b. Goats and Sheep		986	236.64
c. Poultry		9,825	147.39
Annual Production Value of Crops (1986-87)	**Area ('000 acres)**	**Production ('000 tonnes)**	**Production value (million Tk)**
13. Crop			
a. Rice	837	288	3,168.00
Aus	2067	1264	15,642.00
Boro	180	179	2,092.10
Hyu	161	293	3,223.00
b. Wheat	13	13	70.07
c. Jute	42	10	74.29
d. Sugarcane	14	214	158.90
e. All Pulses	335	97	1,150.34
f. All Oilseeds	102	37	412.60
g. All Vegetables	22	405	1671.00
h. All spices	116	97.01	2,052.08
i. Cotton	.09	—	
j. Other Temp. Crop	2312	—	
14. Annual Production of			
a. Cottage Industries		98,207.12	
b. Small Industries		325.78	

Note: * Fixed Assets

Source: Regional Study on Greenhouse Effect and its Impact on the Region (Kathmandu: SAARC Secretariat, 1992), pp. 56-58.

Fuel Wood Scarcity

Usage of trees is far greater than regeneration. Fuelwood constitutes a major portion of the domestic energy consumption. Per capita fuel wood consumption stands at 0.07 m at present. Per capita energy consumption in Bangladesh is 140 kg. Oil equivalent (OE) which is very-very low according to the 1990 energy balance sheet of which 73 per cent comes from traditional biomass fuel. Of the total biomass fuel, agricultural residues constitute 63.5 per cent, fuel wood 22.5 per cent, and animal dung 14 per cent respectively.[33] Even at this stage of low rate of energy consumption the supply falls far below the demand. The total forest cover had dwindled from 20 per cent in the 1960s to less than 9 per cent at present.[34] The total extraction of firewood increased from about 152,000 metric tonnes in 1973 to about 318,000 metric tonnes in 1983.[35]

But it cannot keep pace with the growing population. It has been projected that if this trend continues by 2000 AD the annual fuel wood availability in rural areas will plummet to 0.02 m per capita.[36] As forests are destroyed wood becomes scarcer and more expensive and absorbs a chunk of poor families' economies. In the face of wood scarcity, in Bangladesh rural people's dependence on biomass fuel, agricultural residues and dung would increase depriving their soil of the fertility these provide and making it vulnerable to use of more pesticides and fertilizers to the detriment of the people.

Environmental Degradation Causing Health Hazards

Apart from natural causes like cyclone, flood, tornado, man made causes have affected the environment which are often detrimental to human health in Bangladesh. Rapid and unplanned urbanization extensive and wide deforestation, construction of dams, canal barrages, roads, wrongly designed development efforts such as industrialization, use and disposal of chemical and industrial wastes, extraction of gas, water from deep layer and mineral resources, use of chemicals, pesticides and toxic agents in agriculture and above all population explosion have wrought immense adverse impact on the ecology subjecting human health to various hazards.

Most of the people in rural Bangladesh use water from rivers, canals, tanks, wells and other unsafe sources for all purposes, only a small percentage have access to safe drinking water. Environmental pollution as has been dealt with earlier, has led to the proliferation of a number of water borne diseases such as hepatitis, polio myelitis, cancer, tuberculosis, lung inflammation and skin diseases are also the product of this pollution.[37]

Low flows of the Ganges induced high salinity in drinking water in the Khulna zone creating various hazards. Though the permissible limit for drinking water by WHO is only 500 ppm, the people in the area are drinking water of 1200 ppm. This has resulted in the outbreak of widespread diarrhea, cholera and other diseases in the area.[38]

Malnutrition, which is wide spread in Bangladesh, has been a matter of serious concern. In the BBS household survey a chronic malnutrition (stunting) rate of 56.1 per cent and wasting rate of 8.1 per cent was observed indicating acute malnutrition. The highest record of stunting and wasting occurs among rural female children in the 12-13 months age group which is 63.3 per cent and 23 per cent respectively.[39] This reflects the national economic situation.

The immediate economic impact has been the steady decline in the fish production which affects in the long-term the nutrition and health of children. The infant mortality rate in Bangladesh is 140 per 1000 children and 39 per cent of all deaths are due to infant mortality. 80 per cent of all illness is linked to water borne diseases these being associated with 20 per cent of all child mortality.[40]

Decreased Industrial Production

The Third Five Year Plan of Bangladesh from 1985-90 marked a growth rate of 4.32 per cent for the industrial sector against the target of 10.1 per cent per annum.[41] The primary factor for such a sluggish growth in industrial productivity is the environmental degradation in Bangladesh. Since most of the industries are agro-based, any shortfall in agricultural productivity is bound to affect the industrial growth. Adding to this the uncertainty about the continued supply of raw materials and disruption in communication and transport due to natural calamities like flood and cyclone looms large.

Overuse and depletion of forest resources have created a situation of resource scarcity for the wood-based industries. Reduced water flow and excessive extraction of water beyond the limit as discussed above, and consequent salinity have slowed the regenerating process of forest cover. All jute, textile, paper, pulp and food based industries in Bangladesh are subject to this kind of threat from the very processes of environmental degradation. It is seen that the industries in the Ganges catchment areas suffer a decline in production due to reduced water flow and increased salinity. The Goalpara thermal power station since its commissioning is said to have incurred a heavy financial loss of Tk 30 million for the year 1989 due to a reduced water level and increased salinity. The Khulana Newsprint Mill stated to have operated at half the capacity as like chloride contents of the water used has increased by more than 20 per cent.[42]

Displacement of Population

It has already been noted earlier that one of the consequences of the interaction of the sources of environmental scarcity of resources whether human or nature induced is the migration of the people from one region to another region within a state or from one state to other neighbouring states as environmental refugees with destabilizing effects on both domestic order and international stability.[43]

In 1985, the United Nations Environment Programme introduced the concept of environmental refugees who were defined as those people who have been forced to leave their traditional habitat temporarily or permanently because of marked environmental disruption. This is due to reasons both natural and anthropogenic that jeopardized their existence and/or seriously affected the quality of their life.[44] So it has been a major and predominant cause of flight or migration of people whether intra or interstate.[45] Among a complex web of factors responsible for migration, environmental degradation may act as a precipitating event that "disrupts the normal functioning of the system and thus destroys the capacity of a population to survive under the prevailing conditions."[46] Environmental degradation in the natural processes by human activities in the face of what Giddens calls the "high consequences of modernity",[47] may collapse the very social systems which provide people with an ongoing sense of ontological security. Not only environmental scarcity of resources but their consequences in the form of global warming, greenhouse effect, sea level rise, floods, cyclones, storms and droughts have impelled flight of people as environmental refugees and will continue to do so in future.[48]

In Bangladesh the magnitude of rural poverty and rate of migration to the urban areas would show the extent and intensity of environmental degradation and its social effects all over the country. In Bangladesh there has been continued impoverishment of the present cultivators and share croppers, increasing landlessness, gradual marginalization of the small landowners and peasant families, increasingly skewed land ownership distribution, agricultural indebtedness and pauperization of the small peasantry. In 1964, the rural population living below the poverty line was 50.8 per cent which increased to an all time high of 77.8 per cent in 1982, and came down further due to various alleviating programmes to 51 per cent in 1986. At present the figure is more than 51 per cent and the rural poor is estimated at nearly 50 million.[49] This is more than the South Asian average which at present stands at 49 per cent.[50] The pattern of land distribution and land ownership has been one of the important reasons accounting for the incidence of poverty in Bangladesh. Nearly 50 per cent of the households in the rural areas are landless. It is estimated that landlessness is growing faster than population. It is projected by the United Nations that Bangladesh's current population of 120 million will nearly double to 235 million by the year 2025.[51] Cropland which stands at 0.08 hectare per capita has already become scarce. Population density is over 939 people per square kilometre. with all of country's good agricultural land being exhausted to the hilt, the ever growing population is projected to cut in half the amount of crop land available per capita by 2025.[52] Inheritance customs and population growth have combined to produce scarcity and poverty. With each generation land becomes scarcer and scarcer being subdivided into fragments. Land which is the most fertile and main source of sustenance can no longer be able to support the growing population[53]. Poverty prevails not being able to invest more in soil conservation. Apart from this, as stated by Bangladesh the direct result of water withdrawal by India has been loss of seasonal work of millions who cannot find sufficient surface and ground water to sustain their livelihood during the dry season. Apart from the farmers, the fishermen suffered a lot due to reduced catches and boat men have lost their livelihood as navigability was seriously affected. This has resulted in increased unemployment and poverty among the poor people.[54] Fallow lands are left uncultivated. Poorest eventually leave for urban centres, or hill slopes or neighbouring Indian states.[55] In Bangladesh, landlessness combined with natural hazards like storm and cyclone, and river bank erosion push the landless rural to urban centres and Indian states where opportunities real or perceived appear as pull factors. Also they move to the hill slopes and hill sides like the plain people to CHT in Bangladesh. Here they clear the forest to begin farming anew to exhaust the land in a few years.

Adding to these factors, floods and cyclones have contributed to population displacement in Bangladesh. In case of severe floods like the ones in 1988 and 1989 the rate of displacement was large. 30 million people were displaced due to the 1988 flood.[56] The flood of 1989 displaced nearly 45 million people as per an estimate apart from other huge damages to human lives, livestock, land and agriculture.[57] According to Bangladesh Bureau of Statistics 3 million rural housing structures were damaged in the 1988 flood, belonging to the poor. More than 2 million hectares of crops were damaged.[58] The loss of industrial assets stood at 80 per cent. The incidence of diarrheal diseases went up to 80,000 cases per day in September 1988. All these people were treated in relief camps who had migrated from Faridpur, Dhaka, Comilla, Barisal, Noakhali, Mymensing and Potuakhali to the urban centres especially in Dhaka city. The single harmful environmental factor in the country according to Atiur Rahman is flooding which has led to temporary and permanent migrations, not only across districts but also across international frontiers.[60]

The cyclones of 1970 and 1991 were the two severest cyclones destroying the coastal areas of the country. The 1970 storm with range in the height of 4.5 to 9.0 metres killed 500,000 people, destroyed 4,000,000 houses and 3800 educational institutions. Standing crops of the entire coastal areas were destroyed and the following years marked a declining tendency in the agricultural productivity due to intrusion of saline water into the agricultural land.[61] The 1991 cyclone with a tidal surge ranging from 6 to 10 metres destroyed agriculture of 110,965 ha area of land, houses of the number of 642,552 and killed 138,000 people.[62] Peoples of these coastal areas were consequently settled in Chittagong Hill Tracts.[63]

Table 3.4. Erosion and Population Displacement from May to July 1992

Date	River bank erosion	Population displaced
3 May 1992	Brahmaputra and Teesta	50,000 erosion hit people living in embankment
20 May 1992	Jamuna	100,000 people by devouring 12 villages.
31 May 1992	Padma	20,000
11 July 1992	Brahmaputra	Hundreds homeless in Jamalpur Rangpur.
11 July, 1992	Jamuna	800 people homeless.
16 July, 1992	Jamuna and old Brahmaputra	15,000 families

Riverbank erosion due to environmental degradation has been a primary factor for population movement in Bangladesh. The rivers Padma, Jamuna, Meghna are vulnerable to erosion. The river Jamuna is stated to have shifted upto 19 km. towards the right, Sariakandi, Kazipur and Sirajganj are the most affected by the erosion of the river Jamuna. As estimated, within a period from 1974-81 17,632 persons have become environmental refugees in Kazipur alone. More particularly, Bhairab Railway bridge, Maniknagar, Eklashpur of Chandpur district and Hymehar have been affected by the river Meghna bank erosion from time to time.[65] Table 3.4 shows the extent of erosion and population displacement with a period from May to July 1992 even when there was no danger of flood.[66]

In 1990, 26 per cent of the South Asian population lived in urban areas compared to 50 per cent for the world, and 77 per cent in higher income nations. Within the South Asian region, Bangladesh had the fastest growth from 1965-1980, though the period 1980-90, marked a decline which stood at 6.2 per cent just below Nepal's 7.3 per cent.[67] This rapid growth of urbanization in Bangladesh is not due to the prospects of certain economic booms. It is rather symptomatic of a complete erosion and scarcity of Bangladesh's resource base.

According to a study made in 1981, the natural increase of urbanization in Dhaka was 18 per cent from 1961-74, while immigration was 74 per cent. During the same period, the natural increase of Chittagong city was 28 per cent while 43 per cent was through immigration. In Khulna the natural increase was 27 per cent and through immigration 73 per cent, in Rajshahi the natural increase of urbanization was 30 per cent against 36 per cent through immigration.[68] The floods of 1987, 1988 and the cyclone in 1991 must have swelled the numbers further though no statistics are available. It is estimated that about one and a half million people of Dhaka live in slums and squatter colonies, which comes to about 25 per cent of the total population and increased to 6 million in 1991.[69]

As seen above, sea level rise as a result of global warming would further intensify the population displacement. As predicted, 65 per cent of greater Khulna, 99 per cent of Barisal, 100 per cent of Patuakhali, 44 per cent of Noakhali and 12 per cent of Faridpur will be inundated destroying 13.74 per cent of the net cropped area and 401,600 ha of mangrove forest along with all its resources and displacing 10 per cent of the country's 110.8 million people[70] to the unaffected urban areas and neighbouring Indian states.

This population displacement is not confined to the territory of Bangladesh. Over the last four decades, millions have migrated and continued to migrate to the neighbouring Indian states of Assam, Tripura, West Bengal and Orissa.There has not been any consensus on the exact number of refugees settling in various part of India. It has been calculated at 12 to 17 million with 7 million alone in Assam. These refugees have added to its current total of 22 million. Apart from this the migration of Chakmas in CHT who have been outnumbered by the non-tribal people from coastal plains, to Indian states, due to increasing land man ratio, scarcity of resources and ethnic conflict will show the causative importance of environmental scarcity of resources in displacing people from their homelands. To dilute the disruptive forces in CHT the Government of Bangladesh encouraged settlement from the plain and also the distressed people affected by flood and cyclone were rehabilitated there.

Contrary to the denials by the Bangladesh government, Bangladeshi refugees are found in large numbers in New Delhi and Mumbai. While the Government of India declares that there are about 1,00,000 Bangladeshi migrants in Delhi, intelligence estimates the figure at 200,000. A slum neighbourhood in East Delhi is reported to have housed nearly 3000 Bangladeshi migrant families.[72]

As projected from the continued migration from Bangladesh to India, by the year 2020, there will be 220 million Bangladeshis and one billion Indians competing for land and job.[73]

Domestic Problems And Differences

Economic decline and population movement induced by the environmental scarcity of resources along with other factors, have been responsible for creation of many fissures and cleavages in the social and political structure of the South Asian states. South Asia has already been a region of ethnically divided societies. The existing differences and ethnic conflict involving states and rising security concerns among states, both economy and environment of the region have taken downward turn in recent years.

Ethnic Divides

The ethnic crisis that exists between the tribal Chakmas and the non-tribal Bengalis in the Chittagong Hill Tracts of Bangladesh has had its roots in history dating from the British rule. The Chittagong Hill Tracts

Regulation of 1900 awarded a special exclusive status to the tribal of CHT. Though aimed at stemming the tide of Bengalization, it marked the onset of a process of enslavement.[74] It subjected the hill people to all kinds of subordination and exploitation by their British overlords and was far from being a charter for regional autonomy. [75] The policy of the subsequent Pakistan and Bangladesh governments by abolishing this special excluded status, opened up the resourceful CHT to all kinds of economic and political penetration of the non-tribal Bengalis. The people from the cyclone and flood affected low lying areas of the plains continue to migrate to CHT in large numbers. However, in the earlier period a deliberate policy of depopulation was undertaken by the government in order to dilute their tribal identity which was mustering strong.[76] This was "by encouraging massive influx of plain people into the bountiful CHT. The resettlement and rehabilitation of disaster prone and affected people from the plains resulted in outnumbering the original tribals to the utter disenchantment of the latter. Adding to these woes of being reduced to a minority in their own land, the Kaptai hydroelectricity project which displaced more than 100,000 tribal people as refugees and inundated 1036 sq. km of CHT.[77] and the establishment of other industries like Paper Mills, Timber and Ply Wood Industries, and Rayon and Chemicals Ltd, attracted outsiders. This stoked the fire of discontentment against the Bangladesh Government in the CHT area. All these resulted in reduced land man ratio and declining scope for employment and economic sustenance in an ambience of stiff competition and challenges forged by the plain migrants. According to an estimate, the ratio of tribal and non-tribal, which was 90.9:9.1 in 1951 plummeted to 67.1: 33.9 in 1980.[78] Thus, continuing resource scarcity due to massive migration, lack of access to power and economic livelihood of the tribal people, combined together to turn their long history of passive resistance against the state into an open armed rebellion against the government of Bangladesh.[79]

Socio-economic Divides, Financial Crisis and Growing State Incapability

Bangladesh inherited two colonial masters who largely defined its state structure. When it was within undivided India, it was under British colonialism and after partition of India, it remained a part of Pakistan despite geographical incongruity. It was economically and politically exploited by the West Pakistanis who dominated and controlled the helm of affairs of the state. Thus, external dependence and political and economic distortions with state dominating all affairs, largely defined the extent and nature of allocation, distribution and use of productive forces. The state was bolstered up to mediate by the class which had the unrestricted concentration of economic power.

After the creation of Bangladesh, the same trend shows signs of continuance of the apparatus of the state. State remained in the hands of a politico-military bureaucratic and industrial complex in association with the few economically rich class of both urban and rural areas of the state to define the task of allocation and distribution and use of resources.[80]

The search for legitimacy for the government and its stability also finds its expression in social cleavages. After independence huge amount of financial help and aid streamed to Bangladesh. In order to perpetuate themselves in power different regimes found it expedient to use aid resources for reinforcing their control over developmental process through a coalesce of an urban and rural economic rich class. While populist slogans and concerns for the upliftment of the poor continue to constitute the rhetoric of the regimes, specifically the new military regime after the coup de tat overthrowing the elected government in 1975, to enlarge its acceptability among the people, the urban rich was given economic largesse in terms of transfer of nationalized industries to private hands, increasing bank credit and accommodation for contractors, indentors and importers. Economic resources and political power remain concentrated in this particular urban rich group while the inequality yawned further in terms of number of peoples remaining below the poverty line and migrating to urban slums and shanty towns. In this scenario the urban poor and slum dwellers have been denied basic amenities like water, air, sanitation and electricity. The infant mortality rate is highest in the slum areas, i.e., 152 per 1000, compared to the national average of 124 per 1000.[81]

Nearly 5 per cent of the households are functionally landless and it is estimated that the extent of landless has grown faster than the population. In rural Bangladesh the distribution of income has tended to become more unequal, the share of the bottom 40 per cent of the households in the income scale has been unchanged, while the top 10 per cent have gained at the expense of a middle 40 per cent.[82] The result has been an emergence of patron-client relationship between the landowners and landless. According to Muninul Islam, the alliance of the military bureaucracy and the merchant capitalists continue to plunder the country under the guise of popular democracy with active, and quite often overbearing guidance of the donor countries and aid organizations. The meagre domestic savings, according to him, are not invested for any productive purpose while institutional credit is siphoned off by merchants and diverted to smuggling and black marketing. He notes that capital flight is rampant, poverty alleviation only gets lip service in this scenario and that the system rests on the exploitation of the poor. The increasing concentration and centralization of ownership in rural areas according to him, result in rapid rural to urban migration and dwelling urban centres.[83]

The number of people in absolute poverty is staggering in South Asian region. In Bangladesh 86 per cent of the population lives in absolute poverty. In India 40 per cent of the urban population lives below the poverty line.[84] The region's sustained GDP growth rates for the last decade have not been translated into a better life for the majority of the population.

The mechanism of economic growth in South Asian countries has been such that while poverty increases, the crisis in economic structure manifests itself increasingly in the form of a financial crisis.[85] While the percentage below the poverty line remains high, the budget deficit increases rapidly as does the deficit in the balance of payments. For example, in India the budget deficit as a percentage of total government revenue increased from 29.9 per cent in 1976 to 48.9 per cent in 1986.[86]

There is a similar sharp rise in the balance of trade deficit in these countries. For example, during the period 1970-1984 the trade deficit increased in Bangladesh from US $ 426 million to US $ 1690 million. The rapidly rising budget and balance of trade deficit have created problems of debt servicing—the ratio of debt services to export earnings from goods and services has remained in Bangladesh at 18 per cent. The level of debt servicing in this country is so high that substantial reserve resource flow is beginning to take place. Over the period 1975 to 1985, capital intensity of manufacturing increased from 24 per cent to 35 per cent in Bangladesh.These changes indicate a declining employment generation capability of the economy for given growth rates of GNP. It is unlikely in Bangladesh, that the declining employment elasticity with respect to output can be compensated by accelerating growth in GNP in an attempt to increase employments. There seems to be a tendency for increasing unemployment.

This is further compounded by the growing population and labour force profile of Bangladesh. It is characterized by the predominance of young people. The percentage distribution of population by age group in 1988 shows that the below 15 age group accounts for 46 per cent in Bangladesh.[88] According to a projection, the distribution of population by age would change over time. A recent World Bank Report shows the people in the age group 15-64 seeking jobs in 1993 are 52 per cent in

Bangladesh.[89] It seems by the year 2025, Bangladesh age structure will change in favour of the older groups. The country will have more people in the age group 15-64, meaning there will be more pressure for jobs. In Bangladesh, it will be 68.4 per cent. Bangladesh is also characterized by widespread poverty and unacceptably low standard of living for many of its people.[90] The increase in the number of people in this category over the period was 47 per cent. In both categories, not only was there an increase in the number of people but an increase in the percentage of the population below the poverty line.[91]

The state of health of the majority of the population of Bangladesh can be judged by the fact that a majority of its population does not have access over safe drinking water. As seen above, a large number of people are dying due to various water borne diseases such as cholera, typhoid, dysentery, etc.[92]

The proportion of population in the working age bracket in South Asia in 1990 stood at 57.7 per cent compared to 61.1 per cent for the world and 67.2 per cent for high income economics. Within the region the proportion in Bangladesh was much lower than the average 51.6 per cent.[93] But largely due to varying female labour force participating rates not all of those of working age join the labour force. Bangladesh has a very low labour force participation rates –29.1 per cent in 1989.[94]

The above analysis is suggestive of the fact that the majority of the people in Bangladesh remain deprived of the basic human needs and necessities. Poverty, malnutrition, unemployment are on the increase. This further shows that the demands of the people on the states would be mounting in future. The states with their national indebtedness reaching intolerably high levels, spending excessively on their apparatuses, military and bureaucratic establishments would be balked in their efforts to ameliorate the deplorable economic derivation of the people due to a plethora of reasons of which environmental degradation and environmental scarcity of resources are preponderant factors. As the environmental management experts have noted "some of the most serious and pervasive environmental problems facing developing countries tend to be both a cause and effect of poverty.[95] Poverty increases vulnerability to effects of environmental degradation and on the other hand environmental degradation or environmental scarcity of resources contribute to the continuation of poverty. Poverty and environmental degradation are, thus mutually reinforcing. Given the limited availability of sufficient job creation and income generation opportunities in the agricultural sector, industrial growth becomes essential in Bangladesh. Development process that has taken a complex pattern of industrialized agriculture, industrialization and urbanization instead of decreasing vulnerabilities to the effects of environmental degradation, more often increase these vulnerabilities.[96] For example, industrialization will increase greenhouse gases and disaster proneness. Improved human and animal health and nutrition have been one cause of over population in some regions resulting in overgrazing and land depletion to the point of environmental deterioration and ecological crisis. Populations have moved to urban centres for possible productive employment but, because of lack of proper planning and necessary wherewithals they have inhabited lands which are susceptible to flooding and other health, sanitary and settlement problems. Thus, environment has become often the point of interface between development and programming and vulnerabilities to disasters[97] and other effects of environmental degradation. So this growing incapability of Bangladesh to meet their people's burgeoning aspirations and demand, is added considerable political instability where much of economic and political wherewithals necessary for development, are spent by their respective governments to perpetuate themselves in power. So growing discrepancy between the state capability and the increased demands of the population for basic human needs on the former would create conditions for civil violence and conflict.

Effects of Indian Diversion at Farakka on Bangladesh

Reduced River Flow

As all the rivers except for one small river in Bangladesh, have their origin outside the country, the impact of the main diversion of water through the Farakka Barrage by India has been disastrous on the balance of the riverine eco-system of Bangladesh. South-west Bangladesh dependent exclusively on Ganges water could have been affected by the reduced flows of the river Ganges. Two distributaries, the Gorai and Arial Khan rivers withdrawing water from the Ganges in Bangladesh are affected by Indian diversion. But as opined by Crow, "the relationship between the flow in the river Ganges and the flow in its major tributaries may not be direct".[98] Natural events in the upper catchments can result in low flows in the Gorai. The low flows recorded in the river Gorai during the years 1975-76 and 1976-77, according to Special Studies, are more due to Indian diversion, than due to natural events. But the causal linkage between the two cannot be so firmly established.

Flood

There are many causes of flooding in Bangladesh of which could be the deforestation in the Himalayas, bad agricultural practice in the catchment areas of the Ganges, Brahmaputra and Meghna, in India and Nepal melting of the Himalayan snow and above all, various obstructions created within Bangladesh. As alleged, the Farakka as well as other barrages and dams over the common rivers in India, have contributed largely to its intensity and frequency. Release of silt from water into the upstream pushing a vast amount of silt into the downstream has decreased the carrying capacity of the rivers. As studies show, 30 per cent of the country is subjected to flood due to the spill over from major rivers. While 40 per cent of the country is flooded from small rivers[99]. More than 80 per cent of the flood run off is brought from outside the country of which 90 per cent is contributed by major rivers.[100] Decreased forest cover may have contributed to increased flooding and decreased dry season flood, but the extent to which sedimentation and flooding can be attributed to recent changes in forest cover is debatable.[101] As Bangladesh Government stated, the intensity and duration of flooding in the Ganges in Bangladesh has increased since the operation of Farakka Barrage in comparison to the pre-Farakka Barrage conditions.[102]

Salinity Intrusion

It is alleged that the south-western region of Bangladesh is seriously affected by higher soil salinity, as marked increase in salinity both in surface and ground waters is caused by upstream diversion of the Ganges waters. Report by the Bangladesh government is of the view that "the salinity of Khulna area shot up from 380 micro-mhos/cm in the pre-diversion period to about 29,500 micro-mhos/cm in April 1992". At present, as the report goes on, more than 25,900 sq km. is devastatingly affected by salinity, covering the districts of Kushtia, Jessore, Khulna, Faridpur and Barisal.[103]

The damaging effects of increased salinity have been in terms of crop damage and diminishing agricultural products increasing incidence of water borne diseases and disruption in industrial operations around the Khulna belt.

Decline in Agricultural Productivity

The Indian withdrawal at Farakka has hit Bangladesh's agriculture worst, Ganges-Kodhadak project has already lost its pumping capacity by 60 per cent, due to non-availability of water. Soil moisture deficiency in the south-west region has already resulted in yield reduction. As studies show, "the direct losses caused in agriculture sector due to soil moisture depletion, delayed planting and increased salinity at 1991 price level exceeded Tk. 5000 million per annum.[104] To the contrary, India held these allegations untenable.[105] The Special Studies[106] and White Paper[107] affirm the damaging consequences of Farakka diversion for the agriculture of the region.

Decline in Fish Catch

Due to change in hydrological and hydrobiological conditions to the lower reaches of the Ganges and its distributaries, fish production has seriously declined. Bangladesh claimed that the Indian diversion dwindled the fish catches "probably because of the disturbance of the historic food chain and inability of the fish to tolerate shallow depths and the unprecedented levels of salinity."[108] India refuted this saying hilsa catch could not have been affected because it took place during these monsoons when the barrage did not divert water from the Ganges.[109] According to the recent report published by the Bangladesh government, Hilsa was affected the most and its catch dwindled alarmingly over the years in the post Farakka era".[110]

Decreased Forest Cover

Degradation of the coastal ecosystem is the direct consequence of increased salinity due to Indian diversion. Increased salinity has spelled disaster to the generation and regeneration of Sundari trees accounting for 60 per cent of the total marketable timber of the Sundarbans. The wild life, aquatic habitats, various species of plants and trees are facing extinction due to increase in soil salinity as a result of which the delicate ecological balance of this largest natural mangrove forest has been affected. The Indian government's "The Farakka Barrage" commented that its withdrawal had no effect on Sundarbans.[111] But the evidences suggest that there is a close causal linkage between Indian diversion and decline in Sundarbans forest cover in Bangladesh.[112]

Reduced Ground Water

The south-west region dependent on Ganges water is seriously affected by a fast lowering of the ground water table due to Indian diversion. A survey conducted on the status of ground water level in 1992 in 3300 unions of Bangladesh indicated that, the water table comes down below 10 metre from the pre-diversion levels by 100 per cent in Rajshahi, 80 per cent in Pabna and 64 per cent in Faridpur.[113] But the Special Studies suggested that there were significant changes in the ground water levels in the years in question due to various reasons, but the blame could not be entirely put on Indian diversion.[114]

Disruption in Navigation

According to Bangladesh government, the Indian diversion at Farakka made navigation difficult or impossible in many of the river channels of south-west Bangladesh. The reduction of the Ganges flows have made more than 350 km. of navigable route completely inoperative during the dry months.[115]

Healths Hazards

The reduction of the Ganges flows has resulted in the outbreak of widespread diarrhoea, cholera and other diseases in the areas dependent on the Ganges water. Low flows of the Ganges induced high salinity in drinking water in the Khulna zone creating various hazards. Though the permissible limit for drinking water by WHO is only 500 ppm. The people in the area are drinking water of 1200 ppm.

Disruption in Industrial Sector

In its White Paper, the Bangladesh government claimed that the increased salinity had affected seriously the industrial sector. Serious industrial disruption occurred because power stations, paper mills and jute processors were unable to use highly saline water. The consequences have been in terms of closing down industries in this area forcing many thousands out of their jobs and incurring a heavy financial loss.

Dispute over Land Formation

With the decreasing river depth, land formation in the coastal areas has increased largely due to the absence of strong water flow that pushes the sediment far away in the sea from the coast.[116] Formation of Talpatty/ New Moore island is partly due to this reason and the question of control over it has been a point of conflict between India and Bangladesh.

Dispute over Territory due to Shifting of Rivers

Decreasing river depth has resulted in shifting of river bank erosion and shifting of the mid-channel considered as the boundary line between India and Bangladesh during flood. Erosion of the river bank of the Bangladesh side expands the claim of India to a great extent within the territory of Bangladesh. This applies in the case of the bordering rivers like Kushiara, Muhuri, Feni, Ichamati and Gumti, etc. This has been a bone of contention between India and Bangladesh. The damages in different sectors during the post diversion period from 1976-1994 due to Indian diversion, according to Bangladesh government have been pegged at Tk 117,460 million.[117]

There may be a complex array of causes of environmental degradation in Bangladesh. But the Indian diversion at Farakka has also a major share in damaging the environment in various sectors, as outlined above fig. 3.3 and 3.4 point out the consequence of Indian diversion at Farakka.

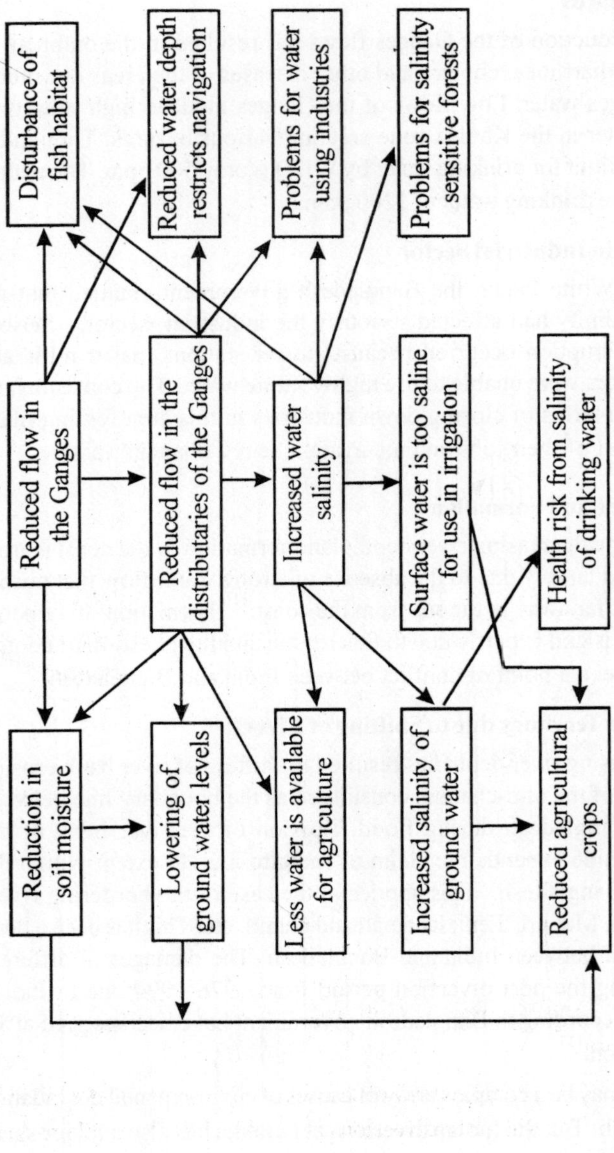

Fig. 3.3. Impact of Reduced Ganges Flow.

Source : White Paper on the Ganges Water Dispute.

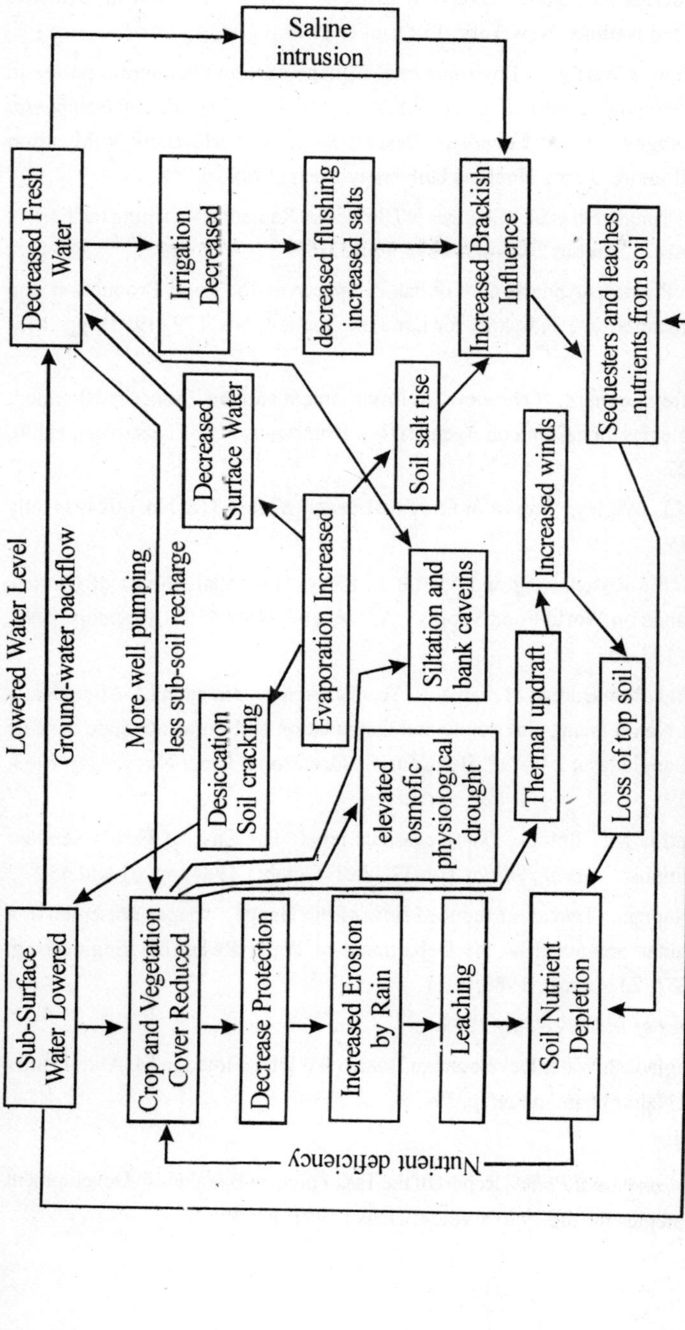

Figure 3.4. More far-reaching claims of the consequences of reduced Ganges flows.

Source : Special Stuides.

References

1. Frederick Krimgold, "Overview of the Priority Area", *Natural Disaster*, United Nations, New York, 15 October 1976.

2. Jeremy J.Warford, "Environmental management and economic policy in developing countries" in G. Schramm and J. J.Warford, *Environmental Management and Economic Development*, A World Bank Publication (Baltimore: Johns Hopkins University Press, 1989) p. 7.2.

3. J.D. Longstreth et.al. "Changes in Ultraviolet Radiation Reaching the Earth's Surface", Ambio 24, No.3, 1995, pp.153-65.

4. Per Pinstrup-Anderson, "Global Perspectives for Food Production and Consumption", Tidsskrift for Land okonomi, 4, No. 179 (1992), pp. 145-69.

5. Jeffrey Leonard, "Overview" in Environment and the Poor : Development Strategies for a Common Agenda (New Brunswick, N.J.: Transaction, 1989), p. 27.

6. T.M.L. Wigley, "Impact of Extreme Events" *Nature* 316, No. 6024, 11 July 1985.

7. Cynthia Rosenzweig and Martin L. Parry, "Potential Impact of Climate Change on World Food Supply", *Nature* 367, No. 6459, 13 January 1994, pp. 133-38.

8. Bangladesh Bureau of Statistics, Year Book, also quoted in M. Abdul Hafiz and Nahid Islam, Environmental Degradation and Intra/Interstate conflict in Bangladesh, *ENCOP*, Bern/Zurich, Occasional Paper No. 6, May 1993, p. 39.

9. Cynthia McClintock, "Why peasants rebel: The Case of Peru's Sendero Luminoso" *World Politics* Vol. 37, No.1, October 1984, pp. 61 and 63.

10. A Hannan, "Impact of reduced flow of the Ganges", paper presented at a seminar organized by the Department of Water Resources Engineering, *BUET*, 23 August, 1980, p. 11.

11. *Times of India*, 28 July 1993.

12. Bangladesh Water Development Board (BWDB) quoted in M. Abdul Hafiz and Nahid Islam, *op.cit*, p. 39.

13. *Ibid*

14. *Environmental Policy*, Report of the Task Force on Bangladesh Development Strategies for the 1990's Vol. 4, Dhaka 1991, p. 64.

15. Bangladesh–Recent Economic Development and Short Term Prospect, Document of the World Bank, Report No.7596-BD, 13 March 1989, p. 35.

16. BWDB 1987 and MOT 1988, Ministry of Irrigation, Water Development and Blood Control, 1987 and 1988, Dhaka 1987 and 1988.

17. *Ibid.*

18. *Disaster Mitigation in Asia and the Pacific*, Manila, Asian Development Bank, 1991, p. 92.

19. M.Imhoff et.al., "Monsoon flood boundary delineation and damage assessment using space borne imaging radar and land sat data", *Photogrametric Engineering and Remote Sensing* 53, 1986, pp. 405-413.

20. Managing the Development Process, *Report of the Task Force on Bangladesh Development Strategies for the 1990's* Vol. II (Dhaka: UPL. 1991), p. 137

21. *Ibid.*

22. *UN. ESCAP, ST/ESCAP* 618 : Coastal Environmental Management Plan for Bangladesh Vol. 2, Final Report, Bangkok.

23. "Impact on Bangladesh due to withdrawals at Farakka of dry season Ganges flow", A Report received from Farroq Shovan, the Foreign Secretary of People's Republic of Bangladesh on October 1995.

24. *Environmental Policy*, op.cit., p. 101.

25. Government of the People's Republic of Bangladesh, Study on the Causes and Consequences of Natural Disasters and Protection and Preservation of the Environment, Dhaka, December 1989, Chapter 3, p. 14.

26. *Regional Study on Greenhouse Effect and Its Impact on the Region.* SAARC, Kathmandu, December, 1992, p. 54.

27. R.Peters and T.Lovejoy, ed. *Global Warming and Biological Diversity* (New Haven: Yale University Press, 1992).

28. F.U.Mahtab, *Effects of Climate Changes and Sea Level Rise on Bangladesh* (London: Commonwealth Secretariat, 1989), pp. 1-10.

29. "Impact on Bangladesh due to withdrawals at Farakka of dry season Ganges flow", *op.cit.*

30. *Environmental Policy*, *op. cit.*, p. 160.

31. *Ibid.*

32. Bangladesh Environment and Natural Resources Assessment Final Report, prepared for the US Development and Washington D.C. 1992, p. 22.

33. M. Abdul Hafiz and Nahid Islam, *op.cit.* p. 42.

34. Shaukat Hassan, "Environmental Issues and Security in South Asia", Adelphi Papers No. 262, 1991, p. 13.
35. Environmental Policy, *op.cit.*, p. 23
36. *Ibid.*, p. 126.
37. See for details, Government of the People's Republic of Bangladesh, *op.cit.*, chapter 9, pp. 1-5.
38. Impact on Bangladesh due to Withdrawal at Farakka of dry season Ganges flows, *op.cit.*, p. 18.
39. *Ibid.*, pp. 4-5.
40. A Atiq Rahman, Salimul Haque and Gordon R. Conway, *Environmental Aspect of Surface Water System of Bangladesh* (Dhaka, UPL, 1990), p. 180.
41. Managing the Development Process, Report of the Task Force on Bangladesh Development Strategies for the 1990's, Vol. II.
42. Government of Bangladesh, "Deadlock on the Ganges, cited in Khursida Begum", *Tension over the Farakka Barrage : A Techno-Political Tangle in South Asia* (Dhaka: UPL, 1987), p. 143.
43. Norman Myers, "Environment and security", *Foreign Policy*, No. 81, 1991: Thomas Homer Dixon "On the threshold: Environmental Changes as Causes of Acute Conflict", *International Security* 16: 2, 1991, p. 77.
44. E. El. Hinnawi, *Environmental Refugees*, UN Environmental Programme, Nairobi (Kenya) 1985, p. 4.
45. N. Meyers, "Environmental dimension to security issues", Environmentalist 6, 1986, pp. 251-57 : A.H. Westing, "Environmental refugees: A growing category of displaced person" *Environmental Conservation* (Geneva) 19(3) Autumn 1992 pp. 201-7 : J. Widgren, "International migration and regional stability", *International Affairs* (Cambridge) 66, 1990, pp. 149-66.
46. Anthony H.Richmond, "Reactive Migration: Sociological Perspectives on Refugee Movements", *Journal of Refugee Studies* Vol. 6, No.1, 1993, p. 16.
47. A. Giddens, *The Consequences of Modernity* (Cambridge: Polity Press, 1991), p. 171.
48. V. Suhrke and A. Vinsentin, "The environmental refugee : A new approach", *Ecodecision*, September 1991, pp. 73-74.
49. *Developing the Infrastructure*, Report of the Task Force on Bangladesh Development Strategy for the 1990's Vol. 3 (Dhaka: UPL, 1991), p. 426.
50. *World Bank Development Report 1992* (Oxford: Oxford University Press, 1992) Poverty in the Developing World 1985-2000.

51. Nafis Sadik, *The State of the World Population 1991* (New York: United Nations Population Fund, 1991) p. 43.

52. Homer Dixon, "Environmental scarcities and violent conflict: Evidence from cases", *International Security* Vol. 19, No. 1, Summer 1994, p. 21.

53. James Boyce, *Agrarian Impasse in Bengal : Institutional Constraints to Technological Change* (Oxford : Oxford University Press, 1987), p. 9.

54. Impact on Bangladesh due to withdrawal at Farakka of dry season Ganges flows, *op.cit.*

55. Elizabeth Abbott, "Where Ganges run flows", *Equinox* Vol. 10, No. 59, (September-October, 1991), p. 43.

56. World Bank Document No.7597/BD, 13 March 1989, p. 19.

57. *Ibid.*, p. 35.

58. *Ibid.*, p. 19.

59. M. Abdul Hafiz and Nahid Islam, *ENCOP, op.cit.*, p. 47.

60. Atiur Rahman, *Impact of Riverbank Erosion : Survival Strategies of Displacees* (Dhaka: Bangladesh Institute of Development Studies, 1985), p. 11.

61. Monirul Qader Mirza and Subroto Pal, Centre for Environmental Studies and Research (Dhaka, February 1992), p. 104.

62. *Ibid.*

63. Shaukat Hassan, *op. cit.*

64. M.K. Elahi, River Bank Erosion, Flood and Population Displacement, A Report on River Bank Impact Study, Dhaka, 1990, cited in Monirul Qader and Subroto PaL, *op. cit.*

65. *Ibid.*

66. *The Daily Star* (National Daily, 3 May, 20 May, 31 May, 11 July, 16 July) 1992.

67. *World Bank Development Report*, 1992, *op.cit.*, p.45.

68. *Developing the Infrastructure*, *op. cit.*, p. 416.

69. P.P. Majumdar, "Basti Jibaner Gatishilata o Sthabirata" (Bengali) Bangladesh *Unnayan Samikka*, BIDs, Dhaka 1992, pp. 71-92.

70. *Environmental Policy*, *op.cit.*, p. 179. See also Regional Study, op.cit., p. 53.

71. See Homer Dixon, *op.cit.*, p. 22, Robert G. Gosselink, Minority rights and ethnic conflict in Assam, India", *Boston College Third World Law Journal,*

Vol. XIV, No.1 Winter 1994, pp. 90-91. Amulya Ganguly, "Bangladeshi lebensraum", *Times of India*, 13 July 1992: Sanjoy Hazarika, "Bangladesh and Assam: Land pressures, migration and ethnic conflict". Occasional Paper No. 3, *Project on Environmental Change and Acute Conflict*, A Joint Project of the University of Totonto and the American Academy of Arts and Sciences, March, 1993, pp. 52-54.

72. Sanjoy Hazarika, *Ibid.*, p. 54.
73. *Ibid.*, p. 61.
74. Edward H. Spicer, quoted in George P. Castille and Gilbert Kushner ed., *Persistent Peoples: Cultural Enclaves in Perspective* (Tucson: University of Arizona Press, 1981).
75. R.H.Sneyd Hutchinson, *An Account of the Chittagong Hill Tracts* (Calcutta: Bengal Secretariat Book Depot 1906), p. 32.
76. G. Rizvi, "Bangladesh: Insurgency in the Hills", *The Round Table*, 305, 1988, p. 42.
77. Bangladesh District Gazetteers, *Chittagong Hill Tracts* 42, (Dacca : Bangladesh Government Press, 1971). See also Almut Mey and Wolfgang Mey, quoted in Willem Van Schendel, "The invention of the Jummas: State formation and ethnicity in Southeastern Bangladesh", *Modern Asian Studies*, (26), 1, 1992, p. 117. See also Nafis Ahmed, *A New Economy Geography of Bangladesh* (Delhi: Vikas, 1976), p. 123.
78. M. Abdul Hafiz et.al., *op.cit.*, p. 50.
79. See Ratan Lal Chakravarty, "Chakma Resistance to Early British Rule", *Bangladesh Historical Studies*, 2, 1997, pp. 133-56, Sirajul Islam, "Tribal Resistance in Chittagong Hill Tracts", in Nishit Ranjan Ray, ed., *Saga of Freedom* (Delhi: People's Publishing House, 1983), pp. 122-129.
80. Rural Poverty in Bangladesh: A Report to the Like Minded Group (Dhaka: UPL 1990), p. 109.
81. *Bangladesh Environment and Natural Resources Assessment*, Final Report, prepared for the US Agency for International Development by the World Resource Institute, Center for International Development and Environment, Washington, D.C. 1992, p. 23.
82. Environment Policy, *op.cit.*, p. 19.
83. Muinul Islam, "Natural calamities and environmental refugees in Bangladesh", *Refugee* Vol. 12, No.1, June 1992, p. 9.
84. *The State of the World's Children 1987* (New York UNICEF, 1987).

85. A. Hussain, "Is our crisis financial or real ?" *The Monthly Herald*, August 1989, Karachi.

86. M. S. Ahluwalia, N.G. Carter and H.B. Chenery, "Growth and poverty in developing countries", *Journal of Development Economics* Vol. 6, No. 3, 1979, Table 1, *World Bank, World Development Report 1987* (New York: Oxford University Press, 1987) Table 3, UNIDO *Industry and Development Global Report 1987*, Vienna, 1987, UNCTAD, *Handbook of International Trade and Development Statistics*, New York, UN 1987, Table 6.2.

87. Akmal Hussain, *Resource Depletion and Sustainable Development in South Asia*. Asia Panel Meetings of IUCN, The World Conservation Union, Perth, Australia, 26-27 November 1990, p. 5.

88. ESCAP, *Population Data Sheet 1985* (Bangkok: ESCAP), and Population Projections.

89. Structure of population in South Asia and other regions, See *World Development Report 1992* (Oxford: Oxford University Press, 1992), quoted in Atique Rahman, et.al., *Exploding the Population Myth*, *op.cit.*, p. 53. *World Development Report 1985*, p. 210, Table 2.

90. World Bank, *World Development Report 1994* (Oxford : Oxford University Press, 1994), p. 95.

91. Quoted in Akmal Hussain, *op.cit.*, Table 9, p. 28.

92. Akmal Hussain, *Strategic Issues in Pakistan's Economic Policy, 1988, Introductory Essay : Is Pakistan's Growth Plan Sustainable ?* (Lahore: Progressive Publishers, 1988).

93. *World Development Report 1995*, *op.cit.*, Table 25, p. 210.

94. *World Development Report 1992*, *op.cit.*

95. Gunter Schramm and Jeremy J.Warford, "Introduction" to volume on *Environmental Management and Economic Development*, A World Bank Publication, *ibid*, p. 1.

96. See Mary B.Anderson, "A reconceptualization of the linkages between disasters and development", *Disasters: The International Journal of Disaster Studies and Practices*, Harvard Supplement Vol. 9, 1995, p. 46.

97. *Ibid.*, "Analysing the costs and benefits of natural disaster responses in the context of development", *Environment Working Paper*, No. 29, May 1990, World Bank, Environment Department, p. 4.

98. Ben Crow et.al., *Sharing the Ganges: The Politics and Technology of River Development* (London: Thousand Oaks, 1995), p. 131.

99. Md. N. Huda and J.U. Chowdhury, Floods and Erosion, paper presented at a regional conference on Floods and Erosion, Dhaka, 7-10 September 1989, p. 9.

100. Amjad H. Khan, Flood Problems and Prospects—A Regional Overview, Keynote Address on a Regional Conference on Flood and Erosion, Dhaka, 7-10 September, 1989.

101. See J. Ives "Floods in Bangladesh: Who is to blame ?" *New Scientist*, 13 April, 1991.

102. People's Republic of Bangladesh, Impact on Bangladesh Due to Withdrawals at Farakka of Dry Season Ganges Flows, a report received from Foreign Secretary, Peoples Republic of Bangladesh, on 30 October 1995.

103. *Ibid.*

104. *Ibid.*

105. External Publicity Division, Ministry of External Affairs, Government of India, New Delhi, *The Farakka Barrage*, September 1976.

106. People's Republic of Bangladesh, Bangladesh Water Development Board (BWDB) International Engineering Co. Ltd (IECO, San Francisco and Dhaka) and Special Studies Directorate of the BWDB, September 1977.

107. Government of the People's Republic of Bangladesh, A Summary Deadlock on the Ganges, September 1976, pp. 6-8.

108. Bangladesh, *White Paper on the Ganges Water Dispute*, Dhaka, September 1976, pp. 14-15.

109. India, Ministry of External Affairs, *Farakka Barrage*, New Delhi, 1976, pp. 14-15.

110. People's Republic of Bangladesh, *Impact on Bangladesh, op.cit.*

111. India, Ministry of External Affairs, *The Farakka Barrage*, *op.cit.*, p. 15.

112. See Ben Crow, *op. cit.*, p. 154.

113. People's Republic of Bangladesh, *Impact on Bangladesh, op.cit.*

114. Special Studies, op.cit, Vol. B, p. V-41.

115. People's Republic of Bangladesh, *Impact on Bangladesh, op. cit.*

116. M. Abdul Hafiz and Nahid Islam, "Environmental Degradation and Intra-interstate Conflict in Bangladesh", ENCOP *Occasional Paper* No. 6, May 1993, Bern/Zurich, pp. 15-16.

117. People's Republic of Bangladesh, *Impact on Bangladesh, op.cit.*

4

Environmental Conflict : Intra-Inter State

The conflicts arising or showing signs of having erupted from a host of social effects due to environmental degradation or environmental scarcity of resources, can come under this category. For example, if a group of people migrating from one region to another region within a country or from one country to another country meet an indigenous group of different ethnic and religious origin, a clash may occur between the two which may appear as ethnic or religious on the surface, but underneath their movement lies environmental degradation, resulting in what is called as group identity conflict.[1]

Neither the Chittagong Hill Tracts (CHT) nor its 700,000 indigenous peoples are widely known. In terms of physical geography the CHT's 13221 square kilometres are part of a much larger, heavily forested but largely inaccessible and remote mountain range, stretching for 1800 kilometres from western Burma to an area where it merges with the eastern Himalayas in China. Its present-day incorporation within Bangladesh is the historical product of the post 1860 British advance to the east and northeast of Bengal, in order to provide a buffer zone, (a) less famous equivalent of its North-West Frontier) for its burgeoning Indian empire. This artificial boundary demarcation prefigured the political separation of the CHT at the end of British rule, in 1947, from Myanmar(Burma) to the south, and the Indian states of Tripura and Mizoram to the north and east. Despite their close ethnic-cultural affinities with other peoples of Sino-Tibetan origin in these states, and the lack of ethnic or religious identity with Bengalis, the Chakma, Marma, Tripura and nine or 10 other ethnographically diverse tribal peoples of the CHT found themselves instead in (East) Pakistan.[2]

It is what has been happening to these peoples since 1947, and more particularly since the Bengali secession from Pakistan to form an independent Bangladesh in 1971. A number of concerned nongovernmental organizations (NGOs) have closely monitored their situation and in more than one instance have unequivocally accused the Bangladeshi government of committing genocide against the jummas—the term of collective self-identification used by CHT peoples in recent years.[3] Survival International, which works for tribal peoples worldwide, has noted their extreme plight claiming a figure of 125000 fatalities since 1947. The International Labour Organisation has spoken of the calculated annihilation of the tribals. In 1984 the Anti-slavery Society forecast that genocide would result if nothing was done.

Amnesty International, always more circumspect in its choice of terms, nevertheless issued a report at the height of the killings in 1986, which charged genocide in all but name. Scholars, notably the anthropologist Wolfgang Mey, have added their voice.[4] With little evidence that the 1989 change from military government to democratic rule had tangibly improved jumma fortunes, and by this time with an estimated 10 per cent of the refugees in neighbouring Tripura, a number of agencies came together as the CHT Commission to investigate the situation fully at first hand. Their report "Life is Not Ours", published in May 1991, spoke of a genocidal process[5] which two sequels appeared to confirm as a long-term trend.

By contrast, the Bangladeshi government has vigorously refuted these charges as totally baseless and preposterous allegations a claim founded on the counter charge that their source was 'disgruntled', 'misguided' or 'miscreant' 'troublemakers'[6] This has usually been a shorthand for the Parbottya Chattagram Jana Sanghati Samiti (JSS), the largely Chakma-recruited Chittagong Hill Tracts Peoples Solidarity Association which the Bangladeshi government has consistently accused of working in the interests of a foreign power', namely India.[7] If the implication here is that the NGOs are credulous Western do-gooders who have been unscrupulously duped into meddling in matters which they do not understand, the Bangladeshi government is not alone in arguing that the threat to the Jummas has been exaggerated. At the first conference of the Association of Genocide Scholars in 1995. Ted Gurr entirely excluded them from a long list of South East Asian minorities in danger, more recently placing them in a medium risk or even residual category only. Neither do the jummas appear in Harff and Gurr's list of genocide and politicide victims since 1945, nor in the recent global survey by Helen Fein.[8]

Adjudicating on which story to believe is not helped by the fact that the CHT has been a militarily controlled area, mostly off-limits to would be independent observers, since 1964. Reports of atrocities and massacres reach the outside world either via the JSS which might be argued to have a vested interest in their exposure, or a Bangladeshi government obversely intent on denying that anything of the kind took place or, if it did, blaming it on the Shanti Bahini (literally 'Peace Force'), the jumma guerrilla army closely linked to the JSS. But the problem is seriously compounded by Western perceptions of Bangladesh. A new state founded in 1971 out of an extremely bloody secession from Pakistan, Bangladesh has always been considered in the camp of the 'victims' not the 'perpetrators', 1971 itself, with its mass rapes and murders to the tune of possibly three million fatalities, began this process.[9] This genocidal trauma was succeeded by a series of other 'natural' disasters which led to the death or economic ruination of further millions. With a massive population increase, insufficient industrial capacity with which to absorb the excess and 85 per cent of its development funds coming from Western aid.[10] Bangladesh has often been treated as a basket case which, in the circumstances, could be excused its proclivity towards authoritarian military rule. What happened in the CHT especially in the late 1970s and early 1980s, was thus clouded not simply by Bangladeshi but also Western agendas to commence radical remedial programmes aimed at pulling the country clear of the dependency trap.

Bangladesh operates on the notion that it is a nationally homogeneous and hence unitary state, a statement which would be true were it not for the relatively small number of adivasi ('tribal' peoples) which include the jumma of the CHT in the east, as well as other groups such as the Garo and Santal peoples in the north. Yet while Bengali ethnic prejudice against the adivasi as a whole is an element in the genocidal equation, it is notable that the Garo and Santal, despite their acute degradation and marginalisation, have not been targeted for elimination.[11] The jummas, dubious distinction lies in the fact that they traditionally inhabit and claim land rights in the CHT which amount to 10 per cent of Bangladesh's territory and whose assets the state specifically wishes to realise and consolidate in the interests of its nation and state building. Or, as two senior army officers are alleged to have proclaimed at a public meeting in Panchari in 1979. We want the land and not the people of the CHT.[12]

It is Bangladesh's developmental agenda rather than the specific attributes or ideological leanings of particular military or civil administrations, which have determined that the state's long-term objective with regard to the CHT includes 'getting rid' of the Jumma. But different actors, especially during the period of military rule from 1975 to 1989, with varying formulations of how most rapidly and effectively to achieve this goal, have shaped its increasingly genocidal tendencies. The contradictions in the situation are as follows. First, the state officially considers all citizens of Bangladesh as full members of the Bengali nation. But it acknowledges that the adivasis are culturally distinct and so proposes to resolve the discrepancy by leading them rapidly into the mainstream.[13] 'Getting rid' of the jumma, in other words, has always been intended to follow the least toxic, least genocidal but nevertheless compulsory path-assimilation. Second, at no time, even during the worst years of military atrocity in the CHT between 1979 and 1986, has there been a sustained moment of genocide. Although there has been no single 'moment' of genocide and though successive governments behaviour with regard to the CHT has been complicated by intermittent, usually clandestine (and more recently official) negotiations for a settlement with the JSS or Shanti Bahini, the overall situation has been one of more than 20 years sustained crisis in which the state has employed the gamut of genocidal strategies. These include the militarisation of the whole region, swamping it with Bengali immigrants, placing the Jummas in cluster villages under military surveillance and denying them access to the commons and forests to sustain their livelihood and life integrity, persistent human rights violations, including disappearances, repeated rape, vandalisation and desecration of religious (especially Buddhist) sites and shrines, destruction of villages and property, physical and mental abuse of individuals, repeated killings, especially though not exclusively of known Jumma activists, leaders, professionals, monks and nuns and finally some 13 major massacres extended over the period 1980 to 1993. These actions taken together would certainly constitute genocide within the meaning of the 1948 convention.[14]

Kuper, Fein, Dadrian, Harff and Gurr have all treated genocidal attacks on indigenous peoples as a distinct category within their various typologies, Fein, for instance, calling this category 'developmental' genocide.[15] These scholars do not seek, hierarchically, to order the annihilation of indigenous peoples as less significant or less noteworthy than other genocides, and indeed in some instances have compiled detailed 'fourth world' case studies.

Indigenous peoples in the Indian subcontinent and beyond have been the subject of received wisdom largely emanating from 19th century anthropologists. These claim for the 'tribes'– itself a patronising and problematic term an originality to—their inhabitated region (quite false in the Jumma case) plus evolutionist notions which stereotype them as the remnant or residue of the oldest, most primitive elements of humankind. If this depiction, on the one hand, would have them 'closer to nature' and even 'noble' in their savagery, on the other, it denotes them to the bottom of the civilisational heap, at best as exotic anachronisms, at worst as backward but marginal obstacles in the path of an ineluctable progress. This essentially Western narrative is, however, closely mirrored in a Bengali counterpart. In this, the 'innocence' and 'naivety', of the hill tribes is clearly indicated by jhuming, the shifting cultivations using slash and burn techniques traditionally practiced in the CHT forests. The alleged evolutionist gap between this 'inefficient' economic mode and the more 'advanced' plough cultivation of the plains in turn provides the rationale for a specifically Bengali version of a mission civilisation in which the childlike and jangli natives are offered the guiding, not to say uplifting, hand of their more sophisticated neighbours as they are inducted into the benefits of civilisation and modernity.[17] Implicit in both Western and Bengali narratives is the assumption that tribal cultures are doomed in the face of modernity and that servival for their members is dependent on the rapid abandonment of their traditional ways of life. Indeed, translated into a debate on genocide, some scholars have gone further, by claiming that the destruction of native societies is inevitable.

Tony Barta, for instance, attempting to apply Marxist analysis to conflict in the Australian outback, has argued that the impact of white captialist settlers on hunter-gathering aborigines precludes coexistence between the two, leading only to relations of destruction. His assertion that 'incompatible forms of economy and society are at the root of the problem shifts responsibility for aboriginal extermination from the state to the dominant settlers who usually initiate exterminatory action, often 'out of private animosities'.[18] But if the state is relegated to the background or if the killing happens without any one authority consciously or deliberately willing it, where is the genocide? The UN convention is clear that intention must be involved and although it is silent on the role of the state, it is difficult to imagine a systematic onslaught on a population which does not involve its resources and capabilities. Theirs, in fact, is a minority view. But the scholars who emphasise intent in their analyses provide little guidance as to how tribal annihilation is part of the main plot.

One weakness with the 'inevitability thesis is that it fails to take account of examples where, at least to date, the resource demands of the dominant society or state have not been overriding, as has been the case with the Garo and Santal in Bangladesh or where, as in neighbouring India, the state has found a pluralistic, albeit precarious accommodation with its many scores of 'scheduled tribes'. Another more telling failing with the thesis is its rather one-dimensional underestimation of the indigenous peoples themselves. The vibrancy, resilience and self-assertion of India's adivasi against 'developmental' encroachment has been a crucial factor in the state's recognition of their group rights.[19] In Bangladesh by contrast, it is the Jummas' very refusal to cave in under similar pressures which provides one key to the genocide.

Mark Cocker, recently writing of the turn of the century German annihilation of the Herero in South West Africa (Namibia), has noted how 'paradoxically the critical factor driving them towards a genocidal policy was a concern that these tribal peoples had shown a potential well beyond their allotted station.'[20] This has been exactly the story with the Jumma. Far from behaving according to a supposed 'passive' tribal type, they have not only absorbed and adopted the language and tools of modernity in order to make good their perceived ancestral claim to the CHT but, where this has clearly been a losing battle against greater odds, have tenaciously struggled, sometimes violently, to impede the state and dominant community's political, cultural and demographic penetration of it. Indeed, the struggle of the Jumma is directly comparable with that of the Mayan Indians of Guatemala, the Kurds in Iraq, the Tibetans, the peoples of East Timor and Irian Jaya (West Papua) as well as, looking back a century, that of the remaining unsubdued Indian tribes in "the USA. All these societies have historically or contemporaneously a commonality in their evolving sense of collective peoplehood and identity forged in the crucible of another more dominant society's state and nation building programme. The demands of each for national recognition or even national self determination on the territory which they inhabit have thus not simply collided with the state's assumption as to its primacy but with its very definition of what constitutes the 'nation'. In none of these instances, did the state set out to exterminate these people simply on the grounds of their ethnic difference or 'otherness'. That they have increasingly done so, in part bears witness to these communities, obdurate refusal to be coerced into the national mainstream on terms determined by the state, combined with their coherent political and political-military resistance to deny it hegemonic control over the land and resources which they consider to be theirs. It is this state-community dynamic which has led, in each instance, through a series of state strategies characterised here as a 'genocidal process' to their culmination, at some stage, in the actuality of genocide. In the case of the Jummas, the only distinction lies in the fact that this actuality is difficult to isolate to a single sequence of events.

Indeed, in terms of typology, Jumma resistance, would certainly qualify the CHT to be placed within Fein's category of 'retributive' genocide, in addition to her 'developmental' category, while examination of the perpetrator's agenda might equally enclose it for consideration within her 'ideological' category. Equally, Harff and Gurr's hegemonial genocide or repressive/hegemonial politicide categories would fit the CHT case history. Modern genocide is rooted in general patterns of development. But the reason why it occurs in some situations and not in others is very much a byproduct of a state's specific developmental agenda, often focusing on a geographical arena where its desire for rapid implementation confronts the people, usually its notional 'citizens', who happen to live there. Understanding not condoning - a genocidal outcome thus requires an examination of the motives of the perpetrators as well as the cries of the victims.

CHT : The View from Bangladesh

The successful secession of Bangladesh from Pakistan in 1971 was seen by its political elites as a prelude to a process of rapid nation and state building which would enable the new country to take its rightful place in the international community. Its progress towards this goal would be gauged by economic indices evaluating its growth and vitality and by the creation of an institutional and juridical framework confirming its political stability. These, at least, would be the primary criteria of the dominating Western powers and major fiscal institutions in the global political economy. Yet the country's ability to engage with let alone compete in such a system was from the start confounded by basic structural, environmental and above all demographic weaknesses.

The population of Bangladesh, the eighth largest in the world, ought to have been its chief asset. But numbering 128 million today compared with 40 million in the 1950s and estimated to double again from its present figure in the space of the next 40 years, possibly not stabilising until it reaches the 340 million mark, its growth represents not simply a drain on the economy but a portent of absolute disaster. Historically, the land of the immensely fertile riverine delta area which constitutes most of a country only the size of Nicaragua, provided for a large agriculturally based population. But this traditional resource base is now rapidly shrinking, the most dramatic symptoms of which have been a series of floods and cyclones, which, in 1988 for instance, displaced some 40 per cent of the population. The two major long term causes of these ecological and climatic changes however, can be traced to the deforestation of the up-river Himalayan states, leading to severe land erosion in downstream Bangladesh, as well as to global warming, the effects of which even with a mere one metre rise in sea level, could turn some 10 per cent of its population into permanent environmental refugees.[21] Even the most optimistic projections could not hope to absorb more than a fraction of the many millions of peasantry already displaced via industrial or post-industrial enterprise. There has been some development of this kind, particularly recently, but unlike many other South East Asian states, no obvious economic take-off. One of the poorest nations in the world, with 80 per cent of its population below the poverty line, the economic prospects of Bangladesh have been described as 'elusive', while its efforts to 'catch up' have resulted in a $16,135 billion external debt, costing $700 million to service in 1991.[22]

None of this grim outlook necessarily on its own accounts for the country's chronic political instability, although it may do much to explain why the CHT has remained a subject of consistent fascination, not to say obsession, among its political elite. At 10 per cent of the country's total land mass, yet with a physical geography in utter contrast to the alluvial monsoon-flooded plains, the deeply forested ravines and valleys of the CHT represent the nearest thing Bangladesh has to a wild west, a 'final frontier', even an EI Dorado. The CHT supposedly has a 'huge potential for development,[23] A recent government sponsored report claims that its 'forest and mineral resources' make it 'vital in a geo-political sense' while its 147 inhabitants per square mile, compared with 1567 per square mile in the rest of the country, demand that its future 'should be viewed from a total national perspective'.[24]

The implication of these comments is clear, while on a level of social engineering the CHT is proposed as an at least part solution to Bangladesh's overpopulation, via a mass relocation of plains people to the hills, on another more obviously economic one, its supposed untapped wealth, particularly in the form of oil and gas, is represented as an opportunity (and possibly a final one) of reversing the country's fortunes in favour of a major breakthrough. What is missing from this picture is the indigenous population. This seems strange in the light of a (then Pakistani) government-commissioned study which in 1967 confirmed that the CHT was in practice 'as constrained as the most thickly populated district' in

Bengal.[25] According to Mark Levene, yet if the received wisdom states that the supposed emptiness of the CHT is 'a myth' the perceived wisdom holds firmly to the notion that it is a territorium nullius, i.e., unoccupied land crying out for industrious Bengalis to inhabit and develop it. The discrepancy is itself instructive, under scoring a state leadership preference to believe what it wants to believe because the alternative, namely coming to some power-sharing accommodation with the Jumma, would mean relinquishing its much cherished dreams of national fulfillment.[26]

This is not, however, a simple case of collective wish-fulfillment persisting in unreason. It is grounded in an acute sense of historical injustice done to Bengalis, contrasting with a single moment of good fortune which all good Bangladeshi nationalists would claim as their birthright and inheritance. This was in 1947 at the time of partition and involved a decision by the British commissioner. Sir Cyril Radcliffe, to award the CHT to Muslim Pakistan rather than to India in his settlement of boundaries between the two states.[27] The CHT in other words, was a windfall from colonialism. This is interesting for no other reason than the fact that Bangladeshi nationalists blame colonialism, either British or Pakistani, for most of the problems that have afflicted their country since independence, especially in the CHT. Yet it was these same colonialisms which provided the conception, direction and parameters for the development of the region which subsequently shape the Bangladeshi period of administration. By ignoring the inconvenient fact that Bangladesh is a willing successor to these colonialisms, beginning when the CHT was brought for the first time, through its annexation to British India, firmly within the Bengali political sphere of influence, this Bangladeshi version would seek to claim that it was these same colonialisms which stymied the development of the region in its legitimate Bengali interest. In this version, however, the Jumma are less 'invisitble' and more the pawns of colonial or other outside powers intent on malevolent disruption of this correct trajectory.

Accordingly, phase one of the Bangladeshi version—the period of British rule from 1860 to 1947—emphasises the way the imperial power sought to isolate and exclude the CHT from the rest of Bengal'. From the beginning, the British did in fact operate a special administrative status for the region, codified and made legally binding in its 1900 'Regulations', affirmed again in its 1920 declaration of the region as a 'backward tract' and confirmed again in its 1935 classification of it as 'a totally excluded area'[28]. According to Mark Levene, this nationalists argument, was mistaken and dangerous on two counts. It unbalanced the traditional economic and social interplay between hill and plains, impeding Bengali entrepreneurial development of the region and fossilising outmoded economic practices based on jhuming, which thereby prevented what should have been the natural absorption of the hill tribes into the more advanced society and polity of the plains. Second, the British gave to the 'tribes' especially the chiefs whose power they had advanced in order to administer the Regulations and collect taxes on their behalf, the erroneous notion that they had provided for a special autonomous status for the region as present day Jummas continue to contend.[29] This was doubly misplaced because not only were the Regulations entirely self-interested—in typical imperial fashion they were designed to divide and rule, keep other parties out, while preserving the region's forest assets for the British but also it was these very same Regulations which struck at the heart of the tribes' self-sufficiency. As this was dependent on traditional usufruct rights to the forests which, under the terms of the Regulations, had been largely sequestered as crown property, the tribes found that the practice of jhum was no longer sustainable, precipitating a destabilisation of the region which has continued to the present day.[30]

If one strand of this argument is to point out that it is the British not the Bengalis who should be blamed for the decline of the hill tribes, another is to lament the willingness of their leadership, nonetheless, to be the imperial power's dupes. And, as if this was not bad enough, they kept on repeating the mistake in the post colonial experience by aligning them—selves with those most inimical to the future Bangladeshi nation. It happened in 1947 itself when tribesmen attempted to resist CHT incorporation in Pakistan by running up the Indian flag in the main towns, thereby embedding in Bengali consciousness the conviction that the Jumma as a whole were a pro-Indian fifth column, while in 1971, when Bangladesh was struggling for its very existence, a number of Chakma and Manna chiefs advertised their hostility by allowing themselves to be recruited as rakajars-irregulars-on the side of the Pakistan military. This apparent alignment with Pakistan was not only unforgivable in the light of the genocidal massacres then being perpetrated against Bengalis but because the whole period from 1947 to 1971 was conceived of by Bengalis as phase two of a rampant—this time internal-colonialism in which Bengal and its CHT hinterland were utterly subordinated to the political and economic will of Islamabad. Indeed, in this view, Islambad's policy with regard to the CHT demonstrated the regime's single minded marginalisation of the Bengali interest at its most egregious.

Although Pakistan's military dictator, Ayub Khan, retained the special status of the CHT until 1962, its designation by him in the late

1950s as a concession area which would be opened up to international finance, pointedly excluded the involvement of Bengali administrative and financial elites. At the core of the regime's developmental agenda was a plan to throw a dam across the Karnaphuli river, at the region's heart, in order to create a huge hydroelectric project. The completion of the Kaptai dam in 1963 was thus intended as the infrastructural baseline for a rapid industrial take off.[32] However, not only was this seen by Bengalis as being for the benefit of the Pakistani regime rather than for the national development of its eastern part, the economic and environmental impact on the region itself, as the government sponsored Forestal report later acknowledged, was both massive and devastating. Forty per cent (or 54,000 acres) of its prime agricultural land was submerged, displacing 100,000 indigenous, mostly Chakma people. Not only were they not consulted about the dam they were not compensated either financially or with other land. In fact, there was no other obvious land to offer to these sedentary rice-growing farmers, only a vastly oversubscribed residual forest area where jhuming was proving unsustainable. The Bangladeshi verdict on Pakistani rule in the CHT is thus to blame it for errors and mismanagement which turned almost one-sixth of the population into environmental refugees, militarizing it and opening up the sale of its land to outsiders.[33] However, righting these wrongs would not be brought about by an end to development per se but rather by the region's full integration into an independent Bangladesh. Only this could save its indigenous tribes from complete destitution.

Bangladeshi self-justification with regard to the treatment of the Jumma would thus begin with the vociferous denial that they intended any harm to their physical well-being or cultural existence. On the contrary, the independent state of Sheik Mujibur Rahman and his successors might be composed mostly of Muslims, might celebrate its near-linguistic and cultural homogeneity, but its constitution guaranteed equality before the law economic and educational opportunity, as well as the free practice of the religion of one's choice, regardless of ethnic background.[34] The implicit message to the peoples of the CHT was that there would be no distinction between them and the Bengali majority and nothing to prevent their full access to the social and political life of the country. What wrecked this proffered embrace was the recalcitrance and hostility of the tribal chiefs them selves. It was they who demanded a renegotiation of the status of the CHT within Bangladesh as an 'autonomous tribal zone' they who wanted a return to the anachronism of the British imposed Regulations; they who took up arms against the state in 'a conspiracy against Bangladeshi sovereignty.'[35] If the nascent state's military responded with search and destroy missions in the CHT, this was because the tribal leaders had brought them upon themselves. If these operations turned into a long-term counter-insurgency, this was because the Shanti Bahini, from its formation in 1973, not only violently challenged the integrity and cohesion of the state but did so with the covert assistance of a foreign power. India, which, after its initial patronage of Bangladesh, had turned into its main enemy. The Shanti Bahini's guerrilla war, its repeated violent attacks on army outposts and later on Bengali settlers, conclusively proved that it was not the Bangladeshi state but the Shanti Bahini which was culpable of provocation. In the circumstances, Bangladesh was entitled to respond as would any sovereign state in legitimate self-defence of the body-politic.

Weaknesses in the Bangladeshi Version

The Bangladeshi version of the CHT problem cannot be simply dismissed out of hand, not least because there are elements of the overall picture here. In addition, it offers an important insight into the workings, including the anxieties, of the Bangladeshi state mind. The flaw lies in its assumption that the obstructive behaviour of many Jummas is primarily a matter of political manipulation by a mischievous leadership and not a legitimate response to impossible developmental pressures which, moreover, represent not a repudiation of the British and Pakistan programmes in the CHT but rather their intensification by Bangladesh.

The wanton destruction of the subcontinent's forests by the British forced them to reconsider their policy in the late 19th century in an attempt to preserve this depleted resources. Their creation of 'reserved forest', as in the CHT, was aimed at maintaining a market economy of profit and not a moral economy of survival. From the first, therefore, the British were not interested to its people or their jhuming culture which, interfering with their monopoiy, they vigorously attempted to destroy or shift in the direction of settled agriculture.[36]

The Pakistani regime followed this same trajectory but with the added remit to their Canadian consultants, Forestal Inc. to create 'a master plan for the integrated-development of the area, based on 'optimum land-use possibilities. Interestingly, Forestal's report noted that under optimum conditions jhuming was highly sustainable.[37] However, its recommendation proposed that it should be phased out in favour of industrial development in the vicinity of the dam, and fruit production elsewhere as the best way of maximizing the region's resource potential.

Since 1971 there have been various modifications to this agenda, including plans for afforestation, rubber plantations and fruit farming, interspersed with more recent talk of 'ecological biodiversity', as Bangladesh has increasingly sought to promote itself to Western financial institutions.[38] However, its basic thrust has not changed. It assumes the termination of a sustainable, localised economy, based on a long-term human adaption to the forest environment, in favour of 'a fundamental switchover from both wet rice and shifting cultivation technology to a modern agro-industrial technology'.[39] In practice, this has meant not only the coercion of the tribal peoples in order to make them relinquish jhum but also the reconfiguring of the very lands they inhabit in favour of fruit gardens or rubber plantations owned or controlled by the state or its nominees. 'Forced into a dependency on the market economy', their only remaining role, so far as one exists at all, is as sharecroppers or day labourers in this system. This, avows the CHT Commission, is at the root of the 'structural violence' in the territory.[40]

One might wish to reply that this sort of social engineering is hardly peculiar to the CHT. Millions of rural people, especially in today's Third World, have suffered exactly this sort of economic strangulation and consequent social degradation as their usually post-colonial governments have struggled to enter the global marketplace in the interests of state-building and development. Almost by their very nature, these top-down, state-led programmes, whether capitalist or socialist, have demanded a politically neutralised, pliant and, where necessary, moveable labour force. The 'inevitability' argument is also strong. The popular Bengali writer, Abdus Sattar, for instance, claimed in the 1970s that the CHT tribes were living an antediluvian and timeless existence, protected by their sylvan isolation from the realms of history and the ways of the world; the implication being that, even if brought kicking and screaming into it, what was being done for them was, like with children, for their own good.[41] Even the most egregious facets of this process, such as the Jummas, forcible eviction from their native homes and subsequent resettlement in military-supervised joutha kamars - cluster villages - are neither unique to the CHT nor, in themselves, genocidal. However, to view these features in isolation from the broader contours of Bangladesh's state-building ambitions would be mistaken. Indeed, the great paradox - and hence danger - of the pivotal role allotted to the CHT in its developmental programme lies in the enormous gulf between the aspiration and the actual ability to implement it. Or put another way, the Bangladeshi lurch towards genocide in the CHT has been less the result of incluctable forces of modernisation per se and more the result of an extremely weak state striving to realise what may well be unrealisable.

From its inception through almost to the present day, the most visible symptoms of this weakness have been factional and extremely fractious party politics, a lack of democracy, lawlessness and endemic violence, governments which have repeatedly abused their office through corruption and nepotism, bloody coups and, above all, between 1975 and 1989, dictatorial military rule, first under General Zia and then, after his assassination, under General Ershad. The speed with which a post-liberation, populist-based polity, which had no notable military tradition and whose armed forces represented only a tiny fraction of the population went down this praetorian route is itself noteworthy, as is the close similarity between these military regimes and those of Pakistan. However, the generals moved into the driving seat in the power structure of the nascent state and took on the mantle of custodian and shaper of its national destiny not only because a specific civil regime was weak but because of much deeper structural problems.[42]

Unlike Pakistan, Bangladesh lacked a strong bourgeoisie with which to develop major industrial or commercial enterprises or to provide native capital for key infrastructural programmes. From the first, the state was required to be 'the leading sector for capital accumulation and development.'[43] This entailed foreign primarily Western aid and investment which would only begin to flow once conditions of stability and prospects for repayment were ensured. Sheik Mujib's initial Awami League regime failed to provide these preconditions, while the radical politics and internecine strife of the other party machines offered no obvious grounds for confidence. However, the Bangladesh Defence Forces (BDF) were unusually placed to provide the necessary guarantees. Their organisational capabilities were already pivotal as the only body in the country capable of mounting post-cyclone or flood relief operations. And, given the lack of credible alternatives, their supervision of a dirigible style state capitalist development seemed plausible. Their commitment to this course, enshrined in Zia's slogan 'develop or perish, was not in doubt.[44] Nor, as it turned out, was their ability to tap external developmental funds. It is no accident that the attempted rapid development of the CHT, with its concomitant creeping genocide came in the years of the generals.

But it is erroneous to read into this outcome an out-of-control military putschism or a distinct but narrow 'hard regime' ideology. The generals' power rested on and indeed was closely intermeshed with the dominant social forces in the state : the zamindar class of rich landowning families who monopolised patronage in the countryside and the large urban lower middle class who had provided the backbone of the national independence movement. Because these social forces were themselves relatively weak, their reliance on the military regimes to enrich them through patronage, status and jobs was consequently all the more pronounced.[45] Yet if private gain acted as a partial goal to develop the region, perceived national imperatives shared by the civilian elites as much as the military were its primary catalyst. Certainly the generals were at the helm as the CHT campaign took on an accelerated forced pace momentum and as the struggle with the Shanti Bahini intensified. But the generals also gave responsibility for the formulation of development strategy to a bureaucratic and technocratic elite, many of whom had held senior positions under the previous Pakistani administration and now dominated policy and decision making in key institutions such as the National Economic Council and Planning Commission, as well as in advisory and governmental rules in the President's secretariat and cabinet.[46]

It was thus a civil-military bureaucratic regime with a united sense of its leading role as guardian of the interests of the Bangladeshi nation-state that in 1976 launched the CHT Developmental Board (CHTDB) with a declared aim of 'boosting the socio-economic uplift of the region' through its designation as a 'special economic zone'.[47] This sounded not dissimilar to previous Pakistani plans. The difference was that this agenda was now an urgent priority with the aim of fully and finally consolidating the peripheral region and its resources into the life of Bangladesh. This was signalled in Zia's creation of a special presidential-led Cabinet Committee for the CHT which, as the highest decision making body on matters pertaining to it, continues to function to the present day of civilian democratic administration, and is still advised by the army chiefs, including the GOC Divisional Commander in Chittagong, who also acts as CHTDB chairman.[48]

This close military supervision of the CHT's development programme underscores the degree to which its post 1976 implementation was being seriously opposed by the Shanti Bahini, who also gave the conflict an increasingly geopolitical dimension as it became apparent that they were above to make raids into the CHT and then escape to bases either in Burma or more particularly, across the Feni river into the Indian state of Tripura. In response, what was broadcast by the government as legitimate efforts to seal these borders in order to isolate and defeat the insurgents, masked not only a military build up in the CHT- to an estimated 115,000 army personnel or almost one soldier for every five or six tribals [49]—but a government counter-insurgency campaign in which all Jummas were potential targets.

The View from the Jummas

Rumours were rife among the Jummas in the late 1970s that President Zia intended to make them a minority in their own land. But the actual relocation agenda suggested starker prospects still. Under military supervision the most fertile valleys would be repopulated with Bengalis, as would the remote borders. Neutralised through this demographic force majeure, the hill tribes would have to submit to the will of the Bangladeshi nation-state and accept their own relocation into joutha khamars where their ultimate fate would be determined by the BDP.[50] How should this agenda be interpreted ? The aim was for Jumma integration into the life of the nation-perhaps 'encapsulation' might be a most appropriate description[51] not extermination. But another way of approaching this official version might be to hypothesise that what actually was being asked of them was to 'disappear' and that what was at stake by 1980 was the manner in which this would happen.

One important consideration is to note the apparent absence of alternative or lateral options. Back in 1947 the CHT tribal chiefs had petitioned the British against incorporation in Pakistan, proposing instead of confederation of Indian-led tribal states linking the CHT with neighbouring Tripura, Assam and Cooch Behar. There were obvious ethnic and religious reasons for this request, not least because, in terms of the Muslim-Hindu divide which propelled the drive towards partition, the Jumma as a mix of Hindu. Buddhists, animists and Christians clearly fell on one side of it and not the other. This did not necessarily point towards the inevitability of some Kulturkampf between Muslim Bengalis and tribal peoples. The historic relationship between them has been described as one of 'uneasy symbiosis',[52] while good inter-communal relations in the wake of a smaller wave of plains people settlement in the 1960s suggested that social coexistence was possible.

Clearly this argument has its limits. The frequency with which, from the 1970s Buddhist temples, monasteries and Christian churches were desecrated by gangs of settlers as well as the army, to say nothing of a persistent gender-specific mistreatment of the Jumma in the form of rape, forced marriage and forced conversion, all suggest a racist contempt for the hill people which seems to have intensified with the increasing post-1975 Islamisation of Bangladesh. Yet there are also grounds for arguing that, rather than these attacks being random outpourings of popular settler hostility, they were actually part of a well-orchestrated BDF campaign to emasculate the Jumma politically and socially as a prelude to their complete marginalisation, if not physical annihilation.[53] What all informed commentators agree is that the cause of the Bangladeshi anti-Jumma drive was not about ethnicity per se but only about that ethnicity in the context of control of Jumma-held land.[54] Obversely, the Jumma leadership sought an autonomous status and separate legislature for the CHT based on the 1900 Regulations, not simply to protect their right to be ethnically and culturally different but as the best guarantee for preserving their land rights. So long as the region was within Pakistan, its distance from the power-centre to some extent cushioned the Jumma from the full implications of this dichotomy. When, however, soon after the creation of Bangladesh, 12 tribal leaders sought to plead the autonomy case with Sheik Mujib, his notoriously brusque response—'We are all Bengali ... we cannot have two systems of government ... forget your ethnic identity, be Bengalis'[55]—crystallised not only the new reality but the true nature of the impasse.

Few dominant elites in modern states are prepared to negotiate pluralist power-sharing or special status for subordinate entities, let alone with regard to the demands of usually relatively small groups of native peoples. Nor could the Jumma have derived consolation from the knowledge that new politics in their drive towards social cohesion and development have nearly always treated tribalism, segmental loyalties and intermediate arrangements as at best suspect and at worst directly inimical to national integrity and unity.[56] Manobendra Narayan Larma's formation of the JSS as a political party to campaign exclusively for the interests of CHT indigenous peoples came in the wake both of Sheik Mujib's refusal to consider autonomy and of a series of sweeping and indiscriminate reprisal raids against the CHT for alleged complicity with the Pakistanis. That the JSS in turn spawned a military wing, the Shanti Bahini, under the leadership of Manobendra' s brother, Shantu Lara, only underscores the Jummas' conviction that the Bangladeshi state had ruled out either compromise or coexistence.

However, the emergence of these overtly radical organisations cannot be viewed in isolation. A groundswell of political activism in the CHT had been developing since the 1950s. Paradoxically, the Pakistani and Bangladeshi states had fuelled these tendencies through the creation of schools and technical colleges and in the extension of adult suffrage to the whole population. In this sense, it could be argued that their assimilative promises were as good as their word. On the other hand, the conscious exclusion of Jumma graduates from state office or employment, or the simple lack of openings, helped swell the ranks of the CHT Students Association, the Women's Federation, and the Rangamati Communist Party. Given the pressures the Jumma were then under, as well as the broader political climate of the 1960s and 1970s, it is hardly surprising if these movement took on an increasingly combative Marxist-Leninist or Maoist orientation.[57]

But even if these overtly political mobilisations were largely limited to student or professional circles, they were indicative of a social and cultural shift in the CHT. Traditionally, it was the tribal chiefs, whose power had been advanced and cemented under British rule, who provided the interface between the state and tribal peoples. It was they who had first contested the Radcliffe Award in 1947 and had attempted to set up the first CHT Peoples Association to fight incorporation into Pakistan. Yet while these ideas continued to command broad Jumma support into the Bangladeshi era, the manifest failure of the chiefs to plead their case to either Sheik Mujib or his successors was compounded by the loss of their actual power in favour of a state appointed district commissioner for the region with virtually unlimited powers. Many of the chiefs, moreover, were bought off with largesse channelled through the CHTDB.[58] With the traditional leadership thus discredited, the growing ranks of the JSS sought new strategies with which to combat the social and environmental onslaught threatening to overwhelm tribal society. The collapse of jhum and with it the first reported cases of starvation, the inroads of the BDF and, in the wake of their newly macadamed roads opening up the remote interior, Bengali logging merchants, settlers and foreign company personnel: the flight of thousands of refugees into Tripura: and, finally and most dangerously, the forced relocations into *joutha khamars*, all seemed to demand a more urgent and comprehensive counter-response.

On one level this was supplied by the Shanti Bahini, its active operations, from the mid-1970s, succeeding in containing the BDF to their encampments or to the main towns, while also creating its own administrative, judicial and fiscal framework in 'liberated' areas of the CHT, backed by village militias and financial exactions made from tribespeople and settlers alike. Yet the insurgency was never sufficiently strong numerically or logistically, to take on the BDF in classic military terms, while its very existence arguably represented provocation which made a genocidal backlash against the population it was claiming to defend all the more probable and imminent. If the verdict on the efficacy of the Shanti Bahini is thus mixed, that on its parent organisation, the JSS, is much stronger. In the early 1970s, Manobendra Larmy could publicly voice in Parliament : 'I am a Chakma. A Marma can never be a Chakma. Chakma can never be a Muron and Chakma can never be a Bengali'.[59] Yet within less than a decade a history of disparate, fragmented and often warring tribal or sub-tribal loyalties had been reshaped through the idea of being a jumma (i.e., someone whose CHT roots lay in the practice of jhum) into one not only of shared victimhood but of common historical identity. For the native peoples of the CHT this 'imagined community' represented not only a repudiation of the state's equally 'imagined' notion of a homogeneous Bengali or Bangladeshi people but offered an alternative unitary formula in its stead.[60] Or to take the argument a stage further, the very idea of Jumma nationhood combined with the ability to struggle for it, not only threatened to wreck the developmental agenda of a new but already highly unstable Bangladeshi state but even its theoretical underpinnings.

Group Vs Group

The situation was further exacerbated by the government's resettlement of environmental refugees from the plain areas in the CHT. These Bangladeshis had been affected by natural calamities which occurred in 1970 and 1991. It also included people affected by other environmental caused reasons like soil erosion, landlessness, river bank erosion and salinity. This mounted to extra pressures on the existing resource base of CHT embroiling the tribals and non-tribal migrants in frequent clashes overland. Being basically agrarian, the tribals could not compete with the skilled non-tribals in non-agrarian fields. Due to decreasing food production on tiny plots, the tribals, started to lose their lands through banks for loans for survival and other works. During situations of scarcity and crop failure when the small marginal plots were inadequate to feed them, they were forced to mortgage their lands to get the money to buy food. They, thus fell into debt to the Bengalis, who then foreclosed and took away their land. A series of clashes, violence and conflict between these two groups over resources, as a consequence, ended in favour of the non-tribals further strengthening the tribals' distrust in the state and intensifying their insurgency against the state. The situation worsened as non-tribal migrants were kept under army protection and also given arms to face the onslaught from the tribals.

This group vs group and group vs state dimension of the CHT crisis which appears to be basically an internal affair of Bangladesh took on an international, dimension with India getting involved. India's involvement was due to its proximity and the presence of many transborder ethnic groups. When the Bangladesh government acted against the hill people they fled into the border states of India. The numbers were large enough to become an irritant between the two nations. Bangladesh suspected India of providing covert military and moral assistance to the insurgents. The insurgency in Bangladesh has created movements of people a security issue in the border states of India with their own inherent problems of insurgency being aggravated.[61] Further, the continuing influx was a strain on the social, economic and political infrastructure of these states, showing possible potentials for violent ethnic and group clashes.

As disclosed after the liberation of Bangladesh, under a scheme proposed by the former Soviet Union as South East Asia Security Plan, the Chittagong Hill Tracts was to be liberated. To this end, the Research and Analysis Wing (RAW) of India is suspected to have arranged special radio electronic training for Chakma youths along with several military training centres and camps for operation.[62] This type of support to the Chakmas is purported to have strengthened India's bargaining position against Pakistan during the sixties.[63]

India at the same time accused Bangladesh of supporting the Mizo National Front (MNF) in Tripura. Adding to these allegations is the very fact of India having earlier used and patronized the Chakmas against the Mizo insurgent groups.[64] While rebutting the charges of being involved in the CHT imbroglio, it is alleged, India has internationalized the issue, with international, humanitarian and donor NGOs being urged upon to back off the repatriation deal on account of "extra judicial execution in the CHT".[65]

Cooperation between the two countries which existed during the birth of Bangladesh as a state soon developed to counter insurgencies. The Shanti Bahini in India and the Mizos in CHT were examples of the use of insurgency groups in each others territory. Mujib secretly allowed the Indian army in the forests of CHT to fight out MNF guerrillas and the Razakars, the pro-Pakistani paramilitary forces who were alleged to have received support from Chakmas. This added to the political advantages of Mujib.[66] In the post-Mujib era, the existing cooperation was replaced by distrust developed between the two states with counter allegations arraigned against each other.

At present Tripura, a state of India has received massive influx of Chakmas into its territory disrupting its economy. The presence of nearly 50,000 Chakma refugees in Tripura has brought a demographic change, which the tribals felt, had far reaching socio-economic ramifications. The cordon separating the refugees in camps from the local tribals in recent years has become slack, providing a scope for strengthening family and social ties between the refugees and tribals.[67] South Tripura bears a testimony to the growing commercial and social bond between the refugees and tribals. Resisting this kind of encroachment into their social and economic realm, the tribals have spawned up their revolutionary activities which have already brought them into loggerheads with the refugees and local administration. Unless credible steps are taken to find an immediate return of Chakmas into their home land, the continuing edging of refugees into Tripura's socio-economic realm would spark of the kind of ethnic conflicts, Tripura had been subjected to, in recent years. There is also an equally valid fear that the Chakmas in India would go underground and mobilize to fight the ethnic upsurge.[68]

This disturbed atmosphere on the border has also encouraged its own extreme elements particularly the Tripura National Volunteers (TNV) to carry on their activities from their hideouts across the border. Bangladesh is supposed to have been supplying arms and ammunitions to the Kuki National Front (KNF) in Manipur in their demand for a separate state.[69]

The brunt of Chakma refugees that Tripura faced has resulted in the Indian government having taken a move towards repatriation of refugees which vitiated the relationship between India and Bangladesh. Although according to a direction between the two governments in 1981, 17,000 CHT tribal refugees would be repatriated, it could not be carried out straining further the relations. The situation became worse when after 1985, the Indian government reached an understanding with the MNF to assist the Chakmas to become more adventurous and politically demanding.[70] Besides the launching of a greater Mizoram comprising of Chin Hills of Burma, the Chittagong Hill Tracts of Bangladesh, the Churachandpur area of Manipur and the Jampui Hills of Tripura, under the leadership of Brigadier Thenphunga Sailo, the former Chief Minister and President of People's Conference could complicate the crisis and strain their relationship.[71]

Chakmas who fled the then East Pakistan were settled in Lohit, Changlang, Papumpare districts of Arunachal Pradesh in 1964. In 1967 there were only 57 Chakma families. Today, they number almost 67,000. Ten years later, as feared, they would reach five lakhs and overshadow the original tribals destroying their culture and identity. At present, their population has almost doubled to destroy thousand acres of their forest land, wildlife and trees. The Chakmas in Arunachal Pradesh being accorded titles to the land in tribal areas by the government have already become an intrinsic part of the local commerce, trade, agriculture and business without the benefit of political rights, especially citizenship, though economic rights automatically flow from their titles to the land. This has aroused strong misgivings and violent resentment for having increasingly eaten into their land and forests. The original Chakmas entered into Arunachal Pradesh may be denied citizenship, but their offsprings have a right to citizenship, being born in India.[72] The burgeoning growth of these Indian born Chakmas has upset the demographic, political, economic and social fabric in Arunachal Pradesh.[73] An increasing sense of being marginalized in their home land, by a culturally and ethnically different group has been perceived a security threat to their very existence. On the other hand, coupled with this, pressures and demands of modernization on the indigenous population to assimilate itself into the political, economic, social and environmental space, already eaten into by the ever growing number of Chakmas have been a preponderant factor adding momentum to the growing militancy among the tribals against the Chakmas. In a bid to face these challenges and repatriation movements, the Chakmas have reported to have forged strong links with militant organizations suggesting grave security implications on Indian's political system.

In an all party rally at Itanagar on 20 September 1996, 31 December set as the deadline for deportation of 64,300 Chakmas.[74] The entire political leadership of the state and the students decided to quit national parties on 31 December to protest against the centre's failure to deport these refugees.

The anti-Chakma stir has entered a violent phase with 200 Chakmas being allegedly killed and their houses burnt over the last two years. The Central government's announcement in the Lok Sabha on 29 April 1993 to grant them citizenship added fuel to this violent phase of agitation against the Chakmas. Faced with the threat of deportation, hundreds of Chakmas are said to be getting guerrilla training in Bangladesh. This is likely to turn the crisis into a violent one. If Chakmas are not deported or settled elsewhere this issue is likely to become an Assam like crisis soon, with all the ramifications of an intrastate and interstate conflict between India and

Bangladesh. With the Supreme Court directing the state government not to deport Chakmas and in that context the Chief Minister's declaration to bring the issue back to the people may further complicate the crisis.[75] The crisis of such a magnitude in Aunachal Pradesh near the door step of China may tempt the latter to fish in the troubled waters of India with grave security implications on India.

The problem of repatriation of Chakmas to their own homeland has now become the main contentious issue embittering the bilateral relations between India and Bangladesh. In the absence of any political settlement between the CHT insurgents and Bangladesh, the Indo-Bangladesh relations are bound to be affected adversely. The politicians of Bangladesh have used the issue of India's alleged role in the Chakma problems to secure and strengthen their legitimacy in power. With a porous border existing between India and Bangladesh, the insurgencies and countermilitary crackdown across the border continue to have security implications for the border Indian States. The political stalemate in Bangladesh continues. In the absence of any concrete constructive programmes in Bangladesh assuring the Chakmas regaining of their lost resource base, their measures to attract the Chakmas back to the Hill Tracts, do not cut any ice with the Chakma refugees. Attempt by Indian politicians at downplaying the issue of Chakma refugees and finding in them a potential vote bank by some politicians has long-term security implications.

Enviromental Scarcity of Land Induced Migration and Conflict

Bangladesh represents a Malthusian nightmare "with too little food or too many people on too little land."[76] Landlessness, gradual marginalization of the small land owners and peasant families, increasingly skewed land ownership distribution, agricultural indebtedness and pauperization of the small peasantry.

In 1964 the rural population living below the poverty line was 50.8 per cent which increased to an all time high 77.8 per cent in 1982, and came down further due to various alleviating programmes, to 51 per cent in 1986. At present the figure is more than 51 per cent, and the rural poor is estimated at nearly 50 million.[77] This is more than the South Asia average which at present stands at 49 per cent.[78] The pattern of land distribution and land ownership has been one of the important reasons accounting for the incidence of poverty in Bangladesh. Nearly 50 per cent of the households in the rural areas are landless. It is estimated that landlessness is growing faster than population. It is projected by the United Nations that Bangladesh's current population of 128 million has doubled in the past 30 years and will nearly double to 235 million by the year 2035. It continues to grow at a rate of 2.4 per cent per year. Cropland which stands at 0.08 hectares per capita has already become scarce. Population density of 939 per square kilometre is among the world's highest. With all the country's good agricultural land being fully exploited, the over growing population is projected to cut in half the amount of cropland available per capita by 2025.[79] Inheritance customs and population growth have combined to produce scarcity and poverty. With each generation, land becomes scarcer and scarcer being subdivided into fragments. Thus scarcity of cropland has strongly contributed to this migration. Out of those sources of scarcity demand-induced scarcity brought about by rapid population growth appears to be a direct and major cause. Supply induced scarcity is a secondary cause. As for structural scarcity, although land distribution is highly unequal this distribution has changed little. Consequently, population growth appears to be the consistent driver behind rising land scarcity in Bangladesh in recent decades, and therefore behind the larger migration of people out of the country. This population growth has produced a wide gap between current satisfaction for Bangladeshis and their perceived potential satisfaction elsewhere. Land which is the most fertile and main source of sustenance can no longer be able to support the growing population.[80]

Poverty prevails not being able to invest more in soil conservation. Apart from this, as stated by Bangladesh, the direct result of water withdrawal by India has been loss of seasonal work of millions who cannot find sufficient surface and ground water to sustain their livelihood during the dry season. Apart from the farmers, the fishermen suffered a lot due to reduced catches and boatmen have lost their livelihood as navigability was seriously affected. This has resulted in increased unemployment and poverty among the poor people. Fallow lands are left uncultivated. The poorest eventually leave for urban centres or hill slopes or neighbouring Indian states. As pointed out by a poor Bangladeshi, debts grow, families grow, but incomes from land holdings and the buying power of the Bangladeshi currency shrink leaving no option but to migrate to Assam.[81] In Bangladesh, landlessness along with degradation of soil, water and forest and natural hazards like storm and cyclone and river bank erosion push the landless rural poor to urban centres and Indian states where opportunities real or perceived appear as pull factors. Also they move to the hill slopes and hill sides like the plain people to CHT in Bangladesh. Here they clear the forest to begin farming anew to exhaust the land in a few years. Migrants often identify the flooding and cyclone as the immediate cause but in most of the cases flooding causes people to move because population growth has already critically limited per capita access to land.

The supply and demand pressures on cropland can be said as a simple Malthusian explanation of poverty in Bangladesh. But Boyce is not in agreement with this kind of conclusion.[82] According to him though marginal agricultural product may have declined in the 1970's and 1980's this outcome cannot be attributed to simply land scarcity. Yields of rice per hectare were among the lowest in the world, average yields were about one-third of those obtained in China or Taiwan. Boyce notes that there was extraordinary potential for increased labour productivity despite the scarcity of land. According to him, the population growth actually induced agricultural innovations during the 1970s and 1980s and helped increase agricultural product. But growth in yields was not fast enough to compensate for the population's increasing food demands. The necessary institutional innovation to provide effective control of flood and irrigation waters was impeded by struggles among social groups over the distribution of power and wealth. The government efforts to mobilise local resource for water through construction of tanks, wells and irrigation canals were distorted to benefit the landowner. Landlords sought to control well to permit monopoly pricing and to gain rights to adjacent cropland. According to him, the distributional inequalities and the inheritance practices were the main reasons to account for poverty in Bangladesh. Since Boyce concluded his study, there has been improvement in Bangladesh's situation because of fall in birth rate and introduction of free market and free trade economists. Though the overall gain deficit has substantially reduced, according to Goletti, "in comparison with other low income Asian countries, Bangladesh has one of the lowest record in terms of agricultural growth."[83]

As said above, such contextual factors include inheritance practices that cause families to divide cropland into smaller plots with each generation, and national and water community water control institutions. These institutions have sharply limited agricultural output and precluded peasants from gaining full benefit from some of the most fertile land in the world.[84] According to Homer Dixon, "although such contextual factors are important, they cannot obscure the fact that land scarcity in Bangladesh has been a powerful force behind migration to neighbouring regions".[85]

Sea level rise as a result of global warming would further intensify the population displacement. As predicted, 65 per cent of greater Khulna, 99 per cent of Barisal, 100 per cent of Patuakhali, 44 per cent of Noakhali and 12 per cent of Faridpur will be inundated destroying 13.74 per cent of the net cropped area and 401.600 ha of mangrove forest along with all its resources and displacing 10 per cent of the country's 110.8 million people, to the unaffected urban areas and neighbouring Indian states.

This population displacement is not confined to the territory of Bangladesh. Over the last four decades, millions have migrated and continued to migrate to the neighbouring Indian states of Assam, Tripura, West Bengal. The attractions of more thinly lands across the borders are immense. The population densities of India's north-eastern states compare very favourly : Assam has about 300 people per sq. kilometre, Meghalaya 78, Tripura 262 and Mizoram 33 sq. km. The economic and resources of these states are not ideal but better than Bangladesh's. There has not been any consensus on the exact number of refugees settling in various part of India. It has been calculated at 12 to 17 million with 7 million alone in Assam. These refugees having added to its current total of 22 million.[87]

Contrary to the denials by the Bangladesh government, Bangladeshi refugees are found in large numbers in New Delhi and Mumbai. While the Government of India declares that there are about 100,000 Bangladeshi migrants in Delhi, intelligence estimates the figure at 200,000.

Enviromental Conflict

The conflicts arising, or showing signs of having erupted from a host of social effects due to environmental degradation and scarcity of resources, can come under this category. For example, if a group of people migrating from one region to another region within a country or from one country to another country meet an indigenous group of different ethnic and religious origin, a clash may occur between the two which may appear as ethnic or religious on the surface; but underneath their movement lies environmental degradation, resulting in what is called as group identity conflict.[88]

Induced by poverty due to environmental scarcity of land between 12 to 17 million landless poor people in their search for land and economic livelihood, have been migrating to neighbouring states of India viz. Assam,

West Bengal, Tripura, Orissa and Urban centres like Delhi and Mumbai creating "a sub nation, the size of Australia within India". Though Bangladesh continues to proclaim that it has no illegal aliens in India Bangladeshi communities have sprung up in New Delhi and Mumbai under the shelter of flyovers and in Muslim dominated regions. The political parties in India resort to political use of the Bangladeshi settlers as potential vote bank. While the Government of India put the Bangladeshi migrant figures at about 100,000, the intelligence sources estimate it at 200,000.[90] Providing political advantage to political parties during hustings, these refugees received patronage in terms of education, development and health facilities even at the cost of the local inhabitants. This contains the seeds of further local conflicts. It is further reported that these immigrants are involved in robbery, murder and other heinous crimes in Delhi and other parts of India.

An estimate suggests that as many as 1,000 people, a month are coming to West Bengal.[91] The state has atleast 120 lakhs illegal migrants. The situation in its border constituencies - from Cooch Behar and Jaepaiguri in the North to West Dinajpur, Malda, Murshidabad, Nadia and North and South 24 parganas in the South is far worse. Most drift to Kolkata where their living conditions are marked by squalor, overcrowding and abysmal poverty. Many illegal migrants have been fanning out into the rest of India as well. As per latest estimates, while Delhi, Bihar and Tripura have one million strong Bangladeshi populace each, these people have reached in large numbers - 1 lakhs as per latest estimates - into Mumbai and Rajasthan well.[92]

Assam like Situation in Orissa

Orissa, a poor and economically backward state of India is not free from the intrusion of refugees from Bangladesh. In 1956 their number was mere 1250 as registered. But during these 44 years their number has gone up to 1,80,000. They have spread up from Dhamra to Paradeep covering the eastern coast. Rajnagar has been turned into a small Bangladesh. They have destroyed the entire mangrove forest for agricultural purposes which used to be the natural bulwark against cyclone and tidal surge. The recent super cyclone on October 29 and 30, 1999 ravaging the coastal districts of Orissa with the loss of human beings and livestock to the extent of 30,000 and 3,00,000 respectively, blew at unbelievable speed of more than 263 kms per hour. The damage could have been less, if the mangrove forest remained intact and untouched by the Bangladesh refugees. The natural bulwark against cyclone and storms was destroyed by these refugees. The politician are doing nothing except registering them as voters in whom they find a reliable vote bank.[93] Reports of local conflicts over land and intrusion into their homeland are constantly heading the newspapers but to no avail.

Due to the constant stream of migrants from Bangladesh to Assam, "the problem the Assam face today is that it soon may be themselves who constitute an island within a sea of Bengalis."[94] The demographic structure of Assam has already been in a danger of having transformed the once dominant Assamese into a minority within Assam.[95] Assam which has never had local mulims in large numbers is today 32 per cent Muslim, the centre estimates that Assam will become a Muslim majority state in another two decades, if illegal migration continues.

There has been a spate of data raising controversies about the exact number of illegal Bangladeshi migrants settling in Assam. Estimates indicate that Assam's population increased from 14.6 million to 22.9 million during 1970s. This increase of 65.6 per cent in one decade cannot be attributed to a natural population growth alone, especially when the rest of India showed an increase of 24.7 per cent during the same period.[96] Illegal migration is the only reason for that unexpected growth. Conservative estimates put it at over 6 million persons.[97]

Government officials in India estimate that India now has around 18 million plus illegal migrants - most Muslims from Bangladesh of whom several millions have registered in the electoral rolls. At least 3 lakhs continue to come in each year.[98] The Bangladesh government, for political reasons has been down playing the number which it is not in a position to take them back. Taking into account many expert estimates, another study is of the view that the Bangladesh refugees have expanded the population of the neighboring Indian states by 12 to 17 million of which 1 to 2 million may be caused by the 1971 war. The population of Assam has gone up by at least 7 million people to its current total of 22 million.[99] Some accounts put the figure as high as 13 million and accuse the Bangladesh government of pursuing a policy of lebensraum in north-east India.[100]

The Assam people however reluctantly accepted these migrants so long as the latter preferred to be mere labourers. Social tensions and violent conflict soon began to erupt when the migrants made serious inroads into their economy by occupying their land and began to prosper. Along with this, the Assamese fear of being reduced to a minority within their own homeland leading to the extinction of their culture and identity, accentuated the problems.

The Assamese legitimate fears, discontentment and lowered standard of living was accompanied by the failure of both the central and state government's disinclination to stem the tide of flow of Bangladeshis who were settled by them for their votes. This led to the first popular movement by the All Assam Students Union (AASU) against these illegal immigration. Their main demands were mainly the detection of foreign nations on the basis of the 1951 National Register of Citizens, their disenfranchisement and deportation. Strikes, demonstrations, blockades, civil disobedience and boycott of elections paralysed the administration. A series of governments rose and fell, political instability continued to invite the intervention of central government and its direct rule. From 1981 to 1983, illegal immigrants swelled in numbers in Assam from Bangladesh resulting in a number of communal clashes and riots killing hundred and thousands of people. The initial ethnic tension simmered for years due to the government's negligence and continued Bangladesh influx and suddenly turned into a fury of human carnage. It was the worst ethnic riot in India since independence and the number of human lives lost in these riots surpassed even the anti Sikh riots of 1984 or the anti Muslim riots of Mumbai in January 1993 or religious rioting in 1990 and 1992 over the Babri Mosque conflict in Northern India.[101] The holding of elections in Assam in 1983 without fulfilling the AASU's demands resulted in extreme violence claiming lives of many thousands. A study of the reasons behind the riots underlines a common factor, i.e., the scarcity of land between Bangladesh and north-east India.[102]

Despite the 1985 Assam Accord the problem of repatriation of Muslim Bengalis continues to exacerbate the U.L.F. A. and Bodoland movement in Assam, as those who came to power in centre did not show any interest to implement the accord. Renewed agitation by the AASU started again with the United Liberation Front of Assam (ULFA) and Bodo Land tribal movements against the Bengalis joined in making revolutionary demands for balkanization of Assam.

The issue of migration of Bangladeshis has already bedevilled their relations. Erecting a fence along the parts of the border and the forced repatriation of refugees at any point on the border have contributed to the ongoing conflict with Bangladesh. Despite a series of meetings at the ministerial and secretarial levels, illegal migration remains and continues unabated. The killing of 16 Border Security Forces (BSF) of India by Bangladesh Rifles in April 2001 is the result of conflict over land.

The ULFA and Bodoland movements continue in their demand for separatism, being allegedly militarily encouraged by Pakistan and Bangladesh. As Hiteswar Saikia, the former Chief Minister of Assam revealed the underground member of the United Liberation Front of Assam, the Bodo Security Force and other insurgent organisations active in Manipur, Nagaland and Tripura were getting shelter, weapons and arms training in Bangladesh with the help of Pakistan's ISI.[103] The outgoing BSF director general, D.K.Arya of India in his 10 page press release statement disclosed that insurgent groups operating in North East were acquiring sophisticated weapons from Thailand with the active connivance of Bangladesh's intelligence agencies. Bangladesh is providing all possible help in terms of shelter and training and the ISI of Pakistan is also actively involved in encouraging the Indian insurgent groups operating from the Bangladesh soil. This was also corroborated by Indian Home Secretary recently.[104] Recently it came out in newspapers that Bangladesh helped some Bodoland leaders fly to Geneva with its passports.

The press release further accused Bangladesh of stoking the fire of religious fundamentalism and disruptive forces in India and deliberately facilitating migration of its nationals to India. He further implied that the rise of insurgency in North East and growing migration to India with Bangladesh and Pakistan actively involved in encouraging morally and materially, such centrifugal forces have serious implications on India's security and unity.

By the year 2020, there will be 220 million Bangladeshis and one billion Indians competing for land and jobs.[105] If the influx is not stopped, there will be a sharp decline in communal harmony and centre-state relations will be vitiated giving rise to separatist tendencies and ethnic crisis in the north-eastern part of India on a scale larger than what is seen at present. In the absence of any concrete measure to stop the immigration by the Government of India, the insurgent activities by Bodo and ULFAs will increase, as found in recent days, deteriorating law and order situation in Assam. Any kind of inaction on the part of the Government will stoke the fire of separatism in these states. This problem will be further compounded, if all predictions about sea level rise due to global warming come true. Milliman and his colleagues estimate that the sea level will rise as much as 209 centimetres along the Bangladesh coast by 2050. As a consequence, in the worst case scenario 18 per cent of the habitable land would be under water and more than 17 million people could be environmental refugees, edging their ways into Indian territory. By the year 2100, the really worst scenario shows that 35 per cent of the nation's population—some 38 million people will be forced to relocate.[106]

References

1. Homer Dixon, "On the Threshold : Environmental Changes as Causes of Acute Conflict", *International Security* Vol. 16, No. 2. Fall 1991, p. 108.

2. For general background information on the CHT and jumma, see Anti-Slavery Society, The Chittagong Hill Tracts, Militarisation, Oppression and the Hill Tribes, London: Anti-Slavery Society, 1984 : CHT Commission. Life is not Ours: Land And Human Rights in the CHT Bangladesh Copenhagen and Amsterdam. Chittagong Hill Tracts Commission, 1991 and Father R.W.Timm. The Adivasis of Bangladesh, London Minority Rights Group, 1991.

3. Willem van Schendel, "The invention of the ' jummas' state formation and ethnicity in southeastern Bangladesh', unpublished manuscript, Department of History, Rotterdam University, 1990.

4. 'Genocide in Bangladesh', Survival International Review, 43, 1984, pp. 7-35: Timm, Adivasis,p.28: The Anti-slavery Society, Chittagong Hill Tracts, p. 69, Amnesty International, Bangladesh: Unlawful Killings and Torture in the Chittagong Hill Tracts, London: Amnesty International, 1986; Wolfgang Mey, Genocide in Bangladesh the CHT case,' paper presented at the 7th European Conference on Modern South Asian Studies 7-11 July 1981; and Gowher Rizvi, 'Bangladesh Insurgency in the CHT, The Round Table, 305, 1988, pp. 39-44.

5. CHT Commission, Life is not Ours, *op. cit*, p. 57.

6. Bangladeshi submission to the UN Working Group on Indigenous Peoples, August 1985, Cited in Amnesty, Bangladesh, p. 11.

7. Anti-Slavery Society, Chittagong Hill Tracts, pp.7.67 : and Life in the Chittagong Hill Tracts, Probe News Agency, Dhaka, 1994, p. 1, which accuses the JSS of wanting to falsely inflate the number of jumma deaths for NGO or broader international consumption. The claim is also made in Abdul M Hafiz and Nahid Islam, Environmental degradation and intra/interstate conflicts in Bangladesh, Environment and Conflicts Project (ENCOP), Occasional Paper No.6, Zurich, May 1993, p. 74 and in an unspecified government report forwarded by the Bangladeshi High Commissioner in London to the author, 14 August 1995, See EBT-21.6 Refugees Studies Documentation Centre, Oxford, for the JSS reports themselves.

8. Barbara Harff & Ted Robert Gurr, "Victims of the state: genocides, politicides and group repression from 1945 to 1995: in Albert J Jongman (ed), Contemporary Genocides: Causes, Cases, Consequences. The Hague: PIOOM, 1996, p.55: Harff & Gurr, 'Towards empirical theories of genocides and politicides : identification and measurement of cases since 1945 : *International Studies Quarterly*, 32(3), 1988, pp. 359-371: and Helen Fein, "Accounting for genocide after 1945: theories and some findings', *International Journal on Group Rights*, 1, 1993, pp. 79-106.
9. See for example, Ziauddin Ahmed, "The case of Bangladesh bringing to trial the perpetrators of the 1971 genocide," in Jongman, *Contemporary Genocides*, pp. 95-115.
10. Timm, Adivasis, *op. cit.*, p. 71. More generally, see Rahman Sobhan, *The Crisis of External Dependence : The Political Economy of Foreign Aid to Bangladesh* (Dhaka and London, Zed Press, 1982).
11. Julian Burger, Report from the Frontier: The State of the World's Indigenous Peoples (London: Zed Press, 1987), p. 129 and Timm, Adivasis, pp. 10-11.
12. Cited in CHT Commission, Life is not ours, *op. cit.*, p. 41
13. Anti-Slavery Society, Chittagong Hill Tracts pp. 85-88, appendix 6, and. CHT Commission, Life is not Ours, 1994 update, p. 31.
14. Mark Levene, "The Chittagong Hill Tracts: a case Study in the Political Economy of Creeping Genocide", *Third World Quarterly* Vol. 20, No. 2, 1999, p. 344.
15. Helen Fein, 'Scenarios of genocide: models of genocide and critical responses', in Israel W Charny (ed.), Towards the *Understanding and Prevention of Genocide: Proceedings of the International Conference on the Holocaust and Genocide*, (Boulder, Westview Press, 1984), pp. 4-5. See also Vahakn N Dadrian, 'A typology of genocide', *International Review of Modern Sociology*, 5(2), 1975, pp. 201-212.
16. See David Hardiman, *The Coming of the Devi: Adivasi Assertion in Western India* (Oxford: Oxford UniversityPress, 1995), ch. 1 : Ajay Skaria, 'Shades of wildness : tribe, caste and gender in western India, *Journal of Asian Studies*, 56(3), 1997, pp. 726-745 and John H. Bodley, Victims of Progress, Palo Alto, CA: Mayfield, 1982, for further discussion of these themes.
17. Schendel, 'Invention', *op. cit.*, pp. 9-10 and CHT Commission, Life is not Ours, pp. 88-89.
18. Tony Barta 'Relations of genocide: land and lives in the colonization of Australia', in Isidor Wallimann and Michael Dobkowski, ed., *Genocide* and the Modern age (Westport, CT: Greenwood Press, 1987) pp. 237-251: and Harff and Gurr "Towards empirical theory", p. 363.

19. Hardiman, The Coming of the Devi, *op. cit.*, esp. pp. 10-15, 216-217.

20. Mark Cocker, *Rivers of Blood, Rivers of Gold: Europe's Conflict with Tribal Peoples* (London: Jonathan Cape, 1998), p. 348.

21. Hafiz and Islam, " Environmental degradation", op. cit, pp. 31-49. Bernard Nietschmann, 'Indonesia, Bangladesh: disguised invasions of indigenous nations, Third World colonial expansion', *Fourth World Journal*, 1(2), 1985, pp. 96-97: and John Vidal, 'Floods that have brought misery and mayhem to millions the world over', *Guardian*, 19 September 1998.

22. Vidal, 'Foods', *op. cit*, and Timm, *Adivasis*, p. 8.

23. M. Mufazzalul Huq, 'Changing nature of dominant social forces and interventions in the CHT', *Journal of Social Studies* (Dhaka), 56, April 1992, p. 71

24. Life in the Chittagong Hill Tracts, pp. 12, 49.

25. Anti-Slavery Society, Chittagong Hill Tracts, p. 26.

26. Mark Levene, *op. cit.*, p. 348.

27. See Manan Ganguli, "The Chittagong Hill Tracts: before and after Bangladesh', *Fourth World News* (Cambridge) December 1995, pp. 5-8.

28. Mey, 'Genocide', p. 5.

29. Mark Levene, *op. cit.*, p. 349.

30. See Huq, 'Changing nature', pp. 72-75: Schendel, 'Invention', pp. 17-21: and Burger, Report from the Frontier, p. 130, for critical confirmation of these contentions.

31. Huq, 'Changing nature', *op. cit.*, pp. 80, 90.

32. Anti-Slavery Society, Chittagong Hill Tracts, pp. 32-33: Bodley, Victims, p. 8.

33. Mrinal Kanti Chakma, "Counter-insurgency: a multidimensional process of marginalisation of the CHT jummas', unpublished paper, Calcutta Research Group, 1996, pp. 9-10 notes the importance of the land acquisition regulation specific to the CHT of 1958, which provided a definitive break with the region's 'special status'.

34. Timm, *Adivasis*, p. 9.

35. Anti-Slavery Society, Chittagong Hill Tracts, p. 57. quoting Sheik Mujibur Rahman.

36. Madhav Gadgil and Ramachandra Guha, *This Fissured Land: An Ecological History of India*, (Delhi: Oxford University Press), 1992, pp. 116-134, 150-153.

37. Quoted in John H. Bodley, Victims of Progress (Pal0 Alto, CA: Mayfield, 1982), p.8. This contradicts the usual Bangladeshi refrain that the greatest threat to the sustainability of the forest come from jhum itself. See for example, Hafiz and Islam, 'Environmental degradation, p. 20.

38. CHT Commission, Life is not Ours, pp.71-86, Life in the Chittagong Hill Tracts, pp. 50-51.

39. Huq, 'Changing nature', pp. 84-85.

40. *CHT Commission, Life is not Ours*, p. 75.

41. Schendal, 'Invention', p. 10. See also Raja Devasish Roy, 'Forests, forestry and indigenous people in the Chittagong Hill Tracts', Earth Touch, February 1996, p. 40. for his comments on the attitudes of government officials.

42. Veena Kukreja, *Civil-Military Relations in South Asia, Pakistan, Bangladesh and India* (New Delhi: Sage, 1991) ch.4, 'Militarism in Bangladesh'.

43. Huq, 'Changing nature', p. 81: and Kukreja, Civil Military Relations, p. 140.

44. Kukreja, *Civil Military Relations*, p. 164.

45. Two specific examples of this with regard to the CHT were the way the state, despite supposedly strict controls protecting its own monopoly, dispensed direct land grants for large-scale rubber plantations and provided licences and permits for commercial logging. See Huq, 'Changing nature', pp. 81-85.

46. Kukreja, *Civil-Military Relations*, pp. 154-156.

47. United Government of Bangladesh report, quoted in Mark Levene, *op. cit.*,

48. *CHT Commission Life is not Ours*, p. 39.

49. *Ibid.*, p. 41, See Mey, 'Genocide', p. 11, for fuller details on the composition of BDF forces in the CHT.

50. CHT Commission, Life is not Ours, p. 16.

51. See Robert Paine, 'The Claim of the Fourth World', in Jens Brosted et al (eds). *Native Power. The Quest for Autonomy and Nationhood of Indigenous Peoples*, (Oslo: Universitetsflorlaget AS, 1985), pp. 49-66 for this argument.

52. Schendel, 'Invention', p. 13.

53. Sexual humiliation and degradation of Women, especially in the wake of 'ethnic cleansing' in Bosnia, is now well recognised as a major, consciously applied instrument in such 'softening up' processes. See Roger W Smith, 'Women and genocide: notes on an unwritten history', *Holocaust and Genocide Studies*, 8(3), 1994, pp. 315-334. Alexandra Stiglmayer (ed), Mass Rape : The War against Women in Bosnia-Herzegovina, (London: University

of Nebraska Press, 1994). For its specific application and other gender-related crimes in the CHT see *CHT Commission, Life is not Ours*, pp. 106-109.

54. Huq, 'Changing nature', p. 67, *CHT Commission, Life is not Ours*, p. 58. For more general confirmation of this point with regard to other third world state versus community struggles see David Maybury- Lewis, 'Living in Leviathan: ethnic groups and the 'state', in Maybury-Lewis(ed), The Prospects for Plural Societies (Washington, DC: The American Ethnological Society, 1984), pp. 224-225.

55. Quoted in *CHT Commission, Life is not Ours*, p. 14.

56. For development of this theme see chapters by Leo Kuper, Peter Worsley and Maybury- Lewis in Maybury-Lewis, The Prospects for Plural Societies, *op. cit.*

57. See *Anti-Slavery Society, Chittagong Hill Tracts*, pp. 44-54: and *CHT Commission, Life is not Ours*, pp- 16, 103-106 for jumma political developments Mey 'Genocide', p. 15. also noted the Shanti Bahini's links with the non-tribal and outlawed Marist Leninist Sarbohara Party.

58. *CHT Commission, Life is not Ours*, p. 84, and Mey 'Genocide', p. 9.

59. Quoted in Ali Murtaza, 'CHT: tracking the past', *Dhaka Courier*. 18 November 1994.

60. See Benedict Anderson, *Imagined Communities*, (London Verso, 1983), for the general argument: and Schendel Invention, pp. 26-31, for its application to the jumma.

61. Partha S.Ghosh, *Cooperation and Conflict in South Asia* (New Delhi, Manohar, 1989), p. 77.

62. Ittefaq, 15 May 1988, Goran Linkgreen et. al, ed., Peace Processes in the Third World, Report from the 1991 Advanced International Programme Conflict Resolution, Department of Peace and Conflict Research, Uppsala University, Sweden, p'. 245.

63. Shaukat Hassan, *Environmental Issues and Security in South Asia*, Adalphi paper 226, The International Institute for Strategic Studies (London), 1992, p.43.

64. Partha S. Ghosh, *op. cit.*, p. 79.

65. Position Paper on the Chittagong Hill Tracts Bangladesh, Institute of International Studies (BIISS) September 1987, p. 71. Partha S.Ghosh, *op. cit.*, p. 86.

66. Partha S. Ghosh, *op. cit.*
67. *Independent* (Bombay), 25 February 1991 and 22 June 1993.
68. Shika Bose, "Victims of Security Dilemma: Chakmas and Refugees from Bangladesh" in S.D.Muni and Lok Raj Baral, ed. *Refugees and Regional Security in South Asia* (New Delhi: Konark Publisher, 1996), p. 112.
69. *Times of India*, 29 January 1995, p. 11.
70. Partha S.Ghosh, *op. cit.*, p. 86. Greater Mizoram comprised of Parts of Tripura, Manipur, Chittagong Hill Tracts and Chin Hills of Burma.
71. Subir Bhaumik and H. C.Vanlaruata, 'Sailo's grand strategy: The former C.M. has picked up the Greater Mizoram cause to come out of the political wilderness", *Sunday*, 19-25 June 1988, p. 64. Ramesh Menon, 'Mizoram : wild dreams—plans to curve new state", *India Today* Vol. xiii, No. 12, 30 June 1988, pp. 63-67.
72. *Frontline*, 2 July 1994.
73. *Times of India* (New Delhi), 28 July, 1994.
74. See for details of all these accounts, *Times of India*, 1 January 1996.
75. Chief Minister of Arunachal Pradesh, Gegong Apang's Interview, *Times of India*, 3 January and 12 January, 1996..
76. Sanjoy Hazarika, "Bangladesh and Assam: Land Pressures Migration and Ethnic Conflict", occasional paper series of the Project on Environmental Change and Acute Conflict, A joint project of the University of Toronto and the American Academy of Arts and Sciences, No.3, March, 1993, p. 46.
77. Developing the Infrastructure, Report of the Task Force of Bangladesh Development Strategy for the 1990' s Vol.3,(Dhaka,UPL 1991), p. 426.
78. *World Bank Development Report*, 1992 (Oxford, Oxford University Press, 1992) Poverty in the Developing World 1985-2000.
79. Homer Dixon, "Environmental Scarcities and Violent Conflict: Evidence from Cases", *International Security* Vol. 19, No.1, Summer 1994, p. 21.
80. James Boyce, *Agrarian Impasse in Bengal: Institutional Constraints to Technological Change* (Oxford: Oxford University Press, 1987), p. 9.
81. Sanjoy Hazarika, *op. cit.*, p. 76.
82. James Boyce, *op. cit.*
83. Francesco Goletti, The Changing Public Role in a Rice Economy Approaching Self-Sufiliciency. The Case of Bangladesh, IFPRI Research Report 98 (Washington D.C. International Food Policy Research Institute, 1994).

84. James Boyce, *op. cit.*

85. Thomas F. Homer Dixon, *Environment, Scarcity and Violence* (Princeton, New Jersy: Princeton University Press, 1999), p. 96.

86. Environmental Policy, Report of the Task Force on Bangladesh Development Strategies for the 1990's. Vol.4, Dhaka. 1991,p. 179. See also *Regional Study on Greenhouse Effect and its Impact on the Region*, SAARC, Kathmandu, December 1992, p. 53.

87. See Homer Dixon, *op. cit.*, p. 22, Robert G. Gosselink, "Minority Rights and Ethnic Conflict in Assam, India", *Boston College Third World Law Journal* Vol. XIV, No.1, Winter 1994, pp. 90-91. Amulya Ganguly, "Bangladeshi Lebensraum, *Times of India*, 13 July, 1992, Sanjoy Hazarika, *Bangladesh and Assam land Pressures, Migration and Ethnic Conflict, Occasional Paper*, No.3, Project on Environmental Change and Acute Conflict, A Joint Project of the University of Toronto and the American Academy of Arts and Sciences, March 1993, pp. 52, 54.

88. Homer Dixon, *On the Threshold, op. cit.*, p. 108.

89. Sanjoy Hazarika, *Bangladesh and Assam, op. cit.*

90. *Ibid.*, p. 54.

91. Shikha Mukherjee, Special Correspondent of Times of India, Calcutta, December 1992, quoted in Sumit Ganguly, "Ethnoreligious Conflict in South Asia", *Survival*, Vol.35, No. 2, Summer 1993, p. 100.

92. *Times of India* (Eastern India Special), "Videshi headache", 15 September 1999.

93. See for details, *The Prajatantra*, (Orissa), 14 January 2001.

94. Robert G. Gossalink, "Minority Rights and Ethnic Conflict in Assam, India", *Boston College Third World Journal*, Vol. XIV Winter 1994, p. 91.

95. *Times of India*, *op. cit.* n. 92.

96. Amiya Kumar Das, Assam's Agony : A Socio-Economic and Political Analysis, 1982, p. 38 quoted in R.G., Gosselink, *op. cit.*, p. 90.

97. Sanjaya, *Assam : A Crisis of Identity* (1980), p. 10, quoted in Gosselink, *Ibid*, See also *Myron Weiner, Sons of the Soil : Migration and Ethnic Conflict in India* (Delhi : Oxford University Press, 1988), pp. 80-81.

98. *Times of India*, op. cit. n. 92.

99. Thomas F. Homer Dixon, "Environmental Scarcities and Violent Conflict : Evidence from Cases", *International Security* Vol. 19, No.1, Summer 1994, p. 22. See also Sanjoy Hazarika, *op. cit.*, pp. 52-54.

100. Prasun Sonwalker, "Exodus of Bangladeshis to India", *Times of India*, 6 December 1991, p. 4. Amulya Ganguli, "Bangladesh Lebensraum", *Times of India*, 13 July, 1992.
101. Sanjoy Hazarika, "Bangladesh and Assam", *op. cit.*, p. 58.
102. *Ibid.*, p. 59.
103. *Times of India*, 29 August 1995, p. 6.
104. *Times of India*, 1 December, 1995. See Indian Home Secretary Kamal Pandey's statement in Agartala, *Times of India*, 10 June 2000 (Eastern Indian Special).
105. Sanjoy Harzarika, "Bangladesh and Assam", *op. cit.*
106. John D. Milliman, Environmental and Economic Impact cited in Jodi L. Jacobson, Environmental Refugees: A yardstick of habitability, World Watch Paper No. 86, 1988, p. 35.

5

Future Sea Level Rise : Exacerbating Migration and Conflict

Future Sea Level Rise and its Impact Assessment

One of the damaging effects of global warming is sea level rise. Mean sea level (MSL) may change for two reasons : expansion of the oceans due to higher sea temperatures, and changes in the land based ice. Most of the projections of future sea level change agree that as a result of global warming, mean sea level should rise. The most recent projections depict a rise of less than one metre before the end of the next century - a change to which many communities might easily adapt. For instance, the best estimate given by the report of the Intergovernmental Panel on Climate Change (IPCC) is an average rate of rise of 6 millimetres per year (mm/yr) over the next century, if no actions are taken to stem the emissions of greenhouse gases.[1] None the less, the large uncertainties around mount projections suggest that the possibility of a much larger rise cannot be ruled out.

The risks of sea level rise affect many countries with potentially important international implications. With their emissions of CO_2 and other greenhouse gases, the industrialised nations of the world contribute largely to the bulk of the global warming problem. Warming, in turn, affects ice sheets at the extreme high latitudes, glaciers in remote mountain areas, and ocean temperatures worldwide, raising global sea level. The impending threats of environmental and socio-economic impacts have been matter of concern to many small island states and low lying river deltas in developing countries which have so far contributed very negligibly to greenhouse gas emissions.

The irony is that in all international fora starting from Rio to Kyoto when the question of apportioning responsibility arises, the industrialised nations very skillfully have tried to skirt the responsibility and share the burden with those developing South countries who have very little contributed to the emission of greenhouse gases. The use of this double standard logic by the industrialised nation lies at the heart of the problem. Bangladesh is one of the few developing countries worst affected by the sea level rise.

Sea Level Variations and Impact Issues

Bangladesh is one of the poorest of the World's Least Developed Countries (LDCS) with an average per capita GNP of US $ 170 and a low per capita use of fossil fuels. Bangladesh ranks poorly on indicators of development : less than one-third of the population is literate and the population which has already reached 128 m is increasing at an annual rate of 2.4 per cent .With a population of this size and a land area of 1,44,000 km^2 such a growth rate is alarming for a country like Bangladesh. It consists largely of the delta of three major rivers of the world, namely the Ganges, the Brahmaputra and the Meghna. It has been victim of recurrent, climate related natural disasters: the devastating floods of 1987 and 1988 and the unprecedented cyclone of 1991. Bangladesh which is one of the countries least responsible for the causes of climate change has been most vulnerable to the effects of sea level rise.[2]

A number of studies have been carried out for Bangladesh. Milliman, et al (1989)[3] and Broadus (1992)[4] , for instance postulated an inundation of up to one-third of the country due to 1m and 3m rises in relative sea level by estimating the area below the 1m and 3m contour lines. The population, land, and agricultural production within the affected area were then calculated as a basis for estimating impacts. Another study by the Bangladesh Centre for Advanced Studies in association with the Centre for Global Change, University of Maryland (Ali and Huq 1991) followed a similar approach for a 1m rise in a more detailed manner.[5]

Environmental and Socio-economic Implications : Dynamic Influence of Local Natural Systems

Brammer (1989, 1992)[6] believes that due to changes in river gradients, sedimentation and drainage, the primary impact of global mean sea level rise on Bangladesh will be an increase in flooding in the depressed basins upstream rather than only at the coast or within the tidal limits. Given the geomorphological and hydrological nature and structure of Bangladesh, even without the anticipated change in sea level, one could expect considerable physical changes to occur in the delta over the next 50-100 years, as they have occurred in past centuries. The lower Meghna river will continue to eat away its eastern bank and this movement would be aggravated if Ganges were to continue its historical trend.

Increasing Rise of Sediments

It may be expected that increasing quantities of sediments will be delivered to the estuary as degradation and erosion in the Himalayas and the Assam Hill continue to accelerate over the next several decades and as additional flood protection embankments along the major rivers channel increased flood flows through to the estuary.

Inland Effects

The greatest effects of the expected rise in sea level may not be seen near the coast but in inland. On both the young Meghna Estuarine Floodplain and the Ganges Tidal Floodplain land levels may be expected to increase concurrently with sea level as alluvium continues to be deposited on the land at high tide. Inland however a rise in sea level in the Meghna estuary could raise river levels upstream in the delta. In turn, the levels of these levees alongside active river channels would rise to match the increased height of seasonal riverfloods. Associated with this would be corresponding increase in the depth of seasonal flooding over most of the Ganges river flood plains, the Gopalganj Khulna - Bils and Old Meghna-Estuarine Floodplain.[7]

Shift in River Courses

Changes in river channels have been a recurrent phenomenon in Bangladesh. This would further increase with increased flood flows and sediment loads consequent upon increasing degradation of vegetation and soils in the Himalayas and Assam hills. Regardless of any change in sea level, such channel shifts could occur within next half century. According to Brammer, "the most that could be claimed in this respect might be, that of a rise in sea level would increase the risk of such major channel shifts occurring and so might advance their time of occurrence".[8] Such changing river courses would inundate agricultural land and houses forcing many people to flee to safe places. The sea level rise will impede the drainage of the additional run off due to an increase of 100 per cent rainfall and exacerbate flooding conditions in inland Bangladesh.

Intrusion of Salinity

Salinity is a factor of great importance in Bangladesh as the coastal zone is extensively affected by salinity. The affected areas include major urban and industrial centres of Khulna and Chittagang. The situation will be further aggravated with sea level rise.

A direct consequence of sea level rise will be intrusion of salinity with tide through rivers and estuaries. It will be accentuated in the dry season after the rainy season and river flows diminish. In fact this upland progression of saline water during the dry season eliminates surface irrigation potential for significant land in the south-west, south-central and south-east regions. Fresh ground water supply for human and industrial consumption is also affected by salinity. Moreover withdrawal of water from the Ganges upstream has caused considerable penetration of salinity inland.[9] According to an estimate, about 14,000 sq.km. of coastal and offshore areas have saline soils and are vulnerable to tidal flooding with salt water. If some 15 - 16 thousand Km^2 of coastal land is lost from a 45 cm. rise of sea level, the tidal ingress and saline intrusion will be pushed further inland. The present fresh water saline water interface may be pushed inland to as far as central Jessore region. The vulnerability due to saline ingress will be much more accentuated in the event of one metre sea level rise.[10] It may be also noted that high salinity intrusion may affect the power station and industrial water use in the Siddhirganj and Narayanaganj area.

Impact on Agriculture

The net result of sea level rise on agriculture is likely to be negative. The main effect of increasing flood levels in the interior regions would be on the Aus and deep water Aman paddy crops. The land area suitable for cultivating Aus paddy and jute would be reduced and farmers would need to change to lower yielding Aman paddy. Even deep water Aman would possibly be eliminated in some low-lying basins which become perennially wet or subject to flooding too early in the rainy season for reliable crop growth. In the dry season, the slower drainage of basin land implies that there will be increasing areas of land which will be too wet to allow the sowing of dry land crops, e.g., wheat, pulses, and mustard. Boro paddy may gradually be eliminated from some perennially wet land where traditional varieties are grown due to the greater depth of water remaining in the basin centres. The cultivation of modem varieties of Boro paddy with irrigation on low lying land may be jeopardised by the greater depth of water on the land at the time of planting and or by the increased risk of early flooding before the crop can be harvested.[11]

According to an estimate,[12] the existing cropping intensities of the affected area is about 136 per cent and the inundation of 2.915 million acres of net cropped land due to sea level change is expected to cause production losses of more than 2 million tonnes of rice, 13,000 tonnes of wheat, 214,000 tonnes of sugarcane, 405,000 tonnes of vegetables, 10,000 tonnes of jute, 97,000 tonnes of pulses, 37,000 tonnes of oil seeds and 97,000 tonnes of spices. The inundation of 2.915 million acres of cropland in fact will cause a loss of nearly Tk 29.71 billion worth of agricultural crops. Moreover 2.73 million of cattle and buffaloes, 986000 of goats and sheep, and 9.83 million of poultry will be affected. The total loss of assets and production in cottage and small industries are Tk., 1077.7 million and Tk. 98,532.9 million respectively.

Impact on Deforestation

Sea level rise will also affect the Sundarbans (Mangrove forest). Mangrove species are very sensitive to changes in salinity. Changes in species vigour or composition due to changes in salinity in this region could have a considerable economic impact. An adverse impact manifested in dying trees and reduced timber production could lead to public and political demands to release part of this area for agricultural settlement and production. It may be presumed that the Sundarban forest provides vital protection for these settled area in Khulna by acting as a buffer against the force of storm surges. Loss of this buffer could increase the threat of storm surges.

Recent projected demand for energy shows that while biomass demand will move up rather slowly, that for commercial fuels will increase fast. Between 1990 and 2010 biomass demand will increase by only 42 per cent while that for commercial energy will move up by 288 per cent.

The problems will arise due to the expected sea level rise. Under a 45 cm. sea level rise, 75 per cent of the Sunderban will be inundated while under the 1 metre sea level rise the whole of it will vanish. These events will certainly create very severe problems of supply of firewood from the forests. As the Forestry Master Plan has estimated by the year 2013, the total demand for firewood in the country would be 11,533 thousand cubic metres. Of this only about 8.208 cubic metres or 71 per cent only will be supplied leaving an unsatisfied demand for 3,345 thousand cubic metres. What it means is that either prices will rise and the excess demand will be choked off or there will be illegal falling to earn a rent or probably both will happen. If the inundation of the Sundarban becomes a certainty, people will very probably try to discount the future heavily, cut down the mangrove as fast as possible and earn that rent as quickly as possible. In the event of a sea level rise, it may lead to faster depletion of the forests in general and the tree resources in particular with disastrous implication on socio-economic conditions of Bangladesh.[13]

Drinking Water Scarcity and Impact on Health

In Bangladesh surface water which is a main source of water for human consumption including drinking is often polluted by indiscriminate defecation practices and unsanitary disposal of human and other waste. In Bangladesh some 80 per cent of all cases of illness can be traced to water borne diseases. The monsoon floods during the rainy season help the bacteria of diarhoeal diseases like cholera to spread spatially through inter-connected water bodies. The situation may be further exacerbated by frequent floods due to sea level rise which may do so through inter connection between bacteria infested and bacteria free bodies. Flies also get a more hospitable environment for breeding. Also in the absence of an effective eradication programme, the ready availability of breeding grounds due to probable increased drainage congestion caused by heavier rain flood and pending effects of flood embankments, the incidence of malaria could possibly increase.

Impact on Human Habitation and Cropland

The sea level rise is expected to inundate about 5.608 million acres of existing coastal land which is about 15.8 per cent of the total area of Bangladesh. The area comprising of 65 per cent of greater Khulna, 99 per cent of Barisal, 100 per cent of Patuakhali, 44 per cent of Noakhali, and 12% of Faridpur will be inundated. The total of 62 up zilas of 13 new districts out of 64 districts will be affected by one metre sea level change. As a result 13.74 per cent or net cropped area 2.915 million acres, and 28.29 per cent of the forest area 1.304 million acres will be lost due to sea level changes and it will not be possible to replace the cropland as rural areas are already extensively used as such.[14]

Increasing Economic Marginalisation and Poverty

Since cultivators may be slow to modify their existing practices in response to the very slowly changing environment, increasing numbers will probably be marginalised economically by the increasing frequency of crop damage or loss, or by the reduced cropping opportunities. Given the existing unequal social relations and the likelihood of their continuation into the foreseeable future, especially in remote areas, it seems inevitable that poverty will increase and that big land holdings will continue to prevail in areas where they are found today, where small holdings predominate, as on the Old Meghna Estuarine Floodplains, increasing pauperization resulting from deteriorating agricultural environment may be expected to push the increasing numbers of people of the land. The conjectured changes stated above would mere reinforce the trends that are already seen as population pressure on the land throughout the delta mounts.[15]

Environmental Induced Refugees

Milliman and his colleagues[16] estimate that the sea level will rise as much 209 centimetres along the coast by 2050. Half the country lies at elevations of less than 5 metres. Loss of land under the 13 centimetres rise in the best case scenario is minimal, less than one per cent of the country's total. In the 144 centimetre rise in the worst case however 16 per cent of the nation's land would be lost. In the worst case scenario local sea level rise would be 209 centimetres, and 18 per cent of the habitable land would be under water. As a result, more than 17 million people would become environmental refugees. By the year 2100, the really worst case scenario shows that 35 per cent of the nation' s population - some 38 million people will be forced to relocate.

A study shows that the population to be displaced by sea level rise and inundation is estimated as 5 per cent of the national population on the basis of 1991 census, i.e., just 5.5 million people in absolute terms. Under the high sea level rise the respective figures are expected to be 13.5 per cent and 14.8 million. Since population is increasing at 2.4 per cent per annum, the people to be affected in 20 per cent will be several times larger. Even if population grows at a long-term rate of only 1 per cent per annum, the absolute size of the affected population will swell to 12 million and 32 million under the respective sea level rise scenarios.[17] As the coastal region is under the threat of various natural hazards and sea level rise will occur over a considerably long time, the affected people will begin to move out on their own in search of a better life in most of the cases elsewhere. With sea level rise, the struggle for life is going to be tougher still, prompting people to outmigrate in great numbers and proportion to urban areas within and to neighbouring Indian states.

Exacerbating the Crisis in India

Given the trends of migration from Bangladesh to neighbouring Indian states being induced by demand-induced scarcity of land along with its supply induced scarcity, the predicted sea level rise may add many more millions to the already residing 12 to 17 million in India.[18] All between 12 to 35 million evacuated due to sea level rise or its consequences like storm, cyclone, flood, decreased agricultural production and poverty may not be settled in urban areas. Many from plain areas may be settled in CHT as is continuing unsettling many Chakmas and tribals from the homeland. Many more millions not settled in CHT or in urban cities may prefer to migrate to Indian states in the hope of getting a better prospect. Not yet fully settled, the conflict between tribal Chakmas and local plain Bengali people with Bangladesh supporting the latter may be unleased further with greater vigour. In the event of ongoing migration of plain people Chakmas may further migrate to Indian states like Tripura further reinforcing India's involvement in it. The cataclysmic nature of the 1998 flooding underscores the degree to which acute long term environmental degradation in term of sea level rise and population pressures in this region are not respector of internal or international borders. The technically illegal spillover from Bangladesh in recent years, of some millions of plains people into the neighbouring hill states of India notably Assam suggests that the interrelationship between these pressures and national minority conflict in Bangladesh is hardly limited to CHT.[19] Apart from this, the addition of many more to the refugees flowing into Assam and other states will exacerbate the ethnic conflict already having destabilising effects on Indian territory. At present with the current migration, the Government of India has not been able to solve the crisis. In case of the predicted sea level rise, flight of some more millions of Bangladeshis into Indian territory will aggravate the situation making the prospect of group identity conflict in Assam and other North-Eastern states of India more apparent. Massacre, communal riots, ethnic conflict, involvement of immigrants in a spate of robberies and heinous crimes and rise of centrifugal forces against the flow of refugees will be more frequent with a greater possibility of India and Bangladesh being involved. This would create far reaching implications on India's security, federal structure and unity. India's overenthusiastic concern for maintaining neighbourly relations with Bangladesh may not be stretched too far to ignore its own national interests and put a lid over new security implications arising out of the flow of migrants from Bangladesh induced by environmental scarcity of resources such as land and its degradation in the overall context of global warming and sea level rise. It is certain that the coalesce of sea level rise and changing climate thrust on increasing population density and poverty in Bangladesh could exacerbate the political tensions that already exist in the region.

References

1. R.A. Warrick and J. Oerlemans, "Sea level rise" in J.T. Houghton, G.J. Jenkins and J.J. Ephraums, ed., Climate Change: The I.P.C.C. Scientific Assessment (Cambridge: Cambridge University Press, 1990).

2. A.A.Rahman and S. Huq , Greenhouse effect and Bangladesh: A Conceptual Framework. In Proceedings of the Conference on the Greenhouse effect and Coastal Area of Bangladesh, eds. Moudud H., et. al, (Dhaka, 1989).

3. J.D. Milliman, J.M. Broadus and F. Gable "Enviromental and Economic Impacts of Rising Sea Level and Subsiding Deltas: The Nile and Bengal Examples", Ambio, 18(6) 1989, pp. 340-345.

4. J.M. Broadus, "Prossible impacts of and adjustments to sea level rise : the cases of Bangladesh and Egypt" in R.A. Warrick, E.M. Barrow and T.M.L. Wigley ed., Climate and Sea Level Change: Observations, Projections and Implications (Cambridge: Cambridge University Press, 1992).

5. S. I. Ali and S Hug, International Sea Level Rise: A National Assessment of Effects and Possible Responses for Bangladesh, prepared for Centre for Climate Change, University of Maryland, Maryland, 1991 USA.

6. H.Brammer, "Monitoring the evidence of the greenhouse effects and its impact on Bangladesh in H.Mouderd, A. Rahman et al ed., Proceedings of the Conference on the Greenhouse Effect and Coastal Area of Bangladesh. Dhaka, Bangladesh, 1989. H.Branmer, "The complexities of detailed impact assessment for the Ganga-Brahmaputra-Meghna delta of Bangladesh" in R.A. Warrick, E. M. Barrow and T.M.L. Wigley ed., Climate and Sea Level: Observations, Projections and Implications (Cambridge: Cambridge University Press, 1992).

7. H.Brammer op. cit. 1992, p. 256.

8. Ibid., p. 257.

9. Regional Study on Greenhouse Effect and its impact on the Region SAARC, Kathmandu, 1992, p. 62.

10. Climate Change in Asia: Bangladesh, Asian Development Bank, (ABB), Bangkok, July 1994, p. 48.

11. H. Brammer 1992, op. cit, p. 258.

12. Regional Study on Greenhouse effect, op. cit. p. 54.

13. Climate Change in Asia, ADB, op. cit. pp. 55-56.

14. Regional Study, op. cit., p. 53.

15. H. Brammer, 1992, op. cit., pp. 258-59.

16. John D.Milliman, Environmental and Economic Impact cited in Jodi L. Jacobson, Environmental Refugees : A Yardstick of Hitabitability, World Watch Paper no. 86, 1988, p. 35.
17. Climate Change in Asia: op. cit., pp. 47-48. H. Brammer, Geographical complexities of detailed impact assessment far the Ganges-Brahmaputra Meahna delta of Bangladesh, pp. 256-59. In R.A.Warrick, E.M.Barrow and T.M.L. Wigley ed., Climate and Sea Level Change: Projections and Implications (Cambridge: Cambridge University Press, 1993).
18. Thomas F. Homer Dixon, Environment, Scarcity and Violence (Princeton, New Jersey; Princeton University Press, 1999), p. 95.
19. Suzanne Goldenberg, "Immigrants bear brunt of Assam's culture of mutiny", Guardian 17 April 1996; Mark Levene, "The Chattagong Hill Tracts: a case study in the political economy of, creeping genocide", Third World Quarterly vol. 20, No. 2, 1999, pp. 361-62.

6

Floods and Cyclones in Bangladesh : Implications and Consequences, Intra and Interstate

In the developing world three major causes dominate natural disaster process.

- Human vulnerability resulting from poverty and inequality.
- Environmental degradation owing to poor land use.
- Rapid population growth, especially among the poor.[1]

The havoc caused by natural disasters could not be entirely blamed on weather, a natural phenomenon: part of the disaster is due to human negligence.[2]

Thus involvement in natural disaster by international, national and academic institutions have led to a number of definitions of natural disaster. The explicit definitions are those forwarded by academic institutions and of crucial importance for research in the area of natural disasters.

Disasters : Human Linkages

On two broad aspects the definitions on natural disasters can be explicated. The first aspect, which includes definitions forwarded by Cisin and Clark is where, disaster is viewed as an event, which seriously disrupts normal life. On the other hand, Krimgold defines disaster as a crisis event that outstrips the capacity of a society to cope or manage with it at least for a time.[3] The emphasis on normalcy is to see disaster as an extension of everyday life. It also implies that an understanding of the threat of disaster is as important to the comprehension of the disaster as the disaster event itself. Hewitt and Burton (1971) developed this notion of potential threat and accent disaster as a function.[4]

The second important aspect, which requires consideration in a definition of natural disaster, is the dynamic human-environment relationship. To comprehend disaster from this point of view, it is essential to see it as an extreme situation implicit in the everyday condition of the given population. It is necessary to consider the socio-economic conditions in relation to physical environment to understand the everyday condition of a population. In the context of hazards faced, this relationship turns to the notion of vulnerability. Vulnerability is the degree to which different classes in society are differently at risk. This is in terms of both the probability of occurrence of an extreme physical event and the degree to which the community absorbs the effects of these extreme physical events and helps the different classes to recover.[5]

Disaster is defined by World Bank as events, which usually have a 'natural' basis (winds, water, land movement) but which also have human and societal aspects as well. It is the negative impact of a natural phenomenon on human life—its economy, its society and its polity that justifies the term disaster.[6]

Without people there can be no disaster. Natural disaster is, therefore, defined as the interface between an extreme physical event and a vulnerable human population.[7] The most comprehensive definition of what constitutes disaster is provided by a report based on the work undertaken by the Oxford Centre for Disaster Studies - disaster is defined as a serious disruption of the functioning of a society, causing widespread human, material, or environmental losses which exceed the ability of the affected society to cope using its own resources. Thus a natural disaster is seen as the product of a hazard such as flood, cyclones/windstorm or earthquake coinciding with a vulnerable situation, which might include communities, cities or villages. In consonance with this definition hazards are defined as phenomena that pose a threat to people, structures or economic assets, which may cause a disaster. They could be either man-made or naturally occurring in our environment.[8]

Vulnerability is defined as the extent to which a community, structure, service or geographic area is likely to be damaged or disrupted by the impact of particular hazard. This could be on account of their nature, construction and proximity to hazardous terrain or a disaster prone area.[9] The two important components in this definition of natural disaster include hazard and vulnerability or hazard as without vulnerability or hazard there is no natural disaster.

Disaster : Nature and Causes

The varied researches undertaken on natural disasters suggest the following nature and causes of disaster :

- Natural events result basically from interactions between the atmosphere, hydrosphere and lithosphere, i.e., they are geographical processes. Resource depletion and environmental decline change these interactions, which in turn, affect the frequency and magnitude of natural disasters.[10]
- Natural hazards are generated from interaction between natural events system and human use system. Earthquakes would not be hazards if humans did not occupy active seismic zones. This means that natural hazards potentially threaten human society.[11]
- Natural disasters are interaction between natural hazards and their vulnerable conditions (socio-economic, cultural and political), which are usually created by human actions. Thus, the distinction between natural and man-made disasters is blurred by tragic impact of the natural disasters that result from human misuse of resources, inappropriate actions and lack of foresight.[12]
- Natural disaster causes tragic impact, which disrupts established way of life. Some of the impacts such as loss of life, destruction to buildings and infrastructure, and economic losses are quantifiable. Other losses such as loss of opportunities, changes in the community's culture, impact on the environment and socio-economic problems are less easily measured.

The United Nations Centre of Human Settlements (UNCHS) offers a holistic framework for natural disasters in terms of creation, effects, outcomes and responses.

"... A natural disaster can be defined as the interaction between a natural hazard, generated in most cases from sudden and unexpected natural event, and vulnerable conditions which cause severe losses to man and his environment (built and natural)".[13] These losses create suffering and chaos in the normal patterns of life, which lead to socio-economic, cultural and sometimes political disruption. Such a situation requires outside intervention at international and national levels in addition to individual and communal responses.[14]

The above definition entailing social scientists concern (namely impact on society, economy, culture, polity and last but not the least environment) demonstrates a shift from focusing on the technical aspects of the physical phenomena (namely quantifiable impact on people and structures) to a wider perception, that natural disasters are predominantly environmental, social and developmental issues.

As threats are becoming more and more complex and inter-related, the challenge is a better understanding of known natural hazards as also the changing and newly emerging threats as well as their complex inter-relationships. Most disaster policy still puts emphasis on the impact of nature. This has led to the dominance of technical intervention focused on predicting the hazard or modifying its impact. The intent of this kind of intervention has always aimed at according to Anderson, 'merely to get things back to normal as soon as possible'.[15]

Ecological Perspective

The ecological perspective considers natural disasters to be neither unforeseen nor isolated problem, but an integral part of the spectrum of man-environment relations. Humans can indeed instigate natural hazards, directly and indirectly by their inadequate or inappropriate intervention in environment. This results in severe ecological stress namely food shortages, water shortages, heat problems, poor sanitation, crowding environmental pollution and degradation, resource depletion resulting in higher risk to future disasters.[16] Researches in the literature on environmental management and sustainable development suggest that it is the poorer countries that are most vulnerable to the effects of environmental degradation and it tends to be the poorest people in these countries who suffer the most.

The most important factor leading to an aggravation of the risk of disasters at present is deforestation and industrial emissions of green-house gases contributing in its consequent chain to climate change, global warming and sea-level rise threatening inundation of vast areas of our planet. Global warming will increase the frequency and intensity of topical storms, as a high surface temperature of over 27° Celsius of the sea helps in the formation of cyclones. An increase in the sea temperature thus increases the possibility of cyclones. In case of Bangladesh, a global rise of sea level temperature even by one metre will lead to a loss of 22,889 sq. km of land around 15.8 per cent of the total land area and could turn a moderate storm into a catastrophic one.[17]

Socio-Cultural Perspective

In accordance with the socio-cultural perspective, the impact of natural disasters is affected by a society's values and institutions, which shape the development and planning process, the production of goods and distribution of resources and provision of opportunities and socio-economic facilities. These values and institutions influence the vulnerability of the people through land use, housing, infrastructure and emergency planning.[18] Moreover natural disasters also lead to severe social stress resulting in social conflicts, rising rates of crime generated by Durkhemian notion of 'anomie' in society, feeling of social isolation and dissimilarity leading to interpersonal problems. Natural disasters often produce at times an immediate period of altruism and heightened social support. However, the reconstruction and recovery process often outlasts this therapeutic phase. Relocation at times as a result of natural disasters results in stressful psychological conditions and negative mental health effects as strangers find it difficult to create new support networks.[19]

Economic Perspective

The economic perspective considers the impact of natural disasters on human settlements as a result of the failure of human-use system both pre and post-disaster to protect people and their belongings. In the pre-disaster situation, this is directly related, among many other factors, to settlement-growth construction methods, high levels of inequality, urbanisation and its associated problems, absence of planning for mitigation, early warning systems and subsequent vulnerability reduction. In the post-disaster situation, the impact is influenced by the effectiveness or ineffectiveness of relief and emergency operations as well as the availability or unavailability of resources to deal with losses and chaos. The impact of natural disaster is, thus, directly related to the level and type of development of a society, when considered from the developmental perspective.[20]

Political Perspective

The political perspective considers the impact of natural disaster on the political process in terms of the efficiency of the existing regime to cope with the impact on economy, environment and consequent development. The effectiveness of the government in reducing socio-economic inequality is judged from the perspective of providing immediate relief and channelising the available resource inflow to the best possible use both during normal times and during disaster for the disaster affected populace. The stability of political regimes particularly in the developing countries is crucially dependent on government capacity. Disaster management policies need to be effectively integrated with long-term developmental policies in order to effectively and efficiently organize disaster management activities in all its different stages - relief, rehabilitation, reconstruction and future disaster mitigation.

The past historical effectiveness (i.e., state's capacity gauged through its past record of dealing with disasters) and the effects of state autonomy (i.e., independence of the government, its ability to take crucial decisions during emergency situations as also anticipate the required logistics during such situations, coordinate the activities of various key actors involved, etc.) are of crucial importance in the evolution of a comprehensive disaster management strategy. Absence of good governance, non-conducive political decisions and consequent legislation ignoring the interests of the vast majority of the poor in developing countries can themselves trigger disasters such as famine.[21]

Developmental Perspective

The developmental perspective considers the linkage between disaster impact and poverty. Poverty increases disaster vulnerability. The impact of disasters is felt most by the poorer countries. The people who suffer most from disasters are almost always the poor people of any society. At the macro level, the impact of disaster usually results in two major setbacks. Firstly it is the direct loss of existing national assets in various forms. And secondly, it is the diversion of national resources and efforts away from ongoing subsistence and development, in order to achieve satisfactory recovery.[22]

Development activities however, undertaken to redeem the deplorable conditions of the poor, need to be done with caution. This is because most development projects planned without recognition of natural hazards, directly contribute to increased disaster proneness without any consideration of this fact. Development at times leads indirectly to an increase in disaster probability due to environmental deterioration and ecological crisis. Thus environment is often the point of interface between developmental programming and disaster vulnerability.

Developmental programme or project in natural disaster prone countries either increases or decreases the likelihood of disasters. The controversy over construction and utility of embankments for developmental purposes as also a solution to flood management is often criticised for contributing to environmental degradation, namely deforestation, destruction of fisheries and large scale socio-economic problems due to distorted and often half-hearted attempts at rehabilitation of the displaced population.

On the one hand, development investments increase a country's capacity to cope with hazards and contribute to disaster prevention. On the other hand when development spending is undertaken without an awareness of disaster proneness it could create the possibility of a new disaster or could increase the potential negative impact of existing natural crises. As natural disaster interrupts ongoing programmes and diverts resources from their originally planned use, a failure to factor the likelihood of natural crisis into planning can represent a serious mismanagement as well as waste of resources. Despite this linkage between natural disaster and development, disasters are seldom discussed in the development literature. Interestingly, development is discussed as a major issue in all the disasters literature. This is of crucial importance for efficient development planning in disaster prone areas and for reduction of the extent of vulnerability to future disaster.[23]

Thus, disaster as discussed from various perspectives, is the product of hazard coinciding with a vulnerable situation stemming from certain root causes political, economic and social aided by dynamic pressures such as environmental degradation due to a burgeoning population, deforestation, etc.

Disaster : Conceptual Issues

Any social science research on disaster management would remain incomplete without a look into the theoretical discourses in the realm of disasters. Its varied dimensions necessitate a multi-disciplinary management strategy, that would look into :

- Environmental /ecological vulnerability – degradation of the environment and inability to protect it.
- Developmental vulnerability – vulnerability caused through unsustainable practices.
- Educational vulnerability – lack of access to information and knowledge.
- Attitudinal and motivational vulnerability – lack of public awareness.
- Political/system vulnerability – limited access to political power and representation.
- Cultural vulnerability – certain beliefs and customs.
- Physical vulnerability – weak building or weak individuals.

Extent and Nature of Impact

An analysis of the World Disaster Reports of 1997 and 2000 would help assess the regional impact of natural disasters, more specifically, floods and cyclones vis-a-vis the global impact of natural disasters. According to the report the average number of people affected by disasters has been enormous. Asia shows the greatest total number affected reflecting the devastating effects of flooding.

It further states, Asia has been one of the most adversely affected region by natural disaster during the period 1971-95, with 59.5 per cent of the total number of people killed across regions in Africa followed by 34 per cent of the total number of people killed in Asia. In terms of people injured of the total of 89,617. Asia leads with 84.3 per cent of the total injured followed by 10.5 per cent injured in America. In terms of people affected by disasters out of the total of 136,571,548, Asia again seems to lead the list with 87.6 per cent of the total people while Africa has 8.6 per cent . In terms of the different impact that different disasters have had on Asia on a total of 123,972,404, the highest number of people come in the category of affected 96.6 per cent with 3.29 rendered homeless and 0.06 per cent injured and 0.03 per cent killed. This reflects that in all, it is Asia that has suffered the most, in almost all respects, due to natural disasters that took place in the 25 year period under survey.

Thus, from the report it is evident that in the decade of the 1990s, floods were responsible for more than half the total number of people reported affected world-wide. Region-wise study shows that Asia and in particular South Asia has been the worst affected. In Asia, they affected more than 84.2 per cent of the total affected (1753505.56), but earthquakes caused the most economic damage followed closely by floods and cyclones. Droughts affected African population the most in the 1990s, but the most economic damage was caused due to cyclones.

The disastrous impacts of floods at the global level vis-a-vis the Asian region is clearly evident from the analysis of flood disasters as cited in the World Disaster Report 1997 and 2000. Floods have been a major killer responsible for 10.3 per cent of the global death affecting another 36% of the total injured and rendering 68 per cent homeless. Among the natural calamities the impact of floods has thus been to the tune of 45.6% of the total (138732.87).[24]

Among the 2,012 natural disasters (1971-95), 23 instances of flooding alone have occurred in Asia in 1996. Floods have thus been one of the major natural disasters that have affected the Asian region causing insurmountable socio-economic losses.[25]

Impact of Disasters in South Asia and Bangladesh

In South Asia, the number of people reported killed and affected by disasters are extremely high given the vulnerable nature of the majority of the population inhabiting South Asia. According to the World Disaster Report 2001, as shown in the Table-6.1 the total number of people reported killed by disasters amongst the South Asian countries in the 1980s was the highest in India with 46.9 per cent followed by Bangladesh with 44.2 per cent . Whereas in the 1990s the total number of people reported killed in Bangladesh was 67.2 per cent even higher than India's 26.9 per cent . In the 1980s the annual average people reported killed was highest in India with 46.9 per cent followed by Bangladesh with 44.1 per cent . In the 1990s the annual average reported killed was highest in Bangladesh with 67.3 per cent followed by India with 26.9 per cent . In terms of the total number of people reported affected in the 1980s and 1990s India recorded the highest with73.5 per cent and 78 per cent followed by Bangladesh with 25.1 per cent and 16.3 per cent respectively.

The annual average of people reported affected in 1980 and 1990 in India were 77.5 per cent and 78 per cent respectively whereas in Bangladesh it was 25.1 per cent and 16.3 per cent respectively. Compared to the other South Asian countries in terms of geographical extent and population the figures are abysmally high for Bangladesh showing the recurrent vulnerability and consequent loss of the Bangladeshis exposed to frequent natural disasters. In the 1990s, the severe 1991 and 1997 cyclone (in terms of people affected as the death toll was much less compared to the 1991 cyclone) and the 1998 floods can be cited as possible explanations for the high toll both in terms of people killed as well as people affected.

Bangladesh appear amongst the top five countries in terms of death toll and number of people affected from various types of disasters. This is partly because the country is geographically located in the hazard prone area, having a very large economically poor population. Often these are the people who live on the most hazard prone parts of the country with least resources, awareness, knowledge, power or the choices to mobilize the defense against frequent hazards.[26]

Table-6.1 : Comparative Data of People Reported Killed and Affected during the 1980s and 1990s in South Asia

South Asian Countries	*Total Number of people reported killed (1981-1990)*	*Total Number of people reported affected (1981-1990)*	*Annual average of people reported killed (1981-1990)*	*Annual average of people reported affected (1981-1990)*	*Total Number of people reported killed (1991-2000)*	*Total Number of people reported affected (1991-2000)*	*Annual average of people reported killed (1991-2000)*	*Annual average of people reported affected (1991-2000)*	*Total Number of people reported killed (2000)*	*Total Number of people reported affected (2000)*
Bangladesh	27,903 (44.18)	228,794,460 (25.13)	2,790 (44.18)	22,879,446 (25.13)	147,753 (67.25)	90,473,239 (16.34)	14,775 (67.26)	9,047,324 (16.34)	681 (14.45)	2,826,122 (2.06)
India	29,639 (48.93)	669,359,908 (73.54)	2,964 (46.94)	66,935,991 (73.53)	59,132 (26.92)	32,402,751 (78.09)	5,913 (26.92	43,240,275 (78.09)	3,424 (72.67)	131,216,825 (95.69)
Nepal	2,707 (4.29)	937,193 (0.10)	2,271 (4.29)	93,719 (0.10)	3,597 (1.68)	911,727 (0.16)	360 (1.64)	91,173 (0.16)	211 (4.48)	50,070 (0.04)
Pakistan	2,224 (3.52)	1,241,030 (0.13)	222 (3.52)	124,103 (0.14)	8,568 (3.90)	26,202,006 (4.73)	857 (3.90)	2,620,201 (4.73)	348 (7.39)	2,200,171 (1.60)
Maldives	0 (0)	300 (0)	0	30 (0)	10 (0)	23,849 (0)	1 (0)	2,385 (0)	n.a.	n.a.
Srilanka	678 (1.07)	9,842,458 (1.08)	68 (1.08)	984,249 (1.08)	614 (0.28)	3,720,964 (0.67)	61 (0.28)	372,096 (0.67)	48 (1.02)	840,000 (0.61)
Total in '000	63.15	9101.75	6.32	9102.75	219.67	5537.34	21.97	5537.34	4.71	1371.33

Note: (a) percentage within single parenthesis indicates total number of people killed and affected (1981-1990 and 1991-2000), annual average of people killed and affected (1981-1990 and 1991-2000) and total number of people killed and affected (2000) across by various types of disaster (vertical).

n.a.: not available.

Source: World Disasters Report 2001, International Federation of Red Cross and Red Crescent Societies, Geneva, 2001.

Table 6.2 shows the annual average (1991-2000) and total (2000) number of people reported killed and affected in Bangladesh in comparison to the over all figures of people affected and killed in the decade of the 1990s and particularly for the year 2000 in comparison to the Asian region.

Table 6.2

Annual Average (1991-2000) and Total (2000) Number of People Killed and Affected in Bangladesh vis-a-vis Asia

	Annual average killed (1991-2000)	*Annual average Affected (1999-2000)*	*Killed (2000)*	*Affected (2000)*
Asia	59,829	188,822,365	11,056	229,117,986
Bangladesh	14,775 (24.70)	9,047,324 (4.79)	681 (6.16)	2,826,122 (1.23)

Note: Figures within single parenthesis are Bangladesh's percentage share of Asia total.

Source: World Disasters Report,2001. International Federation of Red Cross and Red Crescent Societies, Geneva,2001.

The severe impact of natural disasters, in Bangladesh necessitates, the policy interventions as an effective response system to cope with the interruption of normal ways of life (socio-economic, environmental, cultural and sometimes political disruption). The response system at the international, national, community and individual level suggest the need for an effective coordination and cooperation at all these levels. This is so particularly in the evolution of a well pronged disaster management strategy to redeem the plight of both affected and vulnerable to future disaster.

Natural Disaster in Bangladesh

Bangladesh, lying astride the tropic of Cancer and longitude 90°E, occupies an area of about 1,44,000 sq.km. with a population of more than 129.2 million.[27] Situated in the north-eastern part of the South Asian region between latitude 20°34 and 26°38 N and longitudes 88°01 and 92°41 E, the country has a vast area to the south. The Bay of Bengal has an economic zone of the order of 100,000 sq.km. The average population density in 1995 was about 939 persons per sq.km. Despite considerable diversity of physical conditions that exist within its boundaries, principal efforts of the Bangladesh government apart from population control have only from the middle of 1990s (approximately), been diverted towards environmental management including disaster management as an integral component. This is crucial, in order to ensure rationalised and resource management, prevent deforestation and integrate disaster management within larger developmental plans, for the very survival of Bangladesh.[28]

Floodplains of the Brahmaputra, Ganges, Meghna and some smaller rivers of Bangladesh occupy about 80 per cent[29], three terraces (the Madhupur Tracts, the Barind Tracts and the Lalmai Hill area) occupy 8 per cent and hills occupy 12 per cent of Bangladesh.[30] Relief and soil patterns are often complex. Most floodplain villages have elevation ranges of 1m or more, with permeable loamy soils on the higher parts and impermeable clays in the lower parts. These differences in elevation determine local differences in the depth and duration of seasonal flooding. They also determine cropping patterns. For instance, differences in elevation as low as 30 m high can be highly significant for crops, crop varieties and seasonal rotations in relation to flooding characteristics. Flood-plain gradients are on the other hand also low. The average gradient from north-western coast tip to the coast is 20 cm/km and it averages 1.6 cm/km in south of Dhaka. Overland drainage is often impeded by silted-up old river channels, road and railway embankments lacking adequate bridges and culverts, and cropped rice paddy fields surrounded by bunds. The main river channels are unstable, particularly that of the Brahmaputra-Jamuna.[31]

River-bank erosion and changing of river courses[32] pose a serious problem to constructing flood protection works alongside such rivers.[33] The changing course of Bangladesh's rivers[34] consume around 9000 hectares of fertile land annually, spread them out elsewhere, resulting in the formation of small islands or char or diara (newly formed islands) and affecting a million people annually.[35]

The Ganges-Brahmaputra-Meghna (GBM) catchment area has a predominantly monsoon climate, with heavy rainfall concentrated in 3-6 summer months, particularly May-July. In Bangladesh, mean annual rainfall ranges between 1,250 mm and 55,000mm. Cherrapunji on the Meghalaya plateau overlooking the north-east corner of Bangladesh, has 11,615 mm. However, significant variations occur between years in the monthly and annual rainfalls received, leading to considerable differences between years in peak flood levels and extent of floods ranging from 5,000 sq.km. to 50,000 sq.km.[36]

The major rivers and their tributaries have their headwaters outside Bangladesh. The two major rivers Ganges/ Padma and Brahmaputra/Jamuna flowing through Bangladesh have their headwaters in India and China respectively. Only about 7.5 per cent of their total catchment area of about 1.5 million sq.km lie within Bangladesh. Similarly about 90 per cent of their annual flow originates outside the country. 7.8 per cent of the catchment areas of the Ganges, the Brahmaputra and the Meghna are located within Bangladesh. The remaining 62 per cent are in India, 18 per cent in China, 8 per cent in Nepal and 4 per cent in Bhutan.

Except on land close to major rivers and on piedmont (hill foot) plains, seasonal flooding is mainly by rainwater accumulated on the land when drainage is blocked by high river levels. Silty river water only spreads more extensively over adjoining floodplain land - mainly along distributary channels - in years with high river floods. Embankments can provide protection against river floods, but drainage is required to provide protection against rainwater flooding.[37]

Land Use Pattern

Bangladesh's population lives mainly on its floodplains. Rural population densities exceed 1,000 per sq.km. of cultivable land over wide areas. Agriculture is the pre-dominant sector in the national economy. The country's flood plains are intensively cultivated with a little over 63 per cent of the land area under agriculture. Crop production is possible throughout the year. Production in the more secure dry season has increased rapidly in recent years with the spread of small-scale irrigation from surface water and ground water. Rice occupies about 80 per cent of the cropped area. Other important crops are jute, tea, wheat, oilseeds, pulses, sugarcane, vegetables and spices. Agriculture and fishing contributed 24.6 per cent of real GDP in 1999-2000 and employs over 60 per cent of the labour force.[38]

In addition to meeting Bangladesh's food requirements, agriculture supplies raw materials for the food and manufacturing and agro-processing sectors. Though Bangladesh has achieved food self-sufficiency and has diversified the crop base, unpredictable climatic conditions— flooding and droughts—regularly undermine production plants and targets, disrupt the economy and necessitates food imports. Most non-agricultural raw materials, machinery and equipment have to be imported. Although natural gas production is increasing, Bangladesh still runs a heavy fuel import bill. Attempts are being made to diversify the economic and export base by promoting industries such as information technology and agro-processing, but the opportunities and success of the programmes have been limited.[39]

Considerable floodplain areas have already been provided with flood protection or drainage works. Bangladesh Water Development Board has built 6,850 km, of embankments to keep out river floods along several sections of the major rivers and some eastern rivers. In addition, many thousands of kilometers of embankments have been built along other rivers under local initiative schemes, often assisted by Food for Work programmes. However, a techno-fix approach accompanied by embankment failures are common reducing the extent of land which is effectively protected from flooding. During the last fifteen years from 1984 to 1999, the Gumti embankment (built about 340 years back, 1669) broke eight times, causing floods and destruction. In 1999, for the first time the southern embankment broke causing a loss of Tk.33 crores and displacing about 8,000 people.[40]

Bangladesh has been prone to many kinds of natural disasters. Floods damage crops or property in some part or another of the country almost every year. The severe floods, which attracted international attention in 1987 and 1988 were preceded by serious floods in 1984,1980,1977,1974 and in many earlier years. The 1974 flood was followed by a famine in which about 30,000 deaths were officially reported. Breaches in river embankments sometimes aggravate flooding.

Bank erosion along the rivers and in the Meghna estuary robs many families of their homes and livelihoods every year.[41] Droughts seriously reduced crop production in 1972, 1978-79, and 1989. Tropical cyclones (typhoons), sometimes accompanied by storm surges, occasionally strike coastal areas causing great damage and loss of life. Line-squalls frequently cause localised damage to crops and property in the pre-monsoon season. They are sometimes accompanied by hail and more rarely by tornadoes. Earthquakes with magnitudes between 7.0 and 8.7 on the Richter scale have been experienced but they are rare events.[42]

Bangladesh has been a constant victim of floods and cyclones of unprecedented proportions. This chapter primarily focuses on these two natural disasters and the consequent damages. The April 1991 and the May 1997 cyclones and the 1987-88 and 1998 floods have left thousands dead and rendered millions affected into destitute by the disastrous aftermath. This has always brought a devastating and horrifying consequence for the vulnerable populace. With each disaster precipitated by man or nature, the country and its successive governments have had to depend on international organizations and voluntary agencies for providing quick and effective relief. The long-term reconstruction and rehabilitation, necessary to reduce future vulnerability have been a daunting task for all the internal and external agencies.

The non-availability of adequate literature detailing such damages and the consequent absence of analysis and evaluation of disaster management strategies have affected the direction and contents of policy making in the country. More importantly, there tends to be a totally delinked discourse on the technical and scientific aspects of disasters on the one hand, and its environmental causes, socio-economic fall-out and political ramifications on the other. This has resulted in somewhat partial intervention methods implying a compartmentalization of issues and concerns. Disaster is a comprehensive phenomenon and requires comprehensive interventions. This chapter tries to bring in some kind of alignment among the various dimensions of disasters in Bangladesh so as to understand, assess and analyse them in a comprehensive manner.

Features of Political Economy

Bangladesh's polity has a parliamentary system of government based on universal adult franchise through the 12th amendment of the constitution in 1991. Prior to that there was a Presidential form of government with the army playing a prominent role that started with the liberation war of 1971. The role of the army in politics was continued after a series of military coups since mid 1975 and continued till the ouster of General Ershad in 1990. The return of democracy in Bangladesh since the 1991 elections and the formation of the government led by the Bangladesh Nationalist Party (BNP) was followed by the victory of the Awami League (AL) in June 1996 general election. Again the victory of the BNP led alliance in the general election in 2001 was preceded by protracted confrontational and agitational politics. Nevertheless, all these elections do indicate that a democratic culture is gradually evolving in Bangladesh.[43]

This uneven and often conflictual pattern of political development in Bangladesh has proved detrimental to its economy and society. In Bangladesh, economic and development decisions have often been taken to suit the economic interests of the Bangladeshi political elite. The resulting development fallouts are aggravated further by recurring natural disasters. All these have often impeded fresh developmental initiatives and consolidation of any development process.

Successive governments in Bangladesh have been confronted with the problem of raising of the rate of economic growth against the most daunting backdrop of a substantial proportion of the population living below the subsistence level. According to the World Bank, the incidence of poverty, measured by the cost of basic needs of the poor, declined from 42.7 per cent in 1991-92 to 35.6 per cent in 1995-96. However, using a head count method which measures poverty according to nutrition (daily calorie intake), the poverty rate fell from 47 per cent in 1996 to 44.7 per cent in 1999. These statistics cover the fact that poverty is much more prevalent in the rural areas, where agriculture is the major source of employment The very nature of agricultural production makes seasonal and disguised unemployment higher in the rural areas.[44]

Bangladesh's dependency on foreign aid has declined in recent years with foreign aid as a proportion of GDP falling to 2 per cent in 2000 from 7.6 per cent in 1990 and 10.2 per cent in 1980-81. Immediately after independence in 1972-73 foreign aid amounted to 9.5 per cent of GDP contracted to 4.25 per cent of GDP in 1973-74 but rose to 8.5 per cent of GDP in 1974-75. This was despite world economic crisis. The donors' response in the face of severe floods and famine that hit Bangladesh was tremendous raising the foreign aid contribution around 13.7 per cent of GDP in 1981-82. This decline recorded in very recent years is attributable to increased donor conditionalities and an overall decline in global aid flows.[45]

Moreover, the bulk of aid has traditionally been given primarily to finance the provision of food to the poor. As Bangladesh increasingly moved towards food self-sufficiency in recent years, food aid considerably declined. Thus, the nature of foreign aid has undergone a noticeable change with a decline in food and commodity aid and an increase in project aid,[46] indicating a diminishing access to concessional resource flow. However, the proportion of development projects financed from domestic resources has been erratic, with domestic financing falling from 49 per cent of the

Annual Development Plan (ADP, the governments capital expenditure programme) in 1996-97 to 31per cent in 1998-99 before recovering to 50 per cent in 1999-2000. The sharp fall in 1998-99 was caused by the devastating flood of 1998 that submerged almost two-thirds of the country. The subsequent sharp rise in the domestic flows is also explained by a decline in foreign aid flows.[47]

Economic policies are guided by the five-year plans, although most have failed to achieve their usually unrealistic objectives. Real GDP growth in the 1970s and 1980s averaged around 3.3 per cent, well below target owing to various problems ranging from the oil price shock, severe floods and cyclones, political disorder to inept economic management. In the 1990s, however, real GDP maintained annual growth of around 5per cent. Cyclones accompanied by tidal surges and serious flooding constitute a constant threat to agricultural production, destroying crops, livestock and human lives. This places unforeseeable strains on foreign exchange requirements and exports, particularly when jute or tea crops are damaged.[48]

Floods as Natural Disaster

Flood is the most frequent natural hazard that has been damaging and destroying human life and property since the dawn of civilization. People generally do not comprehend the impact of the hazardous flood process that nature unleashes periodically on the earth.

Impact of Floods

The impact of floods on society are complex making them difficult to trace and measure. Floods, while rendering invaluable benefits to human civilization, can also threaten society with negative consequences, posing grave threats to life, property and environmental assets.[49]

Floods, in terms of their disastrous impact affect both society and the economy. As by definition, they affect both the formal and the informal economies, though tracing the effects on the latter is problematic.

Flood damages are usually categorized into :

(a) Tangible and intangible

(b) Direct and indirect

(c) Primary, secondary and tertiary damages.[50]

Tangible damages are usually perceived to be those, which can be measured in monetary terms such as the damage to a dwelling. Such measurement is hardly ever precise and relies heavily upon estimation procedures, in contrast, intangible losses are those that either defy monetary measured (for example : the loss of an archaeological site through erosion caused by powerful flash flooding) or for which monetary estimates are considered impractical. In some countries, placing a monetary value on life is acceptable while in other countries it is not. As monetary measurement techniques improve, losses previously regarded as intangible may become tangible.

Direct flood losses are those caused by the actual physical contact of flood water with damageable property, whereas in case of indirect losses, these are the results of indirect physical contact of flood water with property. When floods drown livestock, there is a direct loss, but when the income from livestock product sales is lost, this is a consequential indirect loss.

Primary impact are considered to be the first round of impact of flooding, i.e., the immediate effects. Typically, such impact lead to further knock-on ones, which are termed secondary ones. For instance, the physical damage to a grain storage depot is a primary loss, whereas the food shortage, which may follow, is a secondary loss. A feature of a model of flood impact, which attempts to include all categories of impact, is that they envision flood damages, extending well beyond the area physically affected by the flood. As with all disasters, floods set off a series of ripple socio-economic effects, which go much beyond the secondary impact and which economists may attempt to measure as multiplier effects within the economy.[51]

The effect of flood hazard goes well beyond the effects, which flow from a severe flood event. As hazard is an ever-present phenomenon in flood prone areas, where its potential consequences are well-understood (perhaps because of the regular occurrence of extreme events) hazards may have a long-term negative impact upon the development process by presenting uncertainty and insecurity.[52]

Hewitt's analysis, of the concept of hazard as damage that only exists in the presence of a vulnerable human community, is of immense importance in any analysis of impact of flood disasters. The usefulness of Hewitt's concept lies in the idea that altering the vulnerability or the coping capacity of the exposed population can reduce the impact of disaster. The concept of vulnerability is the subject of intense debate in any assessment

Table 6.3 The Typical Range of Flood Impacts in a Developing Country.

Primary impacts			*Secondary impacts (mainly intangible)*	*Tertiary impacts (largely tangible)*
Tangible losses		*Intangible losses*		
Direct flood damage	Indirect flood damage			
amage to all building structure: home,shops, manufacturing premises, public buildings,etc		Acute effects: mortality	Food shortage	'Knock-on' effects refugees, migrations
Damage to the contents of buildings,including food stocks	Loss of industrial and agricultural production	Physical and mental impairment and morbidity	Increased mortality and morbidity	Loss of exports: significant reduction of GDP
Physical damage to infrastructure: roads, rail lines, water supply and sewage plants and networks, electricity installations and power lines, hospitals and health care facilities, other communication networks	Disruption of communication: by road, rail, etc	Destruction and loss of communities	Homelessness	
	Disruption of utility supplies: electricity, water, sewage		Shortage of clean water: reduced hygine, contamination of water supplies	
	Disruption of health		Disease epidemics: water borne disease increased incidence of malaria	
	Loss of crops and livestock		Disruption of health care and social services	

Source: Dennis Parker, Nabiul Islam and Ngai Weng Chan, "Reducing Vulnerability following Flood Disasters", in Andenrelle Awotona, ed., Reconstruction after Disaster: Issues and Practices, Ashgate Publishing Company, London, 1997.

of disaster as also the alternative definitions representing different disciplinary and ideological positions and different end purposes. Several types of vulnerability may be distinguished which provide a broad framework for examining how vulnerability may be reduced in the post disaster phase. It demonstrates how vulnerability extends well beyond the initial and obvious effects of a flood disaster.[53]

The ever-increasing frequency and severity of flood disasters have the capacity to severely decelerate the economic and developmental process of developing countries by years and even decades. They have further exacerbated the already manifest ecological and development crises in the country, stemming from the resultant societal crises. The result is a vicious cyclical process with each crisis contributing to an acceleration of the other. This has further created mass poverty and reduced self-sufficient human beings to dependent objects of the more powerful process. The various developmental projects undertaken to meet societal and civic needs get totally derailed as a result of the recurring disasters. Governmental and non governmental organizations are thus often forced to start work afresh, resulting in not only enormous loss, but severe setback to the existing economic growth and pace of development.[54]

Floods in Bangladesh

The Ganga-Brahmaputra Delta, the largest one in the world, is formed by the rivers Ganga, Bramhaputra and Meghna and falls in the Eastern part of Bangladesh.

Bangladesh has an exceptional hydro-geographical setting. The three rivers have a huge catchment area of some 1.7 million sq.km. spread over Bangladesh, Bhutan, China, India, Nepal of which 7.5 per cent is within the country. The number of rivers, streams and canal in Bangladesh is about 230 with a total length of 24,135 km. They occupy a riverine area of about 9,384 sq.km The delta is characterized by flat terrain, interlaced with an intricate system of rivers and tidal channels, which carry an enormous quantity of sediment-laden water downstream.[55]

Table 6.4 below gives the detailed information of the major rivers in Bangladesh in terms of their catchment area in Bangladesh vis-a-vis the total catchment area. It also indicates the minimum and maximum discharge and the recorded water levels and the ensuing difference. The estimated quantity of water flow through these three rivers is about 1500 billion cubic meters.

The Ganga and Brahmaputra, known as the Padma and Jamuna respectively once they enter Bangladesh form the main river system occupying the delta The Jamuna joins the Padma near Aricha and flows up to Chandpur and the combined flow is called the Meghina, which empties into a large estuary at the north-eastern apex of the Bay of Bengal". The rate of the total outflow to the Bay of Bengal through Bangladesh varies from 103,900 m^3/s in August to 8,780 m^3/s in February. When the holding capacity of rivers, khal, beel and haors, in low-lying land is

Table 6.4

Information of the Major Rivers in Bangladesh

Name of the River	*Total Catchme-nt area (sq km)*	*Catchment Area in Bangladesh (sq km)*	*Maxim-um Dischar-ge (Cusec)*	*Minimun Discharge (Cusec)*	*Recorded Maximum Water Level (m)*	*Recorded Minimum Water Level (m)*	*Difference of Maximum and minimum water levels (m)*
Brahmaputra	552,000	39,100	98,300	2,860	20.620	11.705	8.915
Ganges	1,087,300	46,300	76,000	261	15.045	1220	10.825
Meghna	82,000	35,000	19,800	Tidal in Dry Season	7.660	0.735	6.925

Source: *A.K.M. Shamsul Islam, Flood Forecasting and Warning Systems in Bangladesh, Paper presented of National Disaster Preparedness Day, 31st March 1998.*

exceeded, flood occurs. Floods are more or less recurring phenomena in Bangladesh and often within tolerable limits. Occasionally it becomes devastating. In 1988 and 1998, Bangladesh faced unprecedented floods, causing massive loss of life and property.[56]

Along with the floodwater, huge amount of sediment, estimated to be 2.4 billion tons per year, are carried by the river system in Bangladesh. The sedimentation activity is subjected to coastal dynamic processes, generated mainly by river flow tide and wind actions. The ultimate result, may be additional new land in some places due to accretion and loss of land in other places due to erosion. The problem of sedimentation, e.g. Char (islands) formation or accretion and erosion play an important role in the siltation of water holding capacity of rivers. The deterioration of river system due to siltation is one of the major causes of flooding in Bangladesh. In addition, undesirable chars in the river system threaten inland water navigation and cause erosion of the riverbanks and create other socio-economic problems in the area.[57]

Types of Flood in Bangladesh

The land of Bangladesh was created by flooding and floods remain the dominant force shaping the landscape. There are four main natural types of flooding in Bangladesh, each of which is analyzed separately. In addition there are also some floods, which are a result of human activity. The four main types or natural flood are analysed below :

- Coastal floods/storm surges, which occur during the pre and post monsoon season, are caused by cyclones, which produce storm surges (incorrectly referred to as tidal waves) inundating large areas with saline sea water. Fierce onshore winds combined with low atmospheric pressure, raised sea levels and high tides can generate surges upto 9 m, causing tremendous loss of life and destruction of property. They cause sudden, but temporary, flooding of coastal areas with brackish estuarine water for a few kilometers inland during the passage of cyclones. These are responsible for most of the damages caused by cyclones. In a single event, hundreds and thousands of people can lose their lives. Exceptionally, as in May 1965 storm surges upto 12 feet high passed up the Meghna estuary as far inland as the south Sylhet basin flooding adjoining land with non-saline water. Floods caused by storm surges and the mitigation measures they require differ from those occurring on Bangladesh's river floodplains.[58]

- River floods, on the major rivers, occur during the monsoon season due to heavy monsoon rainfall upstream over the Himalayas, the Assam hills, the Tripura hills and the upper Brahmaputra and the Ganges floodplains outside Bangladesh and snow melting in the summer in the Himalayas. These are slow moving floods taking weeks for the river to rise and overflow their banks and lasting for a long time before the flood-water recede. They particularly affect active river floodplains and flows alongside smaller rivers in other regions.[59]

In the case of an unusual event, when the major rivers peak simultaneously and the river levels rise earlier or higher than normal, river water also extends to varying distances over neighbouring river, meander floodplains that are normally flooded by rainwater. During such times floodwater can inundate half the country, causing destruction of crops and property and dislocating rural population. In the exceptionally high river flood in September 1988 river water spread over virtually the whole of the Jamuna and the Lower Ganges floodplains. However, only some parts of the Old Brahmaputra and the Higher Ganges floodplains were affected.

Parts of the Karatoya-Bangali river floodplain have also experienced severe river floods several times in recent years when the Brahmaputra right embankment breached. Peak flood levels in the Brahmaputra-Jamuna river normally occur a month earlier than those in the Ganges. Floods may affect one river system without affecting the other. High floods in either of these rivers may cause damage downstream alongside the Padma and lower Meghna rivers. Overland flooding is particularly severe in years when high flood peaks in the two major rivers coincide, as they did in 1988.[60]

- Rainwater floods/floods due to intense local rainfall occur during the monsoon season. They are caused by heavy rainfall occurring during over floodplain and terrace areas within Bangladesh. Heavy pre-monsoon rainfall causes local run-off to accumulate in floodplain depressions and in the lower parts of the valleys within the Madhupur tract. Later(June-August), local rainwater is increasingly accumulated on the land by rising water levels in adjoining rivers. Thus the extent and depth of the rainwater flooding vary within the rainy season and from year to year, depending on the amount and intensity of local rainfall and on contemporary water-levels in the major adjoining rivers which control drainage from the land.[61]

The volume of rainfall often exceeds the local drainage capacity and remains accumulated sometimes for weeks and even months, when drainage is exceptionally bad. Drainage can be blocked by the road and railway embankment, flood control embankments or during high river flows when gravity drainage cannot occur.[62]

Rainwater flooding is characteristic of meander flood-plain basins and old piedmont and estuarine floodplains. The serious 1987 flood in north-western parts of Bangladesh was mainly caused by excessive rainfall occurring over the north of the area almost throughout the monsoon season. It was aggravated at times by flash floods[63] passing down the Teesta and other rivers entering from the north-west, and by high levels in the Jamuna and Ganges rivers which blocked outflow from the Hurasagar river which drains about 80 per cent of the north-west region. Drainage of overland flow was also impeded by road and railway embankments with inadequate bridges/culverts and by silted-up minor river channels.[64]

Southern and western parts are flooded by tidal water (where they are not cordoned), Tidal water is mainly fresh in the monsoon season; flooding within polders[65] is by rainwater. Flood damage occurs occasionally at high spring tides especially if the level of salinity in the water is high.

As with river floods, the extent of any crop damage caused by rainwater floods depends mainly on when abnormal depths of water occur on land. The flood periods and the corresponding damages are depicted.

Damage to houses, roads and other property mainly occurs when rainwater floods due to heavy rainfall coincide with high river floods, causing relatively rapid flows of water over the land, over topping of road embankments and inundation of towns and other settlements.

- Flash floods are limited to rivers of the north-eastern (Sylhet) and south-eastem (Chittagong) region and occur generally in the pre-monsoon spring season. They rise and fall rapidly lasting no more than a few days, they are still capable of generating high water velocity, which damages crops and property, They may also flow rapidly along river channels and over the land. Water levels in some eastern rivers can rise by several metres within 24-48 hours. Flash floods are caused by runoff during exceptionally heavy rainfall occurring over neighbouring upland areas of India and Burma. They occur most frequently— sometimes several times a year at the foot of the north-eastern and south-eastern hills. They are also common, but not necessarily occurring every year, along the Teesta, Attai and little Jamuna rivers in the northwest and in valleys within upland regions. At much longer intervals (perhaps 20 or more years), flash floods overwhelm almost the whole of the landscapes they did in 1968,1984,1987 and 1997.[66]

Causes of Flood in Bangladesh

The causes of floods in Bangladesh are varied. On the basis of the available literature it can be suggested that floods are often produced by a combination of factors, which differ for each flood. A key feature of flooding in Bangladesh is that each flood is different.[67] The possible causes of flood in Bangladesh can be attributed to diverse factors both external and internal as analysed Table 6.5.

Table 6.5

Causes of Floods in Bangladesh

General Causes

- Heavy monsoonal rainfall simultaneously over the entire catchment area.
- High River discharge combine with heavy rainfall within Bangladesh.
- Earthquakes and sediment transport .
- Greenhouse effect resulting in higher rainfall, higher temperatures and consequently increased melting of ice in the Himalayas.

Internal Causes

- General flat low lying topography, low channel gradient.
- Geological depressions
- Local heavy rainfall.
- High river discharge
- Overflowing of river beds and irrigation channels
- Synchronisation of the high flows of three major rivers. Backwater effects
- Soil saturation
- Old river course within Bangladesh
- Impeded drainage due to high water levels in the rivers
- Siltation of the river beds
- Changing of river courses and riverbank erosion
- Poorly planned embankments for flood protection or roads and railways within the flood plains, upland development works in Bangladesh
- Breaches of embankments
- Waterlogging due to congestion and failures in drainage systems or sluice gates
- Disappearance of wetlands, the environmental managers of flood plains
- Rising of mean sea level during monsoon period

- High tides

External Causes

- Humid air masses producing orographic rainfall on the slopes of the first Himalayan ridges
- Heavy rainfall in the upper catchment area of the big rivers
- Snowmelt
- Immense extra-territorial inflows
- Deforestation
- Aggravation of the flood situation in Bangladesh through construction of embankments and other structures in India especially between 1960-1980
- Farakka barrage producing higher food peak

Source: Thomas Hoffer, Floods in Bangladesh-A Highland-Lowland Interaction ?. Institute of Geography, University of Berne Switzerland, 1998. Also see H. Brammer, "Flood Hazard Vulnerability and flood Disasters in Bangladesh", in D.J.Parker, ed., floods, Vol. I, Routledge, London and New York, 2000.

The severity and intensity of flooding for a particular year depends on a combination of these factors. In this regard, it is crucial to understand the spatial and temporal differentiation of flooding in the Bangladeshi context.

Table 6.3

Spatial and Temporal Differentiation of flooding in Bangladesh

Spatial differentiation

- There is a difference if there are moving depressions or standing low pressures in the foothills of the Himalayas.
- The Meghna is rainfed whereas the Ganges and Brahmaputra are snowfed
- There are different types of flooding: normal monsoon floods of major rivers with the water level showing a slow rise and fall with pulsations, flash floods, where hydrographs rise and fall sharply(especially in the depressions of Sylhet and Mymensingh), rainfloods, tidal floods
- Rainfall variability within the country is very high. It may happen that the northern part experiences a humid year, the southern part a dry year.
- The amount of rainfall in the Ganges catchment is independent of the rainfall in the Brahmaputra catchment

- Unlike the Ganges and the Brahmaputra rivers in the Meghna catchment show a fast reaction to rainfall. They are flashy rivers.
- The Meghna river encompasses one of the wettest regions on earth and drains steeply into Bangladesh. Intensive rainfall and the short geographical distance between upland and lowlands result frequently in flash flooding
- In the Ganges flood problems are concentrated on the Northern bank. The problem increases from East-West and from South-North.
- North Central Region: Large volumes of excess rainwater accumulate in the depressions and low lying areas, and during the monsoon season (from May to October) the predominantly high water levels in the regional rivers (which convey spills from the Jamuna) prevent the outflow of excess rainfall from the internal floodplains. As long as the commanding water levels in the regional rivers also remain high, the levels in the regional rivers also remain high and the removal of water from (or transfer through) the region is severely inhibited. The Maghna-Padma at the south-west corner is tidal influenced and causes further reduction of drainage in the region, thus keeping flood levels high.

Temporal Differentiation

- Precipitation is highly variable during monsoon season. Heavy precipitation of few days alternates with dry periods of same duration.
- During the monsoon period there is often a break. Depending on the duration of the break it is visible in the discharge hydro graph.
- In August little additional rainfall in the catchment area is needed to produce floods due to soil saturation through previous rainfall.
- The Brahmaputra peaks earlier (June-August) than the Ganges (end of early August-early September)
- Synchronisation of peak flows of Ganges and Brahmaputra is not a rare phenomenon. In 19% cases the time lag is less than 10 days.
- The flood period of the Brahmaputra is usually longer than that of the Ganges.
- Severity of flooding is a factor of timing and areal distribution rather than volume.

Source: Thomas Hoffer, "Floods in Bangladesh-A Highland-Lowland Interaction?". Institute of Geography, University of Berne Switzerland, 1998.

Table 6.7 : Causes for the flood of 1987, 1988 and 1998 in Bangladesh

1987 Floods	1988 Floods	1998 Floods
• Heavy rainfall in Bangladesh. • Constant high runoff potential. • High groundwater level. • Rainfall and river water flowing from the Meghalaya Hills • Imported flood wave from the Tista and Brahmaputra during the main flooding period in Bangladesh • Synchronisation of the three main rivers, the Ganges, the • Brahmaputra and the Meghna. Tide after full moon.	• Gradual accumulation of water before and during the monsoon months. • Flood phase early July, which left the catchment areas well saturated. • Just before and during the main flood period: significant rainfall in the northern and northwestern Bangladesh, in Meghalaya and Assam", combination of internal and external inputs. • High 'base flow' of all the three major rivers in August and September, with the Meghna and the Brahmaputra being more important than the Ganga. • Two peaks of most rivers. • Synchronisation of the above danger level flow of the three major rivers; synchronisation of the annual peak of the Brahmaputra and the Ganges. • High groundwater table at the onset of the first flood phase. • Spring tide producing back water effects	• Synchronised peak flow of the major rivers. • Excessive rainfall within the country and upstream due to El-Nino event affecting temperature and weather pattern through June 1998 followed by La Nino created anomalies in monsoon activities over the subcontinent thereby raising total rainfall by 24% above normal rainfall from June 1988 to September 1988 over Bangladesh. • Deforestation in the upper riparian regions. • Siltation of the river beds. • Persistence of the high tide in the Bay of • Bengal due to strong monsoon current that retarded the normal drainage efficiency during July September, 1998 • During the flooding period 9th to 10th August), an earthquake in the Bey of Bengal produced surges that was also considered by some to have retarded the flood water discharge.(no expert opinion in favour of this theory exists. • Man made barriers like roads, highways

1987 Floods	1988 Floods	1998 Floods
		embankments etc. also prevent the natural flow of water and did contribute considerably to the flooding. • An overall atmospheric ambient temperature that was higher to the extent of 0.5 degree Celsius could according to some experts have contributed to the excessive monsoon activities resulting in flood condition.

Source : Thomas Hoffer, "Floods in Bangladesh: A Highland Lowland Interaction ?". IIED, University of Berne, Switzerland, 1988. Also see MD. Shamsul Islam, "1998 Floods in Bangladesh and Government's Response",IMB Dhaka, 1999. Also see Report on Bangladesh Bloods 1998,compiled by 1MB, Dhaka, 1998.

A statistical review has been given by Miah, showing the flood-affected areas from 1954-1987(Table 6. 8).About 18-20% of the total land area of Bangladesh is prone to normal flooding and increases to about 4O% during major floods.

Table 6.8

Percentage of Land Area Inundated by Floods (1954-1998)

Year	Land Area Inundated (%)
1954	25.64
1955	35.21
1963	29.97
1968	26
1969	28.89
1970	29.61

Year	Land Area Inundated (%)
1971	25.33
1974	36.61
1987	39.92
1998	61
1995	22
1996	26
1998	68

Source: Bangladesh Water Development Board, Ministry of Water Resources Government of Bangladesh, Dhaka, 1989.Also see Mapping the 1998 Floods. EGIS Technical Note Series, Ministry of Water Resources Government of Bangladesh, Dhaka, 1999.

There is no systematic record of flood damage available before 1954. After the consecutive floods of 1954 and 1955 the then Government of Pakistan requested United Nations to look into the severe flood problem of Bangladesh. Krug Mission came in 1956 and recommended the establishment of a water development authority to look after the flood issue. East Pakistan Water and Power Development Authority(EPWDA) was created in 1959 with the task of irrigation, flood control and water development.[68]

Table 6.9 gives glimpse of the flood damage records since 1954. The damages were calculated at the 1969 prices and mostly the direct and indirect losses (mainly agriculture, livestock, roads, railways and waterways, control structures, utilities including underground and aerial telecommunication equipment facilities, industry, health and education, rural water supply, rural housing, urban infrastructures and social services) were considered for damage calculation. The agricultural sector is considered to be the worst affected sector by flooding. According to the classification of MPO(1986), there are 9.35 million ha of agricultural area prone to floods. Already 3.166 million ha have been brought under flood protection up to 1987-88.[69]

Table 6.9 shows that Bangladesh has experienced severe floods in 1954,1955,1961,1962,1968,1969,1970,1971,1974,1987 and 1988. According to official figures the 1974 and 1988 floods claimed 57,000 lives. Unofficial estimates put the death toll above 1,00,000.[70]

Table 6.9

Year.	Flooded area (sq. km)	% of the country area.	Value losses (in 1969 prices in million Taka)
1954	36778	25.54	1,200
1955	38850	26.98	1,240
1956	35483	24.64	2,180
1962	37296	25.90	1,020
1963	35224	24.46	83
1964	31080	21.58	246
1965	28490	19.78	45
1966	33411	23.20	344
1967	25641	17.81	90
1968	37296	25.90	1,645
1969	36260	25.18	330
1970	38332	26.62	1,380
1974	38850	26.98	10,000
1984	25900	17.98	2,500
1987	54390	37.77	15,000
1988	83994	58.93	50,000

Source : M. Monirul Qader Mirza and Mustaque Ahmed, Management of Environmental Disaster of Floods in the Himalayan Region, Proceedings of WCNHR, New Delhi, 10E and WFEO, January, 1992.

The people of Bangladesh have learnt to live with the Annual seasonal floods. While seasonal inundation brings benefits in the form of agricultural bounty and wetlands teeming with fish, floods that assume the proportions of the deluge of 1988 inundating two third of the country take a heavy toll.[71]

Table 6.10 below summarises the major floods and their consequent impact on Bangladesh[1].

Table 6.10 Major Floods and their Consequent Impact on Bangladesh

Date	Events	Nature of Calamity
1974	Flood	Widespread flooding killed over 20,000 people devastated large areas of land.
1987-88	Flood	A series of floods killed 5,000 people and caused widespread damage and devastation.
1980	Flood	Widespread and devastated flooding.
1995-97	Flood	Major floods killed 6,000 and caused widespread damage to livestock and fisheries.
1998	Flood	Devastating floods submerged over 60% of Bangladesh's land area causing an estimated 1,100 deaths. Negative impact on infrastructural and agricultural production. Large inflows of foreign aid and relief poured in to alleviate distress and rebuild infrastructure.

Source: Bangladesh : A Proposed Rural Development Strategy : A World Bank Study, University Press Ltd, Dhaka, 2000.

A study conducted by USAID just before the floods of 1987 and 1988 found that severe floods speed up the process of pauperization, thereby widening social inequality, with few of the rural poor able to improve their situation in the aftermath of severe floods and the majority becoming poorer. Severe floods increase hardships cause death and long periods of starvation, The study found that in the absence of other calamities, floods alone are responsible for straitened circumstances and death. Death by drowning, snake-bites and other accidents occur during floods. More deaths are found to be taking place in the aftermath as water borne diseases like cholera and typhoid claim lives.[72]

Impact of 1988 Floods

The 1988 flood was the most devastating and unprecedented of its kind in recorded history of present day Bangladesh causing colossal damages to crops, life and property. The extent of 1988 flooding was widespread covering more than three fourths of the country.[73] The flood of 1988 is the worst flood of Bangladesh in living memory. About 62% of the land were inundated and about 40 million people were affected. The flood caused an estimated damage of $2 billion in property damage.[74]

Although the human misery was enormous because of the prolonged inundation, the death toll from the flood itself was relatively low. Table-

6.11 indicates the impact of 1988 floods. According to the official count, between 1,517-1,600 people lost their lives, though unofficial estimates were much higher. Almost a million houses were destroyed and another 1.5 million damaged. Crops of more than 1.2 million hectares were ruined and 850,000 hectares were damaged.[75]

Almost half the population of Bangladesh was directly affected by the 1988 flood. Throughout the country people took shelter on rooftops and embankments and road bridges and roofs of various government buildings were converted into flood shelters. The total economic losses in 1988 flood were estimated at US $1.3 billion.[76]

People died by drowning, being crushed by falling walls, bitten by snakes or were electrocuted. These were injuries that people might have survived by getting timely medical attention during the flood (for which figures are not available except records stating that *29%* of deaths were due to diarrhoea). Lack of access to drinking water was an even bigger killer. According to Association of Development Agencies (ADA) Report, 8,677 tubewells were destroyed and 18,361 damaged in the flood. With so many tubewells out of action, water-borne diseases were rampant. The report says that 29% of all deaths related to the 1988 floods were children who succumbed to diarrhoeal diseases,

The economic losses as a result of the 1988 flood were severe. Crops on 2 mha of land were damaged out of a cultivable area of 9.5 mha. Roads, railroads, water control works and social services were seriously disrupted. Flooding reached unprecedented level in Dhaka. The more serious losses were not in normally flood affected areas but in areas where deep flooding is not an annual event and where farmers had taken up cultivation of input intensive and new high yielding rice varieties. This led to a complete loss of crop in some areas. The food-grain loss was about 2 million tonnes (annual food grain production in a normal year being 15 million mt)[77].

Table-6.11 Impact of Flood 1988

Area affected	89,280 sq. km. or 62% of the total area.
No. of affected districts	52
No. of affected thanas	373
No. of affected homesteads	1,030,659 (Fully)/2,265,776 (Partly)
No. of affected population	4,67,00,000

No. of death	1,517-1600 (29% diarrhoeal death)
Damaged crop area	1,474,708 (Fully)/770,432 (Partly)
Loss of cattle head	297,986
Loss of goats	57,000
Loss of poultry	50,056

Source: Government Circular, Ministry of Relief and Rehabilitation, Government of Bangladesh, Dhaka, 23 October 1988. Also see -Joint Survey Report of MRR and ADAB, Dhaka, September 1988. Also see Flood 1988, Caritas Bangladesh, Bulletin no.3. Dhaka, May 1989. Also see Disaster Recovery Report, Caritas Bangladesh, Dhaka,1989.

Table-6.12 shows the sector-wise damage caused to Infrastructures. This includes damages and losses incurred by roads (both metalled and earthern), railways, bridges, culverts and educational institutions.

Table-6.12 Infrastructure Damages

Roads (metalled and earthern) and Highways	73,804 km. (Fully)/22,727 km. (Partly)
Embankments.	2,657 km
Tubewells	8,677
Bridges and Culverts	2,397 km.
Rail Tracks	638 km.
Educational Institutions	2,593 (Fully)/ 6,506 (Partly)

Source: Government Circular, Ministry of Relief and Rehabilitation Government of Bangladesh, Dhaka, 23 October 1988. Also see Joint 'Survey Report of MRR and ADAB, Dhaka, September 1988. Also Flood 1988, Caritas Bangladesh, Bulletin no.3. Dhaka, May 1989. Also see, Disaster Recovery Report, Caritas Bangladesh, Dhaka, 1989.

Features of 1998 flood in Bangladesh

Flood in Bangladesh in 1998 was one of the major disasters for it in this century. As per reports of the Flood Forecasting and Warning Centre of Bangladesh and the Bangladesh Water Development Board, there was a rising trend of water levels in the major river basins of the country during the first week of July, 1998. Following the rising trend, some of the major rivers crossed their danger levels on July 12,1998 and since then flood waters continuously rose till September 14, 1998.[78]

The flood of 1998 broke all previous records:

- Country wise overall flood duration-65 days (12th July to 14th September, 1998);
- Single point longest flood condition (water above danger level)–73 days at Bhagyakul, Padma river.
- Number of points where previous water levels were exceeded–6 points.[79]

Table 6.13 shows the extent of area inundated, the toll and the people affected in terms of their households, crops affected or damaged and the loss of livestock, namely cattle poultry, goats etc. 53 out of the total 64 districts in the country were in the grip of floods and more than two-thirds of the country were inundated for 65 days..The number of flood shelters available and the extent to which they were able to protect and shelter people are conspicuously high compared to the 1988 floods. The need for this was an important lesson learnt from the 1988 flood.

Table–6.13

Impact : Loss and Damage caused by 1998 floods

Area affected	About 1,00,000 sq km., 68% of the country.
No. of affected district	52
No. of afffected thanas	366
No. of affected unions	3323
No. of affected homesteads	9,80,571
No. of affected families	57,11,962
No. of affected population	3,09,16,351
No. of people affected by disease	2,42,500
No. of death	918
No. of flood shelters operated	2,716
No. of people sheltered	10,49525

Damaged crop area	32,31,721 acra (partially and fully)
Damaged fisheries area	2,15,200 hectares
Loss of cattle head	3,928
Loss of goats	7,041
Loss of poultry	3,13,058

Source: DMB Report 1998 Floods, Ehaka, 1998. Also see MD. Shamsul Islam, 1998 Floods in Bangladesh and Government's Response, DMB, Dhaka, June 1999. Also see A.K.M. Shamsul Islam, Flood of 1998, Forecasting and Dissemination and the Role of Media for Flood Loss Mitigation, Seminar Paper for IDNDR Day, Dhaka,1998. Also see Deluge in the Delta: Flood 1998, ADAB Activity Report, Dhaka, 1998. Also see The Devastating Flood of 1998, ADAB Activity Report, Dhaka, 1998. Also see Experiences *of* Deluge: Flood 1998, BRAC Research Monograph Series no. 15, BRAC, Dhaka,1999. Also see Imtiaz Ahmed, ed., Living With Floods, UPL.Dhaka,1999.

The reduced death toll of 918 during the floods of 1998, which according to Ahmed is 1200[80], the result of several factors like diarrhea, drowning, death due to snakebite, electrocution etc. The number of flood-related death due to each of these factors were separately available in the case of 1998 floods of which the death due to diarrhea as in the case of 1988 floods was maximum (Table-6.14.)

Table-6.14
Flood Related Death (Until 4 October 1998)

Cause	Number.	Area
Diarrhoea	540	Sylhet and Sunamganj(60); chandpur(20): Belkuchi Thana(30) Noakhali(31); Nilphamari (8)
Drowning	24	Sarishabari (22 childern)
Snake-bite	5	Sarishabari
Electrocution	21	Munshiganj
Other/cause not specified	610	All Bangladesh
Total	**1200**	

Source: Imtiaz Ahmed, Living With Floods, UPL, Dhaka,1999.

Table 6.15 shows the damages caused to infrastructure, namely roads, railways, educational institutions and also tubewells. Tubewells are of a crucial source of drinking water in Bangladesh and their damage or contamination of groundwater is responsible for the deaths and sufferings due to diarrheal and other waterborne diseases.

Table-6.15
Infrastructure Damages

Road and Highway.	15,927 km.
Embankments	4,528 km.
Bridges and Culverts	6,890 km.
Tubewells	3,00,000
Educational Institutions	1,718

Source: DMB Report 1998 Floods, Dhaka, 1998. Also see MD Shamsul Islam. 1998 Floods in Bangladesh and Government's Response, DMB, Dhaka, June 1999. Also see A.K.M. Shamsul Islam. Flood of 1998, Forecasting and Dissemination and the Role of Media For Flood Loss Mitigation/Seminar Paper for IDNDR Day. Dhaka, 1998.Alao see Deluge in the Delta: Flood 1998, ADAB Activity Report, Dhaka, 1998.Also see The Devastating flood of 1998,ADAB Activity Report. Dhaka, 1998.Also see Experiences of Deluge: Flood 1998,BRAC Research Monograph Series no. 15, BRAC. Dhaka, 1999.

The damages and losses caused by the 1998 flood were colossal (Table-6.16). The losses due to unemployment caused by flood are difficult to estimate.

Table-6.16
Sector-wise Estimated Economic Impact of 1998 Flood

Damage Sector	**Million Taka**
Damage to Crops (rice and others)	33050
Damage to Jute, trees and vegetation	3700
Damage to Livestock	30
Damage to Fisheries	1750
Damage to Forestry	1100
Damage to Tubewells	1830

Damage Sector	Million Taka
Damage to Infrastructure	50000
Damage to Railways	1558
Damage to Telecommunication	234
Other Enviromental effects	100
Damage to industrial units and loss of production.	50000
Relief and Rehabilitation support for affected people.	2200
Power, Gas, Petroleum and Transportation sectors	N/A

Note: In 1998 1 US =Taka 43.

Source: DMB, Report on Bangladesh Floods 1998, Dhaka. Also see MD. Shamsul Islam, 1998 Floods in Bangladesh and Government's Response. DMB Dhaka, June 1999. Also see A,K.M. Shamsul Islam. Flood of 1998, Forecasting and Dissemination and the Role of Media for Flood Loss Mitigation, Seminar Paper for IDNDR Day, Dhaka,1998. Also See Deluge in the Delta: Flood 1998 ADAB Activity Report, Dhaka,1998. Also see The Devastating Flood of 1998, ADAB Activity Report Dhaka, 1998. Also see Experiences of Deluge: Flood 1998, BRAC Research Monograph Series no. 15, BRAC Dhaka, 1999. Also see Imtiaz Ahmed ed., Living With Floods, UPL, Dhaka, 1999.

Cyclones in Bangladesh

Cyclones are seasonally recurring rapid onset natural hazards leaving behind in its trail death and destruction of magnificent proportions. Accompanying the cyclones are violent winds, torrential rainfall and storm surges, which create havoc and lead to massive devastation. Humans have no hand in the occurrence of cyclones, they just happen.[81]

Bangladesh has the worst record of all in the case of cyclones and tidal surges. Cyclones and tidal surges are most frequent in the months of October and November. These disasters destroy crops, cause -widespread damage and health hazards for the people. *They* occur so frequently and in such magnitude in Bangladesh that they have multiplied the problem of poverty and seriously challenged the efforts of the country towards self-reliance.

Origin and formation of Cyclone in Bangladesh

Cyclones in Bangladesh in addition to their impressive and erratic frequency and normal combination of heavy rainfall and cyclonic wind forces are accompanied by devastating storm surges. The combination of low atmospheric pressure and the configuration of Bay of Bengal, which traps and concentrates the surge as it approaches land, form storm surges. The low lying plains of coastal Bangladesh offer least resistance to this catastrophic characteristic.[82]

Among the 60% of all death due to storm surges occurring in the low lying arable coastal areas of the countries bordering the Bay of Bengal and the Andaman Sea, Bangladesh alone accounts for about 40%. Between 1877 and 1980, 63 out of the 392 tropical cyclones formed in the Bay of Bengal had landfall on the Bangladesh coast.

The reasons for the non-uniform distribution and large impact of cyclones and storm surges that have struck Bangladesh are the following :

- The phenomenon of recurvature of tropical cyclones in the Bay of Bengal.
- Shallow continental shelf especially in the eastern part of Bangladesh.
- Converging bay i.e. triangular/V shape at the head of the Bay of Bengal.
- High tidal density.
- Almost sea level orography at the Bangladesh coast.
- High density of population.[84]

As discussed earlier, the genesis of cyclones is most favoured by an ocean temperature of 26°C or more, weak vertical wind shear(between 90 hpa and 200 hpa levels) and other thermo-dynamical and dynamical factors.[85]

As seen from the monthly distribution of cyclonic storms of various intensity that have hit the Bangladesh coast during the period between 1877 and 1990 the formation of cyclones in the Bay of Bengal occurs during two distinct periods pre-monsoon(April-June) and post monsoon (September-December).

It is seen that severe cyclonic storms are maximum in the pre monsoon period during the months of May and June and in the case of post monsoon period during the months of October and November.

The thermo-dynamical conditions, necessary for the development of cyclonic storms exist in the pre-monsoon and post monsoon months. The minimum energy required for the development of a cyclone is available at the air sea interface during -this time. Cyclones, which form during pre-monsoon periods, are most destructive due to the great instability of the atmosphere and weak vertical wind shear. The cyclonic storms that strike Bangladesh, formed during monsoon period known as monsoon depressions, are not so destructive in nature due to large vertical wind shear during southwest monsoon.[86]

The storm surge is not appreciable in deep sea until it reaches the continental shelf, which is 150 km. to 300 km. long near the coastline of Bangladesh, Before the continental shelf there is relatively steeper part of the sea bed, which rises rapidly from a depth of 20 m to a depth of about 200 m at the edge of the shelf. Then the depth decreases gradually towards the coastline. This significantly increases the wind drift effect, which is also important in the generation of a storm surge. The amplification of a cyclonic storm surge in the Bay of Bengal occurs due to long and shallow continental shelf and the converging Bay. Bangladesh is at the top of the inverted V shaped Bay of Bengal. Therefore, storm surges are easily amplified due to the concentration of energy.

When a cyclone moves northeasterly to the north of Chittagong, strong winds blows from off shore to the coast and together witin the suction effect of low pressure, the wind drift effect(amplified by the shallow water depth) brings about a large storm surge along the coast. The displacement of water surface during a cyclonic storm surge also depends on the tide. Tides in the Bay of Bengal originate in the Indian Ocean and get amplified due to non-linear shallow water effect. The average tidal range along the Bangladesh coast varies between 3-6 m. Several studies have estimated the effect of astronomical tides on storm surges. The displacement of water surface is largest when the cyclonic storm surge reaches the coast during spring tide. Such coincidence occurred during cyclones of 12 November 1970, 25 May 1985 and 29 -April 1991.[88]

Cyclones of various intensity as classified by the Bangladesh Meteorological Department in terms of the range of pressure drop indicated by the mercury level and range of wind speed are described in Table 6.17. Depressions that strike the Bangladesh coast have been categorised as storms of the lowest intensity indicated by a pressure drop of 3.0 to less than 3.5 and minimum wind speed of 44 to less than 52. Cyclonic storms of hurricane intensity are the most severe cyclones indicated with a pressure drop of 16.0 or more with a range of 119 and above.

Table-17

Classification and Cyclones in Bangladesh based on their intensity

Cyclone Intensity	**Range of Pressure Drop. (in hb).**	**Range of Maximum Sustained wind Speed (in km./hr)**
Depression	3.0-<3.5	44 to <52
Deep Depression	3.5-<6.0	52 to <63
Cyclonic Storm	6.0-<9.0	63 to <86
Severe Cyclonic Storm	9.0-<16.0	89 to <119
Severe Cyclonic Storm of hurricaneIntensity	16.0 or more	1199 and above.

Source: S.Begum, Storm -Surges and River flooding In Bangladesh, in M.I. Sabh et.al,ed., Land Based Marine Hazards, Kluwer Academic Publications, Netherlands, 1996.

The distribution of occurrence of various classes of cyclones, which hit the three coastal regions, Chittagong-Cox s Bazar coast, Meghna-Delta coast, Barguna-Khulna coast of Bangladesh since 1960, is shown in Table 6.18.

Table-6.18

Intensity of Cyclones in the Coastal Regions

Intensity of Cyclone.	**Chittagong Cox's Bazar Coast.**	**Meghna-Delta Coast**	**Barguna khulna Coast.**
Cyclonic Storm	4	1	5
Severe Cyclonic Storm	3	5	4
Severe Cyclonic Storm with Hurricane Intensity	7	6	2

Source: S.Begum, Storm Surges and River Flooding in Bangladesh, in M.I. Sabh, et.al ed., Land Based Marine Hazards, Kluwer Academic Publications, Netherlands, 1996.

Impact of Cyclones in Bangladesh : Historical Perspective Cyclones in the 16th, 17th and 18th centuries

Severe cyclones have periodically caused serious casualty and property damage in the entire coastal belt of Bangladesh. Earlier reports suggest that severe cyclones occurred in 1584,1790,1822 and 1876. In 1584 about 200,000 people were died in Barisal by cyclonic storm surge. In 1737 another severe cyclone accompanied by high tidal surges took a toll of 300,000. In 1790, severe cyclones occurred in Noakhali. Another cyclone in 1822 killed more than 70,000 people in Barisal and 95 percent of the population of Hatuja. Severe cyclonic storm surge also occurred on Nov. 1,1876, Oct. 1. 1896. Among the cyclones that struck between 1797 and 1897, the May 1822 cyclone that struck the Barisal coast has been the most devastating. This is because it caused the maximum damage to livestock and also in terms of death.[89]

Table 6.19 below provides a chronology of major cyclones in Bangladesh. In terms of the nature of the cyclone and the damage caused due to loss of live and property, a comprehensive review of the various cyclones that have struck the Bangladesh coast from time to time have been provided in the table 6.19 that follows shortly. *This* would help gauge the catastrophic nature of the successive cyclones and judge the extent of calamities that have struck the affected populace. This also indicates future calamities that are liable to occur as an aftermath of a cyclone.

Cyclones in the 20th century

Severe cyclonic storm surges in the early 20th century have occurred on Sep.21,1919 and May 3, 1947. During the period 1960-1970, November(12-13) 1970 cyclone was the worst with storm surges as high as 33 feet. This claimed the lives of 3,00,000 people and caused extensive damage to crops and properties. The May 1985 cyclone with storm surges upto 14ft had a devastating impact though in terms of death toll the number was surprisingly low.[90]

The November 1988 cyclone accompanied by severe storm surge left a huge death toll in terms of both cattle and livestock. The 29 April 1991 cyclone that struck large area of the coastal belt of Bangladesh accounted for a heavy death toll and damage worth billions of dollars. The May 1994 cyclone that hit the Cox area resulted in property loss worth $ 131 million. In terms of human cost and livestock the loss was minimized due to early warning system, timely dissemination, quick relief, rescue and evacuation operations. The 1997 cyclone was an example of a severe cyclone as was the 1991 cyclone. However due to a variety of factors like greater availability of cyclone shelters, prior effective cyclone warning, dissemination and evacuation system, the death toll was significantly reduced though the damage to property and livestock was enormous.[91]

Table-6.19 Chronology of Major Cyclones in Bangladesh

Month and Year	*Affected Areas*	*Nature of Cyclone*	*People Affected*	*People Died*	*Cattle Loss*	*Other Loss/Damage*
May-June 1979	Chittagong	Most Severe	ENA	ENA	ENA	Every hut leveled to ground/two vessels sunk inpart.
May, 1822	Barisal	Most Severe	ENA	40,000	1,00,000	Collectorate records were swept away.
October, 1876	Meghna Estuary Hatiya, Noakhali Ptuakhali, Chittagong Coast	Most Severe strom waves 10-45 ft	ENA	ENA	ENA	Enormous properties lost by tidal bore
October, 1897	Chittagong	Hurricane reached maximums intensity of storm waves	ENA	14,000	ENA	Katubdia Island and villages on mainland swept away.
October 9-10 1960	Eastern Meghna Char Jabbar, Char Amina, Char Bhatti Ramgati, Hatiya and Noakhali	Severe Cyclone 125 miles/hr	ENA	3,000	ENA	—
October 30-31 1960	Chittagong	Severe cyclonic storm, 130-miles/hr. Surge height 20ft.	ENA	8149	ENA	70 % building in Hatiya blown off.2 large ocean liners thrown on mainland, 5-7 vessels capsized in Karaaful river.
May 28-29 1963	Chittagong,	Severe cyclone. Strom wave 8-12 ft. Maximum speed 125 miles/hr.	ENA	11520	ENA	Inundation by strom wave along coast upto 30 miles north of Chittagong.

Month and Year	*Affected Areas*	*Nature of Cyclone*	*People Affected*	*People Died*	*Cattle Loss*	*Other Loss/Damage*
May 11-12 1965	Barisal, Pariapur Khulna, Jessore Noakhali, Chittagong 100 miles/hr	Most severe Maximum speeds	ENA	19,270	ENA	In Barisal alone 14,193 people were killed.
Nov 12-13 1970	Meghna Estuary	Most severe strom surges 10-33ft. Speed of 138 miles/hr.	ENA	3,00,000	ENA	Hurrixane continued for about 9 hours, widespread damage to crop and property.
May 24-25 1985	Cittagoneg, Noakhali Coast,Cox's Bazar, Chittagong, Bazar, Chittagong, Sardwip, Hatiya Urir Char	154 kph. Strom surges 14 ft. Severe cyclone	ENA	11,069	135,033	House damaged = 94.379 Road damaged = 40 miles Trees uprooted = 1200 Embankment damaged 242 miles.
Nov 29, 1988	Chittagong Cox's Bajar, Barisal, Noakhali, Patuakhali, Berguna, Katubdia	Tidal bore speed 120 Wph	ENA	150,000	70,000	Crops damaged Tk. 4300 crores
April 29, 1991	Chittagong, Cox's Bazar, Barisal, Noakhali, Patuakali, Berguna Katubdia.	Tidal bore thunder stroms	ENA	138,00	ENA	Property damage worth $2.5 billion
May 1994	Cox's Bazar	Several cyclone	ENA	150	ENA	Destroyed property $ 131 million
May 1997	Chittagong, cox's Bazar.	–	3,91,981	111	3,118	ENA

ENA: Estimate not available

Source: Jayanthi and Sharma (1986), Murty et.al. 1986, Kasture(1992). Talukdar(1992),Murty and Flather(1994), Synghal (1992), in T.S.Murthy and V.R.Niralla," El-nino and Strom Surges in the Bay of Bengal", in, M.I.E.I. Sabh, ed., Land Based and Marine Hazards, Kluwer Academic Publishers. Netherlands, 1996. Also see Report on May 1997 Cyclone, Bangladesh Meteorological Department, Dhaka, 1997. Also see Bangladesh: A Proposed Rural Development Strategy, University Press Ltd., Dhaka 2000

Cyclones of 12 November 1970, 25 May 1985, 29 April 1991 and 19 May 1997 were the most catastrophic cyclones of the century, ranking highest in terms of wind intensity, storm surge height and the number of deaths.

Features of 29-April 1991 Cyclone

The cyclone that crossed the Bangladesh coast during the night of 29 April 1991 can be described as a super-cyclone. It had a dimension more than two times the size of Bangladesh. The central overcast cloud had a diameter exceeding six hundred kilometres, the maximum windspeed observed at Sandwip was 225 km. per hour. The actual windspeed could have been higher as the wind speed measuring device was blown away after this wind speed was recorded. The maximum windspeed obtained from NOAA-11 at 1338 hours was about 240 km. per hour. The cyclone was first detected as a depression(windspeed not exceeding 62 km. per hour) on the 23 April in the satellite picture taken at SPARRSO from NOAA-11 and GHS-4 satellites. It formed into a cyclonic stows on 25 April.[92]

The cyclone in its initial stage moved slightly north- westwards than northwards. From 28 April it started moving in a north-easterly direction and crossed the Bangladesh coast of Chittagong port during the night of 29 April where it had its windfall. The cyclone started lashing the coastal islands Njhura Dwip, Manpura, Bhola, Sandwip from the evening of that day. The maximum storm surge was estimated to be 6-10 m.[93]

According to official statistics, the cyclone of 29 April 1991, devastated about 2000 sq.km. of coastal area having a coastline of over 400 km; about 1,380,000 million people were killed and more than 2000 families became homeless resulting in an industrial damage of 112,960 millionTaka.[94] Table 2.20 shows that loss and damage caused to lives and property as a result of the devastating cyclone and the inadequacy of the existing cyclone shelters which led to "the staggering loss of lives.

A study of the impact of cyclone, carried out by BCAS 1991, showed:

1. The ph and salinity of soils increased in the affected areas resulting in severe damage to crops and groundwater.
2. Several houses were destroyed or damaged including many school building, hospitals etc.
3. Severe damage to roads, electricity networks, water supply.
4. Sharp Increase in reliance on deep tube wells for drinking water due to visible pollution of pond water.

Table 6.20

Impact: Loss and Damage Caused by the April 1991 Cyclone

People Killed	1,38,00
People affected	1,07,98257
People homeless	2,00,000
Cattle heads lost	0.224 million
Crop affected	295.73 metric tonne
Affected culverts and bridges	6,000
Affected Educational Institutions.	9,590
Maximum wind speed recorded at Cox's Bazar	185 km. per hour
Chittagong (ship observed)	210 km. per hour
Sitakundu	180 km. per hour
Sandwip	225 km. per hour
Strom surge	6-7.6 m. (20-25 ft)
Landfall Area	A little North of Chittagong at 0200 BST of 30 April , 1991
Estimated central pressure	940 hpa
Pressure deficiency at the centre	69 hpa
Maximum sustained windspeed	225 km. per hour

Source: Bangladesh Meteorological Department. Also see Mushtaque Chowdhury, et. al. The Bangladesh Cyclone of 1991: Why so many People Died.Disasters, Vol.. 17,no.4, December 1995. Also see Raana Haider, A Atiq Rahaman and Saleemul Haq. ed., Cyclone 91: An Environmental and Perceptional Study, BCAS, Dhaka, 1991. Also see Marlene Bradford, Robert,S.Carmichael, Natural Disasters, Vol.II, Salem Press, California, 2001. Also see Md.Akram Hossain, Cyclone Warning System in Bangladesh, DMB, Government of Bangladesh, 1997.

5. Severe damage to agriculture and plantations(25-30% of mango and jackfruit trees were found uprooted).
6. Farmers lost their stock of seed, food, livestock and equipment and could not prepare for the next crop.
7. The prey-predator relationship was badly disturbed.

The estimated economic damage to different sectors as a result cf the 1991 cyclone is shown in Table 6.21. The total economic loss due to the cyclone has been estimated by the Government of Bangladesh to be of the extent of Taka 147,919 million(US $ 4,225 million).The property damaged was estimated to be worth $ 2.4 billion.[96]

Table 6.21

Estimated Damages to The Economy due to Cyclone 1991

Sector	Estimated Value of Damages (million Taka)
Agriculture	16,535
Industry	112,970
Transport and Communication	8,856
Socio-Economic Infrastructure	9,358
Others.	200

Note: In 1991 1 US $= 35 Taka

Source: Cyclone Disaster of April 1991 and Relief and Rehabilitation Requirements, Government of the People's Republic of Bangladesh, Ministry of Planning and Ministry of Finance, Dhaka, 1991.

Features of the 19th May 1997 Cyclone

The cyclone was named 'HELEN' and coded `IB BRAVO" It started near the Andaman and Nicobar islands, 1400 W. from Bangladesh as a well marked low detected over Southeast Bay and Adjoining Andaman sea at 0900 UTC of 15 May 1997. It intensified into a deep depression at 1200 UTC on the same day. It intentsified into a deep depression over Southeast Bay at 0300 UTC on 16 May 1997. It moved in a Northerly direction and intensified further into cyclonic storm at 0900 UTC of the same day. It continued to move in a northerly direction and concentrated further into a severe cyclonic storm at 17,0900 UTC. It maintained its northward movement and intensified further into a severe cyclonic storm with a core of Hurricane winds over East, Central and adjoining Bay of Bengal area at 17,1800 UTC It moved northwards slowly and gained energy continuously. It came under the range of Cox's Bazar radio at 19,000 UTC. Finally it moved in north-easterly direction and crossed Chittagong-Feni coast near Sitakundu, 20 miles west of Chittagong at 1430 UTC of 19 May 1997. Then it moved further inland in a north-northeasterly direction and gradually weakened.[97]

A major difference between the 1991 and 1997 cyclone was that in 1997 when the winds were at their peak the normal ocean tide was at the lowest ebb though the period was one-day ahead of the full moon(Buddhha Purnima) unlike the coincidence with full tide in 1991 adding to the tidal surge. The coastal embankments also held firmly though there was saline water intrusion reported only from Anowara island.

Table 6.22 shows the extent of loss and damage in terms of both human lives lost, people affected as well as the damage caused to livestock and essential infrastructure. The total estimated economic loss was to the tune of 1 billion.

Table 6.22

Impact : Loss and Damage caused by the May 1997 Cyclone

People Killed	111
People wounded	10,754
People missing	2
People affected	3,91,981
Cattle heads lost	3,118
House affected	6,79,987
Crops affected	1,85,314 acres of land
Affected culverts and bridges	512
Affected educational institutions	4,239
Damaged roads and embankments	1,445 kms
Maximum wind speed recorded at: Cox's Bazar Chittagong (ship observed) Sitakundu	230 kph 210 kph 232 kph
Strom surge	10 feet
Estimated Central Pressure	965 hpa
Radius of maximum wind	74 kms

Source : Bangladesh Meteorological Department, Government of Bangladesh Dhaka, 2001.

An analysis of the economic damage and destruction, caused by the 1997 cyclone, suggests the port city of Chittagong was worst affected with 50,000 people being affected by the cyclone. The city itself suffered extensive damage where 200 industries, 500 business institutions, 80 schools, 100 mosques and 50 temples were completely destroyed. The port suffered a damage amounting to Taka 30 million. The Urea Fertilizer Factory lost Taka 70-80 million. The Storm disrupted power, telecommunication and water supply. The fishing boats and trawlers that had gone out to the sea were washed away. The Shipping Corporation of Bangladesh and the Inland Water Transport Corporation underwent severe loss amounting to more than Taka 30 million.[98]

Based on the above analysis it is necessary to have an overview of the likely impact and damages that are caused by cyclones in Bangladesh in order to ensure effective and comprehensive disaster management.

The damages caused by cyclone can be grouped as under:

- Structural
- Non structural.

The structural damages arising out of a cyclonic disaster can be further categorized as

- Public property damage.
- Private property damage.

Table 6.23 provides a categorization of damages caused to infrastructure".

Table-23

Damages Caused by Cyclones

Public	**Private**
Roads and Pathways, Bridges	Farming Infrastructure
Sluices and Culvert, Embankments	Planatations Flood Crops.
Rural Electricity Network	Livestock
Forestry	Cattle
Agriculture	Poultry
Cyclone Shelters	Shrimp Culture
Schools	Goat

Public	Private
Water Supply System and Sanitation	Fishing
Markets	Housing
Industries especially Small Scale Industries	
Tourism	
Govt. and other Buildings.	
Hospitals and Health Care Service	
Communication System	

Source: Raana Haider, ed., Cyclone 1991, Revisited, Bangladesh Centre for Advanced Studies, Dhaka 1992.

The structural damages leading to huge public and private property damage result in non-structural damages in the long run. The non-structural losses are evident in the affected areas retarded economic development. In the rural areas loss of people and livestock strike at the very root of the institution of family, rendering a bleak future to millions of children. The result is poverty, unemployment and malnutrition.

The epidemics that strike as a consequence of breakdown of water supply and sanitation system, as also loss of plantation and food crops pose a major threat to the already aggrieved homeless populace. The worst sufferers are the women and minor children who have to bear the brunt of it all.

All these factors make the already affected populace extremely vulnerable to varied calamities including future disasters. The extent and nature of the damages caused by the cyclone make it imperative to undertake a multi-pronged, effective and efficient disaster management strategy. Such a strategy should involve both the public and private organizations at both individual and community level to ensure a consistent and coordinated effort towards pre-cyclonic activities and post cyclonic calamities.

- Disasters are linked to poverty-The foremost reason why development planners should consider disaster proneness in their planning is that poverty increases disaster vulnerability". Most disasters (when defined as events that outstrip the country's capacity to cope) occur in developing countries, and the people who suffer most from disasters are almost always the poor people of any society. Though natural disasters which cause loss of life and property occur in every country, *the* losses when seen relative to the resources which a country represents a higher burden on the developing countries. Even though economic losses from disasters may be absolutely high in the developed countries, the loss of GNP due to disasters is estimated to be about twenty times greater in developing countries than in the developed countries. Thus one basic aspect of the relationship between disasters and development lies in the fact that poverty increases the likelihood that any crisis event will become a disaster.

- Development can increase disaster proneness the second consideration for integrating disaster awareness into development planning is that, under certain circumstances, development itself can increase the likelihood of disasters. Due to the relationship between poverty and disaster proneness it is assumed that investments on decreasing poverty, i.e. investments on development could be thought of as investments on disaster prevention. While this is largely the accepted presumption the reverse too occurs. Certain development projects planned without recognition of local natural hazards, directly contributes to increased disaster proneness without any consideration of this fact. Development sometimes leads indirectly to increase in disaster probability, to cite an example, improved human and animal health and nutrition have been one of the causes of over population in some regions resulting in over grazing and land depletion to the point of environmental deterioration and ecological crisis. In some cases, populations have moved to urban areas for productive employment but because of lack of planning they have inhabited lands which are susceptible to flooding.

Thus, environment is often the point of interface between developmental planning and disaster vulnerability. Development programmes in disaster prone countries either increases or decreases the likelihood of disasters. While development investments increase a country's capacity to cope with natural hazards (to predict, manage, insure against or shore up against them), they also contribute to disaster prevention. When development spending is undertaken without an awareness of disaster proneness it may create the possibility of a new disaster or increase the potential negative impact of existing natural crises.

- Development resources are frequently wasted through failure to consider disaster proneness - this reason is of importance specially in terms of development assistance in understanding the linkages between development and disasters. When development projects are undertaken without regard for disaster potential, scarce development resources are frequently inefficiently allocated. Investments are lost when a project is financed which is later wiped away by a predictable cyclone or flood. Disasters reduce the economic life of development investments. Yet there are many instances of donor-funded development projects in disaster prone areas, in which this has occurred (eg. Community built centres and newly acquired livestock wiped out by a cyclone in Asia) or in which a development investment has increased the likelihood of a disaster.

Disaster-Development Linkages in the Context of Bangladesh—Implications

This necessitates an analysis of the linkages between disaster and development in the context of Bangladesh. The very nature of deltaic formation originating from its meandering river system draining into the Bay of Bengal makes Bangladesh disaster prone.

Amongst natural disasters the annual flood cyclone tends to attract more media coverage. Even though the death toll is usually not high, floods do uproot people from their settlements, damage infrastructure and marginalise people with little resources. River-bank erosion which is less dramatic in pace is particularly devastating at the local level. To cite an example, one million are affected every year by river-bank erosion while at the same tine new land is created. The simultaneous process of erosion and creation causes tremendous economic losses. While engineers and policy makers wish to banish flooding -through technological solutions, the fact remains, that without an annual flood Bangladesh would find itself in serious economic and environmental constrains. Normally, a fifth of the country is covered with surface water yet the fact remains that Bangladesh does not face floods every year. Indeed floods enhance the ground water reserves and facilitate irrigation during the dry season as well as make communication both cheap and easy through rivers and boats.[99]

The policy makers and major donors have searched for single conclusive solutions such as embankment protection from floods and have often ignored the virtue of a broad integrative approach. This stems from a lack of understanding of the relationship between the environment (both natural and social) and development in Bangladesh.[100]

The vulnerability of the poor is exacerbated by spatial demographic factors, which interact with social conditions. Bangladesh's topography, formed by three of the largest river systems of the world, extensive rainfall and its funnel like coast enhance flooding and invites cyclones. Poverty forces people into settlements in vulnerable areas. Although only a minority of the people are gradually being alienated perhaps about 6% in the late 1980s, deprivation is also caused to the majority through loss of livestock and fruit trees and the dwindling of common property resources such as open water bodies, grazing ground and forests. Women in particular are vulnerable to the scarcity of firewood. Poverty limits the ability of people to build houses, which are threatened by natural disasters.[101]

Women headed households are another outcome of poverty. An absence of male members and presence of very young and very old members may mean lower earning capacity. The increase of female headed households is a clear indication of vulnerability in any society.

Decision making in rural Bangladesh follows well-established social and economic lines, which have been monopolised by a small elite. The poor are vulnerable to the manipulation of patronage by traditional leaders and rural elite. This increases the vulnerability of the majority. Within the household, male domination increases the vulnerability of women and children. This has led to a dismantling of the traditional safety net. This has deprived poor people of the little protection or support they previously had. This low level of institutionalisation has encouraged personalised, ad hoc administration, which leads to selective patronage distribution favouring a group of intermediaries. Development has become synonymous with the growth of rural power brokers.[102]

As is shown above, Bangladesh is prone to natural disasters such as floods, cyclones, storms and surges which have serious and deteriorating implications on its socio-economic conditions. Global warming causing sea level rise in Bangladesh has further accelerated the rise of such devastating natural disasters, This will unsettle millions of people from their homeland and compell them to move to safer places either in their own country or to the neighbouring Indian states. Since the Bangladeshis are constantly flowing to Indian states till yet, the scenario of sea level rise resulting in inundation of low lying areas of Bangladesh, and frequency of floods, storm and cyclones, will add many more millions to the continuing flow of refugees to the Indian states. The presence of increasing numbers of Bangladeshis in northeastern states of India, other metropolitan cities and states will stoke the already ethnically aggravated conflagration, with Bangladesh actively providing sanctuary and moral and material help to the rebellious tribal militants such as Bodo and ULFAs. The improving economy and considerable success of Bangladesh government in rehabilitating the people affected by these disasters and mitigating the damage, have not been enough to put a check on the spurt of flow of Bangladeshis into India, The natural disasters and environmental scarcity of resources such as land, as discussed in preceding chapters may act as the push factors prompting the Bangladeshis to leave their homeland. Comparatively a better economic conditions and lack of such calamities in Indian states may have acted as the pull factors attracting the migrants from Bangladesh to Indian states. Homer Dixon, put another theory to understand the current migration from Bangladesh. In his analysis, the real motivator of migration is the gap between the potential migrants' current level of satisfaction and the level they expect to attain in a new land.

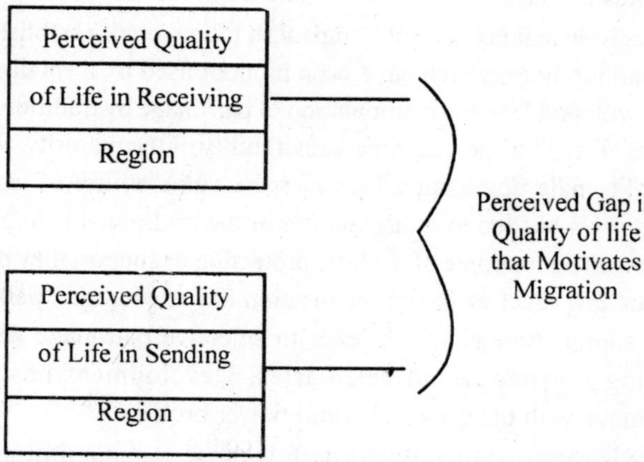

(This figure is taken from Homer Dixon, Environment, Scarcity and Violence (Princeton/New Jersey; Princeton University Press, 1999), p.94).

The larger the gap, the greater is the incentive to migrate. And this gap is not determined by an additive function of push and pull factors but by the relationship between the perceived quality of life in the home region and that in the receiving region. Anything that constrains or depresses the perceived quality of life in the home region, and anything that augments the perceived quality of life in the receiving region, increases the size of the gap.[103] It is in Bangladesh, the frequency of natural disasters along with their devastating repercussions on their economy and the environmental scarcity of cropland constrains or depresses their perceived quality of life. Environmental scarcity of land and decreasing land man ration have played a subtle yet powerful effect in prompting migration to Indian states such as Assam, Tripura, West Bengal and Orissa and other cities.

However successful a country may be in its programmes of disaster management, forecasting, warning and settlement of people before and after the calamities, it cannot prevent disasters as such. Lack of adequate scientific and technological innovation, facilities, computarisation of warning system and monitoring, along with lack of economic and financial wherewithal in a country like Bangladesh where corruption and cornering of resources by elite in administration and business and growing marginalisation of the poor have become a recurrent feature, may add to the problems of alleviating and mitigation measures to combat the catastrophes. The horrors of recurrence, frequency and severity of the catastrophic calamities in Bangladesh loom large in the minds of the affected people. To combat global climate change is not the work of Bangladesh, as its contribution of CO_2 emission to the atmosphere is very negligible. Since it is the responsibility of the rich industrialised North countries the spectre of global warming continues to haunt, with the rejection of Kyoto protocol both by the United States and Russia. In such a situation of uncertainty about the measures to reduce CO_2 emission to the atmosphere, the danger of sea level rise unsettling millions as environmental refugees with the scanario of many more millions fleeing to India, continues to threaten Bangladesh as well as India.

Natural calamities such as floods cyclones, storms and surges are hazardous in the sense that it entails an element of human involvement, A hazardous event that causes unacceptably large number of facilities and/ or overwhelming property or other damages is a natural disaster.[104] Though these calamities have their roots in nature, their frequency and severity is attributable to human activity and their socio-economic political development defined in terms of exploiting the nature. While poverty and dwindling land-man as well as resource ratio are causing the environment to degrade at a faster rate, ecogeographic setting and various physiological and morphological characterstics have made the country extremely vulnerable to natural disaster. Recurring floods, cyclones, tornadoes, storm surges are frequent occurrences which contribute to further degradation of environment in Bangladesh. At the regional level, the country faces environmental degradation due to imbalances in the shared ecosystem i.e. the Himalayan drainage ecosystem. Bangladesh, the lower riparian, is geographically situated in such a position that it is affected by most of the adverse consequences of any disruption of this unified ecosystem caused by various indiscriminate and uncoordinated economic activities of the upper riparians. At the global level also, as discussed in the preceding chapters, Bangladesh faces nightmarish dangers emanating from global warming and sea level rise. Due to the flat nature of terrain, the country is much vulnerable to inundation in case of even a little rise in the sea level together with the series of catastrophes that are related to the warming atmosphere and the rising sea. The destabilizing effect on the country's ecosystem that arises out of various man made factors at the global, regional and national levels, stems from the degraded environment and shrinking natural resources.[105] Situated in the tropical monsoon region, the regional variation in the topography of Bangladesh, as discussed in previous chapters causes environmental degradation. The north west region of the country with an elevation from about 12 meters to 90 meters above sea level is prone to low water rainfall and high water deficiency in the driest month. While the average height of the country i.e. 7.6 meters has made her an easy prey to the 'green house monster location in the Bay of Bengal has made the country a favorite spot for cyclones and tornadoes. In comparison with the neighbouring countries, cyclones approaching the coast of Bangladesh are more disastrous. The reason for this is the funnel shape of the Bay with Bangladesh at the bottom of the funnel where the waters are piling up. In addition to this the sea level in the eastern estuary increases during the monsoon by about 1 meter as a result of upland discharge, strong wind from the southwest and a low barometric pressure. The physiological situation of Bangladesh, its hydrological cycle, and climatic and topographical factors have made it vulnerable and prone to cyclones, surges and floods. The human activities and their concept of development have made their occurrance more frequent and severe in terms of damage to human lives, property, crop and unsettlement of human beings from their homeland and migration to regions within the country or outside. Hence, the fencing of Indo-Bangladesh border with barbed wires by the government of India cannot be effective in halting the escaping into Indian territory of Bangladeshis from the gnawing clutches of death, loss of property or economic livelihood. Hence the spectre of environmental induced migration and migration induced violent group identity or ethnic conflict in Indian states is likely to reign supreme in the minds of the policy makers in India while formulating a national policy to stall migration. It is not the barbed wire but addressing the problems of environmental degradation at the global, regional and national level will herald a permanent solution to the crisis.

References

1. Planning and Management of Disaster Reduction, Report by the United Nations Centre for Human Settlement (UNCHS), Nairobi, 1990, p. 8.

2. Anders Wijkmar and Lloyd Timberlake, Natural disasters: Acts of God or Acts of Man, International Institute for Environment and Development and Swedish Red Cross, Geneva, 1984,p. 21,22,27. Also see P.L.Abbott, Natural Disasters (Dubuque, I.A : William C. Brown 1996), p- 2 - 8

3. Fredrick Krimgold, Overview of the Priority Area: Natural Disaster, United Nations, New York, 1976,p. 1

4. Paul Susman, Phil O.Keefe and Ben Wisner, Global Disaster a Radical Interpretation, pp 263-264. Also see K.Hewitt, "The Idea of Calamity in a Technocratic Age", in K.Hewitt, ed.. Interpretations of Calamity : From the Viewpoint of Human Ecology. (Allen and Unwin, London), pp. 3- 32.

5. Paul Susman, Phil O.Keefe and Ben Wisner, n.4, p.264. Also see Disaster Mitigation in Asia and the Pacific, Asian Development Bank, Manila, 1991, pp.33-35. Also see Piers Blakie, Terry Cannon, Ian Davis and Ben Wisner, At Risk: Natural Hazards, People's Vulnerability and Disasters, Routledge, New York, 1994, pp. 9-12.

6. Mary B. Anderson, Analysing the Cost and Benefits of Natural Disaster Responses in the Context of Development, Environment Paper, No.29, World Bank, Washington,

7. Paul Susman, Phil O. Keefe and Ben Wisner, n.4,p.264.

8. Disaster Preparedness Training Manual, National Red Cross, Philippines, 1994, p.2. Also see Andrew Maskrey, Disaster Mitigation: A Community Based Approach, Development Guidelines, No.3, Oxfam,Oxford, 1989, pp.1-20.

9. United Nations Disaster Management Training Programme, United Nations, New York, 1991, p. 53. ALso see Piers Blakie, et.al., n.5, pp.9-12.

10. Souhil EL- Masri And Graham Tipple "Urbanisation, Poverty and Natural Disasters: Vulnerability of Settlements in Developing Countries", in Andrenelle ed., Reconstruction after Disaster : Issues and Practices,(London : Ashgate Publishing Company, 1997) pp'. 1-2.

11. Ian Burton. R.W.Kates and G.F. White, The Environment as Hazard (New York: Oxford University Press, 1978), p. 150 .

12. Ian Davis, ed., Disasters and the Small Dwelling, Pergamea Press, Oxford. 1981, p.8, Also see James Lewis, "Development, Vulnerability and Disaster Reduction", in Andrenelle Awotona, ed., Reconstruction after Disaster:

Issues and Practices. Ashgate Publishing Company, London, 1997, pp.45-46. Also see Piers Blakie, et.al., n.5, pp. 8-12.

13. United Nations Centre for Human Settlements (UNCHS) Report, United Nations, New York, 1994. pp. 3-10.

14. Anders Wijkman, n.2 ,p.19.

15. Mary B.Anderson, "A Reconceptualisation of the Linkages between Disasters and Development", Disasters: The International Journal of Disaster Studies and Practice, vol,9(Harvard Supplement), 1985,p.46-51. Also see Mary B.Anderson," Vulnerability to Disaster and Sustainable Development: A General Framework for Assessing Vulnerability", in M. Munasinghe and C.Clarke, ed., Disaster Prevention for Sustainable Development: Economic and Policy Issues, IDNDR and the World Bank, Washington D. C. , 1995.

16. Y.F.Aysan,"Vulnerabilitv Assessment", in P.A.Merriam and C.W.A.Browitt, ed.,Natural Disasters: Protecting Vulnerable Communities. Thomas Telford, London, 1993, pp.3. Also see Souhil El-Masri and Graham Tipple n. 10., p.3. ALso see Jasmin K.Riad and Fran H. Norris, "The Influence of Relocation on the Environmental, Social and Psychological Stress experienced by Disaster Victims", in Environment and Behaviour, Vol.28, No. 2, March 1996, p.173.

17. Jermey J.Wadford, "Environmental Management and Economic Policy in Developing Countries", in G.Schramm and J.J. Wardford, Environmental Management and Economic Development, World Bank Publication, John Hopkins University Press, Baltimore, 1989, p.7. Also see Keith Smith, Environmental Hazards: Assessing Risk and Reducing Disaster, Routledge New York, 2001. pp.44-47. Also see Report of the Task forces on Bangladesh Development Strategies for the 1990s. Vol.I, Government of Bangladesh University Press Limited, Dhaka, 1991,pp. , Also see K.Nizamuddin, "Global Warming and its Impact on Bangladesh in K. Nizamuddin, ed., Disaster in Bangladesh, University Press Limited, Dhaka, 2001, pp. 131-136. Also see Dr. Saleemul Huq, "Global Climate Change and the Role of Bangladesh", in People's Report on Bangladesh's Environment 2001, Vol.1, Unnayan Shamannay, University Press Limited, Dhaka, pp. 223-226.

18. Souhil EL. Masri, n.10, p.3.

19. Jasmin K.Riad and Fran H.Norris, n.16, pp. 166-167,173.

20. Souhil EL. Masri, n.10, p.3. Also see Keith Smith, n.17, pp. 44-47.

21. Keith Smith, n.17, p.48.

22. Disaster Management: A Disaster Manager's Handbook, Asian Development Bank, Manila, 1991.

23. Mary,B.Anderson, n.6, pp.3-7. Also see Rita Funaro Cartis, Natural Disasters and the Development Process: A Discussion of Issues, Office of Foreign Disaster Assistance USAID, Washington, D.C.July 1982, p.1. Also see J.Roberto Jovel, Economic and Social Consequences of Natural Disasters in Latin America and the Carribean, United Nations Economic Commission for Latin America and the Carribean (UN ECLAC), Santiago, Chile, 1989,p.18. ALso see Neil Middleton and Phil O'Keefe, Disaster and Development, Pluto Press London, 1998, pp.3-12. ALso see Fredrick Cuny Disaster and Development (Oxford: Oxford University Press, 1983), pp;2-20. Also see Piers Blakie, Terry Cannon, Ian Davis and Ben Wisner, At Risk: Natural Hazards, People's Vulnerability and Disasters, (New York: Routledge, 1994), pp. 8-12.

24. World Disaster Report 1997 and 2000,Geneva.

25. Ibid.

28. Souhil-EL-Masri, n.10,p.4.

27. On the basis of the adjusted population,2001 census in Population Census 2001, Preliminary Report, Bangladesh: Bureau of Statistics, Ministry of Planning,Dhaka, 2001, p.4. Also see Bangladesh Country Profile 2001,Economist Intelligence Unit, London,2001, p. 3. The population was 121 million in 1995 on the basis of estimates based on the adjusted 1991 census as stated in the People's Report on Bangladesh Environment,2001, Vol.I,University Press Limited, Dhaka,2001, p.22.

28. Asian Development Bank, Disaster Mitigation in the Asia and the Pacific, Manila, 1991, p.74. ALso see Regional Study on the Causes and Consequences of Natural Disasters and the Protection and Preservation of the Environment, SAARC Secretariat Report, Kathmandu 1992, pp.138-139. Also see Bangladesh: A Proposed Rural Development Strategy: A World Bank. Study, University Press Ltd. Dhaka, 2000. Also see M.A.H.Pramanik, "Natural Disasters, in A.Atiq Rahman, Saleemul Haq, Raana Haider and Erik G Jansen, ed., Environment and Development in Bangladesh, Vol. 1, University Press Ltd,1994,pp. 134-135. Also see People's Report on Bangladesh Environment 2001, n.1, pp.22-23.

29. H.Brammer, "Floods in Bangladesh, Geographical Background to the 1987 and 1988 floods", The Geographical Journal, Vol.156, no.1, 1990, pp. 12-22.

30. In Bangladesh, the lower course of the Brahmaputra is called the Jamuna and the lower course of the Ganges is called the Padma.

31. Md. Abdur Hob, "Flood Hazards in Bangladesh: Nature, Causes and Control", Asian Profile Vol.18, no.4,1990,pp.365-367. Also see ADB, n.28, p. 75. Also see Pramanik, n.28, pp. 142-143. Also see GIS Map, Government of Bangladesh.
32. M.Hossain, " Siltation of River Bed", and Flood Problem, in M.Ahmad, ed., Flood in Bangladesh, Community Development Library,Dhaka, 1989, pp.78. ALso see "River Erosion" Disaster Report, 1997, Disaster Forum, Dhaka,1998, pp. 17-26.
33. Md.Abdur Rob, n.31, pp. 365-367. Also see ADB, n. 28,p. 75. Also see Pramanik,n.28,pp. 142-143. ALso see GIS Map, Government of Bangladesh.
34. The major rivers of Bangladesh do not flow in the same course for two successive years. Also see M.Abdul Baqee, Responding to Nature's Toll: The Case of Char Islands in K.Nizamuddin, ed., Disaster in Bangladesh, University of Dhaka, Dhaka, 2001, p. 29.
35. World Disaster Report 2001, International- Federation of Red Crescent Societies, Oxford University Press,Geneva, 2001, p.16.
36. ADB.n.28,p.74. Also see B.G.Verghese, Waters of Hope, Integrated Water Resource Development and Regional Cooperation within the Himalayan-Ganga-Brahmaputra-Barak Basin, Academic Publishers, Dhaka, 1990,pp.445-447 Also see P.Rogers, P.Lydon and D.Seckler, Eastern Waters Study: Strategies to Manage flood and Drought in the Ganges Brahmaputra Basin, USAID, Washington D. C.1989, pp. 80-84.
37. ADB, n. 28, p.75. Also see R.Hughes,S. Adnan, B.Clayton- Barry Dalal, Floodplains or Floodplans ? A Review of Approaches to Water Management in Bangladesh, International Institute for Environment and Development Research and Advisory Services, Dhaka 1994,pp.94. Also see Pramanik, n. 28, pp. 140-143.
38. ADB n.28, p.75. Also see Peoples Report on Bangladesh Environment, 2001,n.27, p. 23. Also see Bangladesh Country Profile 2001, n.27, p.23.
39. Bangladesh Country Profile 2001, n 27,p.23. Also see Bangladesh Bureau of Statistics, Statistical Pocketbook of Bangladesh, Government of Bangladesh, Dhaka, Annual., 1998. -Also see Peoples Report on Bangladesh Environment, 2001, n.27,p.23.
40. ADB.n.28, p.75. Also see the Sangbad July 29,1999. Also see the People's Report on Environment,2001,n.27, pp.130. Also see Piers Blakie, Terry Cannon, Ian Davis and Ben Wisner, n. 23, pp. 138-143.
41. H.Brammer, n. 29, pp. 12-22.
42. FAO, Land Resources Appraisal of Bangladesh for Agricultural Development, Report 2, Rome 1988.

43. Rehman Shobhan, Bangladesh: Problems of Governance,New Delhi, Konark Publishers, 1994, pp. 1-20. Also see Lawrence Ziring, Bangladesh from Mujib to Ershad: An Interpretative Study, Karachi, Oxford University Press, 1992, pp.1-10. Also see Moudud Ahmed, Democracy and the Challenge of Development: A Study of Political and Military Interventions in Bangladesh, Dhaka University Press, Dhaka, 1995. pp.5-20

44. World Development Report, Annual, World Bank, Washington, 1999, pp.10. Also see Bangladesh Country Profile,2001, n.27, 2001, p. 25.

45. World Development Report, Annual, World Bank, Washington, 1999, pp. 10. Also see Bangladesh Country Profile, 2001, n.27, p. 25. Also see Rehman Shobhan, The Crisis of External Dependence, University Press Limited Dhaka, 1982, p. 12.

46. Of the total aid flow in 1971-73 of 822.3 million US dollars, food aid accounted for 38%, commodity aid 51.9% and Project aid 10.2%. Since 1980s and more so in the 1990s of the total aid flow steady decline has been witnessed in the share of food and commodity aid compared to an increase in the share of project aid, with food aid accounting for 6.8% commodity aid 17.8% and project aid 75.4% of the total aid flow of 1481.2 million US dollars in 1996-97.

47. C.R, Abrar, and Muhammad Siamsul Huq, Aid Development and Diplomacy, University Press Limited, Dhaka,1999, pp. 1-15. Bangladesh Economic Review, 2001, Ministry of Finance, Dhaka,2001, pp.1-10. Also see Bangladesh Country Profile 2001, n.27,p.25. Also see Rehman Shobhan, " State of the Bangladesh Economy, 1999: An Overview", in Rehman Shobhan, ed., Trends in the Post flood Economy: A Review of Bangladesh's Development 1998-99, CPD, University Press Limited, 2000, pp.1-11.

48. Bangladesh Country Profile 2001, n.27,pp.29-31. Also see Quazi Shahabuddin,"1998 Floods, Post-Flood Agricultural Rehabilitation Programme and Growth Performance", in Rehman Shohhan, ed., Trends in the Post Flood Economy: A Review of Bangladesh's Development 1998-99, CPD, University Press Limited, 2000, pp.59-74. Also see Mustafa K. Mujeri, "Macroeconomic Development in the 1990s" in Abu Abdullah ed., Bangladesh Economy 2000, Bangladesh Institute of Development Studies, Dhaka, 2001, pp. 1-10.

49. Dennis Parker, Nabiul Islam and Ngai Weng Chan, "Reducing Vulnerability following Flood Disasters: Issues and Practices", in Andrenelle Awotona, ed., Reconstruction after Disaster: Issues and. Practices, Ashgate Publishing Company, London, 1997,p.28.

50. D.J.Parker, " Managing Flood Hazards and Disasters",in D.J.Parker, ed., Floods, Vol.II, Routledge, London and New York, 2000, pp.287-306. Also see J.W. Handner, "Flood Hazard and Sustainable Development", in D.J.Parker, ed.,Floods, Vol.II,Routledge, London and New York, 2000, pp. 276-286.

51. Dennis Parker, et.al., n.49,p.26.

52. Dennis Parker, et.al., n.49, p. 26. ALso see D.J.Parker. n.50, pp.287-306.

53. Dennis Parker, et.al., n.49,p.28. Also see James Lewis, Development in Disaster Prone Places: Studies of Vulnerability, Intermediate Technology Publications, New York. 1999, pp.145-149.

54. Piers Blakie, Terry Cannon, Ian Davis and Ben Wisner, n.4O,pp. 138-145. ALso see Fredrick Cuny, Disaster and Development, Oxford University Press, Oxford, 1983,pp. 1-20.

55. B.G.Verghese, R.Rangachari, Q.K.Ahmed, Asit.K.Biswas and M.M.Sanju ed., Ganges-Brahmaputra-Meghna Region: A Framework for sustainable Development, University Press Limited Dhaka, 2001, pp. 105-108.

56. Pramanik, n.28,p. 135. Also see Regional Study on the Causes and Consequences of Natural Disasters and the Protection and Preservation of the Environment, n.28, 1992, pp. 138-139. Also see Thomas Hoffer, Floods in Bangladesh: A Highland-Lowland Interaction ?, Institute of Geography, University of Berne, Switzerland, 1998,p.8.

57 Pramanik, n.28, pp. 135-136. Also see SAARC Secretariat Report, n.28, pp.138-139.

58. Prananik, n.28, p.136. Also see M.M.Miah, Floods in Bangladesh, Academic Publishers, Dhaka, 1988, pp.5-6. ALso see ADB. n.28,pp.77-82. Also see MD.Abdur Rob, n.31, PP.371. ALso see M.Hossain, A.T.M.A.Islam and S.K. Saha ed., Floods in Bangladesh: Recurrent Disaster and People's Survival, Universities Research Centre, Dhaka, 1987, p.104. Also see "Cyclones since 1960" Disaster Report: Bangladesh 1997, Disaster Forum, Dhaka, 1998, pp. 42.

59. N.Huda, "Flood Control Proposal for the Major River Systems of Bangladesh", in M.Ahmad, Flood in Bangladesh Community Development Library, Dhaka, p. 121.

60. H.Brammer,1990,n.29, pp.12-22. Also see Thomas Hoffer, n.56, pp. 8-9.

61. Thomas Hoffer, n.56, pp.8-9. Also see H.Brammer, "The Complexities of Detailed Impact assessment for the Ganges-Brahmaputra-Meghna Delta of Bangladesh "Paper for international -workshop on the effects of climatic change on sea level, severe tropical storms and their associated impacts,

University of East Anglia, Norwich, September 1987, p.22. Also see Hossain, et.al , 1987, n. 58. p.19. ALso see J.D.Ives, "Floods in Bangladesh: Who is to Blame ? " New Scientist, vol. 13,no. 4, p. 37.

62. M.L.Dewan, Floods in Bangladesh: What are the Solutions?, International Society of Bangladesh, Concordia,University of Montreal, Canada, 1989, pp.56.

63. "Flash Flood: 1997", Disaster Report: Bangladesh 1997, Disaster Forum, Dhaka, 1998, pp. 9-11.

64. Thomas Hoffer, n.56, pp.8-9.

65. Polder refers to a low-lying land reclaimed from the sea "by the construction of a perimeter dyke.

66. Flash Flood 1997, n.63, pp.9-11.

67. R.Hughes, n.37, pp. 21-22.

68. M.A.H.Pramanik, n.28, p.145.

69. M.Monirul Qader Mirza and Mushtaqe Ahmed, "Management of Environmental disaster of Floods in the Himalayan Region" Proceedings of WCNHR, New Delhi, 10E and WFEO, January 1992, p. 209.

70. Ibid, p. 209.

71. Mahbuba Nasreen, "Coping With Floods", in Imtiaz Ahmed, ed., Living With Floods: An Exercise in Alternatives, UPL, Dhaka,1999, p.35.

72. See Imtiaz Ahmed, ed., Living With Floods: An Exercise in Alternatives, *UPL,* Ehaka,1999, p.151. Also see USAID, OFDA Annual Report, Office of the Disaster Assistance Agency, Washington, 1988, pp. 110-122.

73. Government Circular Ministry of Relief and Rehabilitation Government of Bangladesh, Dhaka, 23 October 1988. Also see Joint Survey Report of MRR and ADAB, Dhaka, September 1988. Also see Flood 1988, CARITAS, Bangladesh,Bulletin no. 3, Dhaka, May 1989, pp. 1-2. Also see Disaster Recovery Report, CARITAS Bangladesh, Dhaka, 1989,p.4.

74. Selina Begum, "Storm Surges and River flooding in Bangladesh", in M.L.EL Sabh et.al., ed., Land Based and Marine Hazards, Kluwer Academic Press, Netherlands, 1996, p. 117.

75. Also see Selina Begum, n.74, pp. 117.

76. Also see Floods 1988, ADAB Report, Ehaka, 1988, pp. 1-8.

77. Selina Begum, n.74. p. 117. ALso see SAARC Secretariat Report, n.28, p. 144. Also see Flood 1988, n. 73, pp. 1-3. Also see Disaster Recovery Report, n.73, p.4.

78. DMB Report on Floods of 1998, DMB, Dhaka, 1999, pp. 1-6. Also see MD.Shamsul Islam, 1998 Floods in Bangladesh and Government's Response, Dhaka, 1999, pp.4-5.

79. DMB Report, n.78, pp. 4-8.
80. Imtiaz Ahmed, n.72, pp.151.
81. Cyclones, Ministry of I& B, Government of India and Naba Mudra Publishers Ltd, Calcutta, 1972, pp. 1-5. Also see Ian Burton, W.Kates And G.F. White, The Environment As Hazard, Oxford University Press, New York, 1978, pp. 10-25.
82. Selina Begum, n.74, pp.121-122. ALso see Pramanik,n.28, pp.153. Also see MD.Akram Hossain, Cyclone Warning System in Bangladesh, DMB,Government of Bangladesh, 1997. pp.26-32. Also see A.M. Choudhury, "Cyclones in Bangladesh", Bangladesh Quarterly Vol.12, no.1, Autumn 1989, pp.7-12.
83. Selina Begun, n.74,pp 121-122. Also see S. Raghavan and A.K.Sensharma, "Tropical Impacts in India and Neighbourhood" in Roger Pielke Sr., Storms, Vol. I, Routledge, London and New York, 2000, pp. 339-356.
84. Cyclonic Storms", Disaster Report: Bangladesh 1997, Disaster. Forum, Dhaka, 1997, pp.36-37. Also see Selina Begum, n.74, pp. 68, pp. 121-122. Also see A.M. Choudhury, n.82,pp.7-12. Also see MD.Akram Hossain, n. 82, pp.28-30.
85. Selina Begum, n.74, pp.121-122. Also see A. M. Choudhury, n.82, pp.7-12.
86. Selina Begum, n.74, pp.123. Also see, M.A.H.Pramanik, n.28, pp.149, 151.
87. Selina Begum, n.74, pp. 123-124.
88. Selina Begum, n.74, pp. 124-126. Also see A.M.Choudhury, n. 82, pp.7-12. Also see Raana Haider, ed., Cyclone 91 Revisited, Bangladesh Centre for Advanced Studies and University Press Ltd., Dhaka,1992.
89. Selina Begum, n. 74, pp.126-127. Also see Marlene Bradford, Robert S. Carmichael, ed., Natural Disasters, Vol.11, Famines, Hurricanes, Typhoons and Cyclones, Salem Press, California,2001, pp.512-518.
90. Jayanthi and Sharma(i986), Murty et.al. 1986, Kastura (1992), Talukdar (1992), Murty, and Flather (1994), Synghal (1992), in T.S.Murthy and V. R.Niralla, "El-nino and Storm Surges in the Bay of Bengal", in M.I.El,. Sabh, ed., Land Based and Marine Hazards, Kluwer Academic Publishers, Netherlands, 1996. Also see Report on May 1997 Cyclone, Bangladesh Meteorological Department, Dhaka, 1997.
91. Ibid. Also see, Mahendra P.Lama, "Economic Resources and Environmental Concerns in South Asia", in D.D.Khanna, ed., Sustainable Development in South Asia, Macmillan India Ltd., New Delhi, p.246.
92. Raana Haider, et.al, 1992, n.88, p.20. Also see MD.Akram Hossain, n.82, p.35.

93. Ibid.

94. Selina Begum,n.74,pp. 126-127. ALso see Raana Haider, n.88,pp.7-17. Also see A.M.Choudhury,n.82,pp.7-12. Also see Cyclone Disaster of April 1991 and Relief and Rehabilitation/Reconstruction Requirement, GOB, Ministry of Planning and Ministry of Finance, Dhaka,1991, 1-8.

95. Raana Haider, n.88,. p.7-11,35-39. Also see, Mahendra P.Lama, n.91, p.246.

96. Mushtaque Chowdhury, et.al, "The Bangladesh Cyclone of 1991: Why so many People Died", Disasters, Vol.17, no.4, December 1993- p. 291.

97. Bangladesh Meteorological Department, Government of Bangladesh, Dhaka, 1997. Also see May 1997 Cyclone,ADAB Activity Report, Dhaka,1997, pp.1-8.

98. Cyclonic Storms, Disaster Report: Bangladesh 1997, Disaster Forum, Dhaka, p.37.

99. Atiur Rahman, "Disaster and Development: A Study in Institution Building in Bangladesh", in Hameeda Hossain, Cole. P. Dodge and F.H. Abed (Dhaka: University Press Ltd. 1992), p. 352. Also see Atiur Rahman and Rokshana, Disaster and Development: A Study of Human Saga in Bangladesh, Unpublished Work, Dhaka, 1998, pp.4.

100. Atiur Rahman,n.99, p.352.

101. Atiur Rahman, n.99, p.352. Dennis Parker, Naibul Islam and Ngai Weng Chan," Reducing Vulnerability Following Flood Disasters Issues and Practices", in "Andrenelle Awotona ed., Reconstruction after Disaster: Issues and Practices. Ashgate Publishing Company, London, 1997, pp. 23-25. Also see Piers Blakie, Terry Cannon, Ian Davis and Ben Wisner, At Risk: Natural Hazards, People's Vulnerability and Disasters, Routledge, New York:, 1994, pp.9-12.

102. Atiur Rahman, n.99, p.353.

103. Thomas F.Homer Dixon, Environment, Scarcity and Violence (Princeton/ New Jersey: Princeton university Press, 1999), pp. 93-96.

104. Disasters, Planning and Development: Managing Natural Hazards to Reduce Loss, Report by the OFDA-USAID and Organisation of American States, Washington, D. C: 1990, p.7

105. M.Abdul Hafiz and Nahid Islam, "Environmental Degradation and Intra/ Interstate Conflicts in Bangladesh", Environment and Conflict Project (ENCOP), Occasional Paper no.6, May 1993, Centre for Security Studies and Conflict Research, Swiss Federal Institute of Technology and Swiss Peace Foundation, Zurich/Bern, pp. 1-95.

Floods and Cyclones in Bangladesh: Implications and Consequences ... [illegible]

93. Ibid.

94. [illegible] Rahman, *op. cit.*, [illegible] [illegible] [illegible] [illegible] [illegible] "Cyclone" [illegible] [illegible] [illegible] Relief and Rehabilitation [illegible] Reconstruction Requirement ... [illegible] Ministry of Planning and Ministry of Finance, Dhaka, 1991, [illegible]

95. Rehman, *op. cit.*, pp. 74, 35-37. Also see [illegible] and [illegible] [illegible], "The Bangladesh Cyclone of 1991, Why so many People Died", [illegible] Vol. 17, No. 4, December 1993, p. [illegible]

97. Bangladesh [illegible], Government of Bangladesh, Dhaka, 1993. Also see [illegible] 1997 [illegible] ADAB [illegible] Report, Dhaka, 1997, pp. [illegible]

98. [illegible] Bureau [illegible] Report, Bangladesh: 1991 [illegible] Flood [illegible]

99. [illegible] "Disaster and Development Strategy" in [illegible] and [illegible] (eds.), [illegible] [illegible] Ahmed [illegible] [illegible] (1992), [illegible] Also [illegible] and [illegible] [illegible], A Study on Flood [illegible] Bangladesh [illegible], Dhaka, 1991, p. [illegible]

100. Atiur Rahman, *op. cit.*, p. [illegible]

101. Atiur Rahman, *op. cit.*, p. [illegible] [illegible] Rahman and [illegible] "[illegible] Responding Vulnerability [illegible]" and [illegible] Issues and Practices [illegible] [illegible] [illegible] London, [illegible] [illegible] [illegible] [illegible] [illegible] Floods: Perspectives, Vulnerability and Disasters, Routledge, London, 1994, p. [illegible]

102. Atiur Rahman, *op. cit.*, p. [illegible]

103. Thomas Homer-Dixon, *Environment, Scarcity and Violence*, Princeton, New Jersey, Princeton University Press, 1999, pp. [illegible]

104. [illegible] Bangladesh Development [illegible], [illegible] [illegible] [illegible] the [illegible] and Organisation [illegible] Washington, D.C. [illegible]

105. [illegible] and [illegible], "Environmental Degradation and Intrastate Conflicts in Bangladesh", Environment and Conflicts Project (ENCOP) Occasional Paper No. [illegible] [illegible] and Conflicts Research, Swiss Federal Institute of Technology and Swiss Peace Foundation, Zurich, [illegible] pp. [illegible]

7

International Intervention : Questions of Equity, Ethics and Political Will

Though migration has given rise to increasing political tension and conflict between Bangladesh and India, it has not yet resulted in an armed conflict or war between the two. Addition of many more millions due to predicted sea level rise may not likely to end in a war between the two. What lies at the root of the crisis? Part of the crisis remains embedded in the exorbitant emission of greenhouse gases and CO_2 to the atmosphere by the industrialised nations of the world. That is to say, from only 27 of all the sovereign states, accounting for 43% of global land area and 20% of global population. On the contrary, comparatively little of the carbon dioxide emissions today flow from the remaining nations acco nting for 57% of the global land area and 80% of the global population. What comes as a threat to Bangladesh or India or other developing countries in terms of disastrous consequences of sea level rise or climate change is the cumulative effects of emissions of CO_2 by the industrialised north to the atmosphere. Thus the degradation of the environment-atmosphere poses a security threat to millions of people living in low lying areas like Bangladesh in terms of sea level rise and other implications of climate change on health, agriculture and economy.

So the basic question remains who is to be blamed ? Who is to shoulder the responsibility and burden of reducing CO_2 in the atmosphere ? In terms of emission of CO_2 to the atmosphere the industrialised nations should unilaterially share the burden. But what remains at the crux of the matter is the industrialised nation's pleading for sharing the burden with the developing countries on the basis of equity. While denying the same while using the atmosphere as a waste disposal site. This double standard logic at present remains the main issue with US stressing on developing countries' meaningful participation in the reduction of CO_2 emision. The Kyoto Protocol succeeds in super imposing this view of US and its allies on the developing countries through Clean Development Mechanism bypassing the former's major historical emission of CO_2 to the atmosphere.[1]

The only way to stop the doomsday prophecies associated with climate change from coming true, is to reduce emissions by 50 - 70 per cent below 1990 levels, by reducing or even altogether abandoning, the use of carbon based fuels. But in a world where things are never quite this simple, the use of these fuels, and hence carbon emissions, are closely linked to economic growth and life styles. The more prosperous a country's economy and the higher its per capita economy, the higher its fossil fuel consumption for power generation and transport, and the higher its greenhouse gas emission. Industrialised countries owe their current prosperity to years of historical emissions, which have accumulated in the atmosphere since the start of industrial revolution, and also to a high level of current emissions. Developing countries, meanwhile, have only recently set out on the path of industrialisation, and their per capita emissions are still comparatively low. The Green house gas emissions of one US citizen, for instance were equal to 19 Indians, 107 Bangladeshis, 269 Nepalis and 134 Bhutanese in 1996.[2]

Under these circumstances any limit on carbon emissions amounts to a limit on economic growth, turning climate change mitigation into an intensely political issue. International negotiations under the UN Framework Convention on Climate Change (FCCC) aimed at limiting greenhouse gas emissions into the atmosphere, have turned into a tug of war with rich countries unwilling to compromise their lifestyles, and poor countries unwilling to accept a premature cap on their right to basic development. Developing countries have demanded their space to grow while refusing to take on emission into at their current stage of development. The people of industrialised countries have more than used up their share of the absorptive capacity of this atmosphere, through their high emission levels in the past and in the present. To that extent global warming is their creation. So it is only right that they should take the initial responsibility of reducing emissions, while allowing developing countries to achieve at least a basic level of development. Moreover, asking developing countries to reduce carbon emission levels now, amounts to asking them to freeze their standard of living at their current stage of development. As a result of these political complexities, negotiations under FCCC have turned into a game between unequal partners, as seen from Kyoto protocol and subsequent other climate negotiations. The Kyoto Protocol provides for three flexibility mechanisms to assist industrialised countries in achieving their targets at low cost. These are emissions trading (trading of emissions allowances between industrialised countries) joint implementation (industrialised countries can earn credits by financing projects that cut emissions in other industrialised countries) and the Clean Development Mechanism (CDM, a form of joint implementation between industrialised and developing countries). The future of the Kyoto protocol remains shrouded in uncertainly, with US rejecting the treaty, US position not accepted by G-77 and China on the one hand, and European Union on the other.

Issues like use of additional land use, land use change and forestry (LULUCF) activities allowing countries with reduction commitments under Art 3.4 of Kyoto protocol remains controversial. Equally contentious is the issue of whether sinks and nuclear projects should be excluded from CDM. Developing countries India and China came under pressure for allegedly promoting the inclusion of nuclear projects in CDM. If the US has its way, it might increase its emissions and still meet its, Kyoto targets. The umbrella group (US and its allies) fought off restriction on the use of trading mechanism. Industrialised countries are resisting all efforts of having a just and effective compliance regime to ensure that countries meet their commitments under the Kyoto Protocol. Promised funds in articles 4.8 and 4.9 of the Climate Convention to meet the specific needs of the developing countries regarding adverse effects of climate change or impact of steps taken to counter climate change remain elusive and sidelined during negotiations of Conference of Parties to the Climate Change Convention.[3] Without a major move towards zero carbon energy systems by the industrialised countries, and without the acceptance of equity and an equal per capita entitlements, all negotiations towards reducing CO_2 emissions will remain orchestrated to cater to the industrialised North's interests raising the spectre of global warming and sea level rise. This will continue to remain a preponderant factor in the prospects of flow of much more refugees from Bangladesh into India along with its security implications.

Supply of Ingenuity and Institutional Framework: Limitations and Constraints

The economic optimists always stress on the extraordinary ability of human beings to surmount environmental scarcity of resources and improve their lot. According to them, many societies adapt well to scarcity without undue hardship to their populations Since necessity is the mother of invention, the rise of supply of enough ingenuity in the form of new technologies and new and reformed social institutions—like efficient markets, clear and enforced property rights and effective government will alleviate the effects of scarcity. This is opposed by neo-Malthusians - often biologists and ecologists - who claim that finite natural resources place strict limits on the growth of human population and consumption both regionally and globally. If these limits are exceeded, poverty and social breakdown ensue. Though the debate is sterile, each camp contains a portion of the truth.

Optimists and distributionists often commit the mistake of assuming that an adequate supply of ingenuity is always assured. But supply will be constrained by a congeries of factors- unchecked brain drain out of many poor countries, limited access to capital, incompetent and corrupt judiciary, and weak states. Markets do not work well in poor countries -property rights are unclear, prices of water, forests and other common resources do not adjust accurately to reflect rising scarcity. More importantly, however, the supply of ingenuity can be restricted by stresses generated by the very resource crises the ingenuity is needed to solve. Scarcity can engender intense rivalries among interest groups and elites impeding the supply of ingenuity to solve the resource problems. It changes the behaviour of subgroups within societies by changing their profit and loss calculations in ways that can exacerbate political conflict. Thus, the result is that economists cannot be left with the task of predicting the social consequences of severe environmental scarcity. Politics - a power struggle among groups for relative advantage remains a key factor affecting whether or not societies adapt successfully to environmental scarcity.[4] In Bangladesh, for instance, environmental scarcity and shortage of land and the need for control of flood and irrigation waters have inflamed competition among social groups. This competition in turn obstructs technical and institutional reform. Government efforts to mobilise local resources for water control through construction of tanks, wells and irrigation canals were distorted to benefit large land owners. Funds are misappropriated, and projects were badly constructed and poorly maintained because land lords had little direct interest in their success. Landlords sought to control wells to permit monopoly pricing and gain access to adjacent cropland. At the same time, poorer groups threatened by the increased economic and political power of land owners with access to the well water often sabotaged new tube wells. Country's distributional inequalities remain grotesque without a change in inheritance and property rights, which would weaken the rural elites, poverty and economic inequality cannot be mitigated. According to Boyce, such institutional changes are clearly unlikely in "the absence of a broad political mobilisation of the landless and near landless majority in the countryside, and the barriers to this are formidable".[5]

Societies like Bangladesh face a widening "ingenuity gap" as their requirement for ingenuity to deal with environmental scarcity rises , while their supply of ingenuity stagnates or drops.

In the absence of supply of ingenuity in Bangladesh to deal with the environmental scarcity of resources like land and its social effects, which has prompted millions of Bangladeshis to India, the flow of refugees will continue, further aggravated by sea level rise.

South Asia accounts for a slowly rising proportion of global green house gas emissions. In terms of per capita emission, each South Asian contributed 0.18 tonnes of carbon compared to the 5.34 tonnes produced by US consumers and the global average by 1.12 tonnes.[6] According to a Report of the World Resources Institute 1990-91 Bangladesh's contribution to the net carbon dioxide emission to the atmosphere among the South Asian states is 1.61% compared to the 90.72% by India. In order to have meaningful participation in the reduction of green house gases in the atmosphere, these SAARC countries need to adopt strategies to deal with the problem of climate change. Most limitation strategies advocated for stabilising global climate change refer to a mix of strategies of fuel switching to less carbon emitting or no carbon emitting fuels and increased energy efficiency measures. For example, the study on Bangladesh calls for a reduction in the over dependence on biomass fuels and a shift to natural gas and other commercial fuels as biomass fuels are not only adding to the global warming problem but also have other adverse environmental implications for the country. The policy mix chosen to reduce green house gases emission will depend very much on these countries, access to financial and technological resources and their natural resource base. Thus the supply of ingenuity to meet the challenges would be very much stymied by Bangladesh's financial, technological and natural resource crunch.

Movement to alternative energy sources such as hydro, ocean thermal, geothermal, solar and other renewable options is another strategy open to these SAARC countries. The main problem with developing hydropower in these countries, however is their political and social acceptability, with most hydro-projects running into difficulties because of the non-acceptability of the social costs of displacing people and ecological cost of forest submergence. A need for cooperation among India, Bangladesh and Nepal in the Indus-Gangetic Plain for hydro power share of water and control of flood is essential.

But bilateral conflicts and misgivings between India-Nepal on the one hand and between India and Bangladesh over water issue remain potential underneath to affect environmental integration and cooperative strategies, despite treaties signed between them as solution to these problems.

Moreover, this energy source has long gestation periods relative to fossil based energy, and hence less attractive to support from a politician's view point. Long gestation period also means that significant reductions in emissions cannot be obtained before year.[7]

There is an urgent need to restructure the process of energy planning in SAARC economies as a part of limitation strategy. In Bangladesh special consideration is now needed to the integration of energy and land use issues in the planning of development schemes. There needs an urgent attention to developing an energy strategy that responds to short term fuel wood shortage, and to long term needs through appropriate commerical fuel substitutes and needs priority to the efficient management of biomass energy sources.

More stress need to be given on regional rather than national approach to energy planning. What it needs is to note that less Greenhouse gases offending fuels are not equally distributed among the countries within the region and to strongly argue for a case for regional cooperation on energy trade on environment. For example abundant hydropower in Nepal which if harnessed can find a ready market in India and Bangladesh. A similar case for regional trade also exists for natural gas from Bangladesh which would find a market in India.

Any regional cooperation efforts in this field require considerable strong political will and foresight which seems to be lacking among the countries, in spite of many economic measures to be undertaken being signed among these countries in SAARC summits. Outstanding political issues and misgivings among them remain a constraint on accepting limitation strategies for reduction of greenhouse gases emission.

The prevalence of scientific uncertainty about sea level rise and other impacts of climate change make it important to develop and improve monitoring of atmospheric and ocean phenomena to try and detect warning signals, improve predictive capacity and assess climate sensitivity.

India has established considerable capabilities and facilities in the field of atmospheric, geophysical and oceanic sciences as well as in the field of biosphere observations. It has the capability to probe the atmosphere right upto the outer regions of ionosphere and beyond.

Efforts are currently being undertaken to formulate a coordinated plan for minotoring of greenhouse gases in Bangladesh. The lead agencies who are engaged in these activities such as the Department of Environment, Meteorological Department, Bangladesh University of Engineering and Technology, SPAARSO all have miniature laboratory facilities, but are not well equipped to carry out the required studies in a methodical manner. All these agencies and other related ones need adequate financing for upgradation of their lab facilities including field appliances. There is also need for the establishment of the required number of monitoring systems in close association with International Monitoring Networks, for monitoring greenhouse gases, and also for sea level rise.[8]

Facilities for hydro-meteorological forecasting of flood, storms and cyclones do exist the Bangladesh but there are not adequate. With the availability of INSAT based cyclone Disaster Warning Services (DWS), India has an effective early warning system.

These above constraints are very much acting on Bangladesh to adopt strategies to deal with reduction of greenhouse gase emission and consequences of global warming such as sea level rise, cyclone, flood and storms.

Possible intervention and adaptation strategy in Bangladesh : Constraints

It does not mean that the Bangladesh Government will sit idly and will be a spectator to the rising water levels overwhelming the country. An obvious response to the increasing flood hazards is flood control i.e. the erection of embankments and installation of pump drainage. So many factors get involved in such situations that make things turn out for worse -recognising the problem, deciding upon a response, mustering financial support, creating appropriate institutions and executing the infrastructural requirements.

Another constraint is that flood protection works are costly to build, operate and maintain. The cost of pump drainage is also equally exorbitant. Embarkments along the major rivers have been susceptible to constant erosion by the occurrence of shifting of river channels as has happened in the case of the Brahmaputra Right Bank Embankment and the embankment of the Chandpur Irrigation Project. The cost of acquiring land to retire a section of embankment threatened by bank erosion has been very high.

Embankments by themselves cannot provide total flood protection to all the land they supposedly command since the most floodplain land is flooded by ponding of runoff from local rainfall and the raised ground water level when rivers are at peak levels. The vulnerability of embankments will be more severe on the occasion of sea level rise.

Where pump drainage is not provided either tidal sluices are needed or local run off must be allowed to escape through channels behind embankments. The latter solutions may not be available on the old Meghna Estuary Floodplain and Low Ganges River Floodplain where gradients are less than on the Jamuna Floodplain and where the lowest parts lie close to the present mean sea level. It is on these floodplains where the most serious effects of deeper flooding and impeded drainage are predicted to occur in the consequence of a rising sea level.[9]

Even pump drainage does not offer a viable solution to the areas most likely to be adversely affected by rising sea levels. The active channels of Bangladesh's major rivers provide hardly any site where pumping stations can be built. This is because of the shifting river channels and the rapid silting up of outlet channels as has happened in the case of Kobadak Project near Kushtia.

The practicality of pump drainage along the Old Meghna Estuarine Floodplain and the Low Ganges River Floodplain has been subject to controversy. Rainfall in these regions is high and short period intensities can be very high. So in order to protect short term paddy what needs is to evacuate water within 2 or 3 days by increased pump drainage. The effect of such increased drainage has been very much on downstream areas of Tidal Floodplain and the Old and Young Meghna Estuarine Floodplains. It is also held that the construction of double embankments along both sides of mighty rivers by concentrating their flow , increases their erosive capacity and increases flood in downstream areas. The implication of the above is that embankment and drainage do not suggest a possible simple solution to the problems created by increased flood levels in the consequence of a sea level rise.[10] The absence of alternative solutions to the above problems due to sea level rise in Bangladesh keeps the level of flow of refugees to Indian state high.

Conclusion

The influx of refugees into Indian north eastern states has been continuing. This has not shown yet any abetment despite India's efforts to fence the boundary and remain vigilant. While following the Western pattern of development, the developing countries like Bangladesh tend to be more concerned with growth in economics and GNP than with the environment, in its economic planning and policy, environment has not got that priority place to stem the tide of refugees flow into India. On the other hand , as seen above, Indian politicians find a convenient and easy vote bank in refugees naturalising them as citizens. The crisis continues to be worse than before despite both governments taking up the issue in their talks and negotiations. As seen above the crisis finds solution in some concrete steps to be taken up by the rich industrialised North and the world community.

As the study shows, in the event of predicted sea level rise many more million will be added to the existing flow of refugees into the Indian north eastern states raising there the spectre of violent ethnic conflict. According to a latest report of the UK Met Office's Hadley Centre for Climate Prediction and Research, even if greenhouse gas emissions are stabilised which would require an overnight cut of 60-70 per cent in global carbon dioxide emissions, there would be a 1°C rise in atmospheric temperature and a sea level rise of about one metre. The highest emission scenario could lead to 6° C rise in temperature over land by 2100, 2° C higher than the previous estimates.[11]

Another startling revelation by the report is that planting more trees to absorb carbon will not solve the problem. Thus the issues of forest management and afforestation as carbon sinks found in Kyoto Protocol will be more controversial and make the implementation of its provisions more uncertain and contentious.

Keeping in mind the prospect of global warming growing far greater and faster than previous estimates, the policy makers in India and Bangladesh should take concrete steps as regards the limitation and adaptation strategies to stem the tide of the consequences of climate change. At SAARC and global level both countries should work in close cooperation to impress upon the world key players the need to give priority to environmental scarcity in their policy agenda. The poor developing countries like Bangladesh are yet to see the necessary political will and sagacity in the rich industrialised nations to take immediate exemplary steps in this direction realising the growing security threats to the developing countries from the climate change mainly a deed of them. At the same time, the time has come for the South countries to redefine what so far they have held as development following the western pattern.

Added to the political and security complexities of both India and Bangladesh and other South countries is the fact that tracking climate change, predicting the adverse effects with severe degree of reliability and fixing the onus of responsibility require a degree of investment and scientific expertise that is mostly available to the industrialised nations. This leaves developing countries, which have made little effort to expand their scientific capacity dependent on Northern scientists and institutions to tell them the extent and consequences of global warming. According to Centre for Science and Environment, "science has been used several times in the past to implicate developing countries either by showing their future green house gas contributions as increasing and counter productive to industrialised country action, or by making no distinction between the survival emission of the South and the luxury emissions of the North".[12] Very little research has been conducted on the possible impacts of climate change on different countries and regions leaving them totally unprepared to handle the adverse effects of climate change. This kind of silence on this count will cause most damage in the developing countries. If this is true, there is a danger that the incentives for industrialised countries to take action against global warming will be comparatively low. Adding to this kind of scientific uncertainty and confusion, industrial groups with vested interests continue to generate science contesting even the fact that global warming is a threat to the world.[13] As seen above, this is going to be a great constraint on Bangladesh's ability to generate supply of ingenuity and adaptation strategies to deal with the situation.

References

1. Anil Agrawal, et al, ed., Green: Global Environmental Negotiations (New Delhi: Centre for Science and Environment, 1999).

2. Anil Agrawal , Sunita Narain and Anju Sharma, ed., Green: Global Environmental Negotiations 1(New Delhi: Centre for Science and Environment, 1999).

3. Down to Earth, vol. 9, no. 15, December 31, 2000, pp. 30-59.

4. Homer Dixon, Environment, Scarcity and Violence (Princeton/New Jersey: Princeton University Press, 1999), pp. 26-27.

5. James Boyce, Agrarian Impasse in Bengal: Institutional Constraints to Technological Change (Oxford: Oxford University Press), p. 255.

25. World Bank Development Report I992, (Oxford : Oxford University Press, 1992), p. 199.

26. SAARC, "Regional Study on Greenhouse Effect and its Impact", (Kathmandu, SAARC Secretariat, December, 1992), p. 112.

27. Ibid.

28. H.Branmer, The Complexities of detailed impact assessment for the Ganges-Brahamputra-Meghna delta of Bangladesh" in R.A. Warrick. E.M. Barrow and T.M.L. Wigley ed., Climate and Sea Level Change: Observations, Projections and Implications (Cambridge: Cambridge University Press, 1992), p. 259.

29. H. Brammmer, op. cit, p. 261.

30. Down the Earth, vol.9, No.15, 31 December, 2000.

31. Anil Agarwal and Others, Green, op. cit, pp. 20-21.

32. Ibid. p. 20.

8

Conclusion

In the preceding chapters a theory substantiating the causal links between severe environmental scarcity or degradation and violence is established and illustrated with evidence drawn from Bangladesh. As Bangladesh is a poor country, it cannot adapt to severe scarcity. With the environmental scarcity and degradation of renewable resources increasing day by day, the incidence of such violence is likely to augment.

Environmental scarcity or degradation is caused by the degradation and depletion of renewable resources, the increased demand for these resources, and/or their unequal distribution. As seen above, these three sources of scarcity often interact and reinforce one another resulting in resource capture and ecological marginalisation.

Resource capture occurs when degradation and depletion of a renewable resource interacts with population growth encouraging powerful groups within a society to shift resource distribution in their favour. This phenomenon of resource capture intensifies scarcity for poorer and weaker groups in society. Ecological marginalisation takes place when unequal resource access couples with population growth to cause long term migrations of people dependent on renewable resources for their livelihood. They migrate to ecologically vulnerable and fragile regions such as steep upland slopes, areas at risk of desertification, tropical rain forests, and low quality public lands within urban areas. Bangladesh is characterised by these two phenomena. Resource capture occurs due to land owners' distribution of resources in their favour helped by the inheritance laws and state. The plain people affected by flood, cyclone and other natural calamities have been settled in CHT degradating its forest resources and uprooting the tribals from their homeland. This is an illustration of ecological marginlisation.

The environmental scarcities and degradation reinforced by resource capture and ecological marginalisation, as seen in the preceding chapter will lead to multiple social effects in terms of decreased agricultural production, decline in economy, poverty, migration of people and growing incapability of state to meet these challenges. Environmental scarcities also strengthen group identities based on ethnic, class or religious affiliations, a process called social segmentation; strengthened identities intensify competition among groups, reducing social trust and useful inter group interaction. In Bangladesh the conflict between plain Bangladesh muslim people and the CHT tribals illustrates this point.

As seen above, these harmful social effects have led to ethnic conflict or clashes among groups within a state or when the migration has taken place to the neighbouring states, the conflict has been interstate. Migrating groups when come in contact with a different ethnic group of a neighbouring state, group identity or ethnic conflict has taken place, as found in Assam, Tripura and other North eastern Indian states.

Sceptics may claim that environmental scarcity or degradation has never been a powerful cause of violent conflict.[1] In a highly complex, multicausal system, it is an aggravating cause. Political, economic and social factors including failed institutions and policies are much more important contributors to violence. According to sceptics, these political, economic and social factors are in reality the ultimate causes of environmental scarcity. Environmental scarcity is therefore subordinate to these factors and never plays an independent causal role. It is true that environmental scarcity or degradation produces its effects within extremely complex ecological-political systems. It may be, environmental scarcity is not sufficient by itself to cause violence. When it does contribute to violence, it always interacts with other political, economic, and social factors. Environmental scarcity's causal role can never be separated from these contextual factors. As seen in case of Bangladesh, the contextual factors like land distribution, inheritance laws and state controlled by elite have combined with severe environmental scarcity or degradation to produce the disastrous social effects mentioned above. Because the relationship between environmental scarcity and contextual factors is interactive it is often impossible to determine the relative weight or power of environmental scarcity as a cause of violence in specific cases. But this does not mean that environmental scarcity or degradation is always an unimportant cause.

Since a large proportion of the world's population is almost completely dependent on cropland, water and forest supplies for existence, the social effects and stresses produced by the environmental degradation of these resources cannot be underestimated. Besides, environmental scarcity's causal role should not always be subordinated to that of political, economic and social factors. Environmental scarcity often reciprocally influences the political and economic character of social systems-as, for example, when it stimulates resource capture by powerful groups or elites impèding any kind of institutional and policy reform. Land scarcity in Bangladesh has resulted in resource capture by landowners obstructing any kind of institutional reform for equal distribution of land. Second, environmental scarcity is partly a function of the character of a society's physical environment. Bangladesh's physiological and hydrological nature and structure has been such that it is bound to cause environmental degradation and certain disasters like flood, cyclone, storm and shifting of river courses. And third, if severe environmental damage becomes irreversible it can become a permanent source of social stress ; even if the political and economic factors that originally produced the damage are fixed, it remains an independent "burden on the society.[2]

As seen in the preceding chapter, environmental scarcities resulting in various social effects in terms of decreased agricultural production, decline in economy, poverty and natural disasters due to global warming have led to large scale migration to neighbouring Indian states. Bangladesh Government has been continuing with the policy of settling plain muslim population affected by flood, cyclone and storms, and also marginalised by the land owners, in the CHT. This has resulted in uprooting the tribal CHT people from their homeland who have preferred to migrate to Indian states such as Tripura and other North eastern states. This large scale migration of CHT tribal people to Tripura has caused so many social and economic stresses which ultimately resulted in violence between the migrants and the local Indian people with the involvement of both India and Bangladesh. The intra state conflict originally between CHT people and Bangladesh plain people with the Bangladesh government perpetuating genocide on CHT people was transformed into an inter group conflict or inter-state conflict between India and Bangladesh with the migration of CHT people to Indian states.

The insurgency was not crushed the jumma did not 'disappear'. On the contrary the thousands languishing in Indian controlled refugee camps in Tripura further internationalised the issue, while also providing India with a powerful stick with which to beat Bangladesh in favour of its own geostrategic interests. Nor did the Bangladeshi government come anywhere near to completing its agenda inside the CHT. If the majority of the remaining, usually starving, jummas were now in joutha khumars, where they were now dependent on military-supplied food aid, 300000 Bengali settlers found themselves incarcerated in 78 similar 'cluster villages, this being the only way the BDF was able to protect them.[3]

On the one hand, reforms initiated from 1989 onwards suggested that the elimination strategy of previous years had been abandoned, Ershad's division of the CHT into three districts, Rangamati, Khagrachari and Bandarban, each of which was to be run by councils whose powers supposedly amounted to considerable autonomy, sounded promising. Moreover, the subsequent collapse of his regime and its replacement by the first civilian government in 15 years under Begun Khaleda Zia also seemed to offer genuine prospects for a legal jumma participation in an emerging democracy. This changing political climate may have helped persuade the Shanti Bahini to declare a unilateral ceasefire in August 1992, though a more likely cause was the intense international pressure upon the new government to engage in talks with the JSS. After the free elections in June 1996, in which Sheik Hasina Wajed (the daughter of Sheik Mujib) was returned as Prime minister, these talks resulted in a peace deal now in the early stages of implementation.[5]

Yet, if this implicit recognition that the jumma have a case and that there is a possibility that the future of the CHT might involve a partnership with them suggests a major shift in government thinking, the JSS leadership has until recently remained adamant that 'so-called reforms' were nothing more than a cosmetic sop for Western consumption. Thus, the District Councils have been imposed without consultation and, far from offering a special autonomous status, were actually designed to integrate the region more fully into Bangladesh in line with the 61 district councils created by the military regime for the rest of the country. Similarly, Ershad's 1989 annulment of the 1900 Regulations left the jumma with less, not more protection, not least because the real authority in the region remained the military.[6] With 85000 troops in the region, regular firefights despite the supposed ceasefire-with the Shantl Bahini, continued maltreatment and killing of jumma, including three massacres after the advent of 'civilian' rule, one of the,, at Logang village, Khagrachari, in April 1992, the largest single massacre of all, military, if not government intransigence against compromise has remained the rule.[7] In fact, the main superficial difference compared with previous years has been the BDF's operation of its anti-jumma campaign behind proxy bodies. One of these is the Parbatya Gana Parishad, the Hill Tracts Council, a militant organisation for defending Bengali settlers, largely recruited from membership of the fundamentalist Jamat-e-Islami party, Another is the so called Tiger Force, a militia composed of Marma and Mru Tribesmen, whose traditional rivalries with the Chakma and hence Chakma dominated JSS are clearly exploitable.[8] The cataclysmic nature of the 1998 flooding underscores the degree to which acute, long-term environmental and population pressures in the whole sub-Himalayan delta region are no respecter of internal or international borders. The technically illegal spillover from Bangladesh, in recent decades, of some millions of plainspeople into the hill country of neighbouring Indian states, notably Assam, and the dealing of many thousands of these settlers at the hands of hill tribesmen, suggests that the interrelationship between these pressures and national minority conflict is hardly limited to the CHT.[9] Nor has the Bangladeshi government been slow to recognise their importance. 'It seems crazy that aid donors would want to endanger the survival of millions of Bangladeshis just for the sake of the hill tribes - who are 0.5% of our population', said an official spokesperson in 1994.[10]

While endorsing the immensity of its population problem, this analysis has disputed that this factor alone has determined successive regime's response to the CHT either in the recent past or into the foreseeable future. Certainly it is convenient for a government dependent on Western aid to present the issue thus and offer itself as the best hope for a humanitarian solution. Yet in practice no Bangladeshi government has ever shown particular interest in assisting the poorest elements of society, 50% of whom are virtually landless. On the contrary, because of the state's continuing dependence on the zamindari, to whom the poor are heavily in debt, or in other ways beholden, its response to rural peasant mobilisation has always been unremittingly coercive.[11]

Nevertheless, social relations in the Bangali country side do feed into the government's CHT policy in a critical way. The majority of plain settlers there come not from the very poorest strata of society but slightly up the social rung. These marginal farmers have also suffered unrelenting and usually cross generational debt to zamindari from which the offer of resettlement in the CHT has provided an apparently attractive escape route. By Bangladeshi standards not only does this involve relatively generous government assistance, plus the promise of up to five acres of free land, but most importantly, it offers complete release from their debt burden. It could be argued that in this way the government is, after all, attempting to solve something of its population crisis while providing a better future for those fortunate enough to be relocated. Unfortunately, the flaws in this position are manifold. The settlers have not adapted well to hill conditions, which do not favour a replication of lowland agriculture, while their position has become increasingly untenable as jumma resistance has grown. In July 1988, for instance, 233 Bengalis were killed by the Shanti Bahini.[12] Worst of all, the settlers have burnt their bridges to their former homes in the plains by renouncing whatever sharecropping or tenancy rights they formerly possessed, this being the arrangement by which they received their necessary certificate of relocation to the CHT, stamped by their local Union parishad (district) chairman who, very often, was also their landowner.[13]

Thus, cynical as it may sound, resettlement in the CHT has neither been beneficial to the migrants themselves nor to Bangladesh's overall population problem, which is so vast that even the transfer - were it possible -of several million Bengalis to the CHT would make no appreciable difference. However, it has served two closely interrelated interests: that of the dominant class and the state. For the roughly 10% of the population who already own 50% of it, the land transferred by departing migrants has helped consolidate their holdings (as well as their economic control over remaining peasant farmers), as well as giving them a stake and vested interest in CHT exploitation. More importantly, for the state, settlers have provided the necessary malleable fodder with which to strategically swamp the natives and thereby secure control of their land and borders. The figures speak for themselves. In 1951 the ratio of new settlers to native inhabitants was 1:90. By 1981 it was 28:72. In 1994, many years after sponsored settlement had officially ended, the Bengali population in the CHT numbered 468825 or 48% of the region's total of 967 420, Indeed, in two out of the three districts, Khagrachari and Bandarban, the more fecund settlers now outnumber jummas.[14]

Bangladesh is a weak state. But it also desperately desires to be strong. All the more so because its situation is getting worse. Predictions of economic growth, founded in the early 1990s on an emergent, largely self-propelled garment industry, have moved something of a false dawn. Agricultural production has dropped, foreign aid been cut back. Darker clouds beckon still with the advent of global economic instability. If the Bangladeshi economy is really 'coming to a crisis', as one of is leading economists has predicted, the need for some miracle cure may be seen by its elites as all the more urgent and necessary.

This is why the issue of the CHT and with it the genocidal threat to its native peoples is unlikely to go away. For all of its history 'Bangladesh has looked to the territory as a panacea for its economic ills. Much more powerful countries have similarly looked to their supposedly virgin frontiers, or territories beyond in the route by which to transcend mundane limitations on the accomplishment, a great national project. The idea that the CHT could be key to Bangladesh's great leap forward,[16] thus continues to hold elite imagination. With the big western oil companies again queuing up to get back into the CHT.[17] and with renewed prospects for Western aid and investment, the onus on the state and its military arm finally to complete the Bangladeshisation of the territory as its short-cut to economic take off is great. Yet achieving this desired goal is now also complicated by a different set of Western desiderata. Although Bangladesh continues to be a major recipient of Western aid, Western bankers and sponsors have been scrutinising its democratic and more specifically human rights credentials more thoroughly, not least because of its past CHT record. New criteria include the return of the 54000 jumma refugees from Tripura and a peace agreement with the JSS. But there is clearly something schizophrenic here. In the one hand, TNCS want the CHT pacified and insurgent-free, on the other, Western institutions under pressure from NGOS; want Bangladesh to stop killing the people for whom the insurgents have been fighting.

Internally and externally the CHT issue has been fought out through military means by both countries. Exchange of fire and skirmishes between the Bangladesh border forces and border security forces of India is a frequent occurrence. India is accused of supplying arms and ammunition to the insurgent groups of CHT, though India denies this. Similarly Bangladesh is accused of helping insurgent Nagas and other rebels of north eastern states. Despite this militarization of the crisis, at present both India and Bangladesh are trying to resolve the crisis politically. A peaceful atmosphere in the CHT and restoration of their lost land and resources, and repatriation of Chakma refugees have always occupied the front lines in each and every bilateral talk between the two countries. The implementation of agreements could not be worked out successfully either because of the disagreement as to the total number of refugees or because of the absence of a peaceful atmosphere in CHT to start repatriation, Though there are reports of some Chakmas returning to CHT, the trust and faith of the Chakmas in the ability and sincerity of the Bangladesh government has not been stronger enough to woo them back to Bangladesh. So long as Bangladesh follows a policy of intentionally externalizing and exporting the ecological costs of its areas of the country and a comparatively better environment in the CHT will attract people to settle there. At the same time, the frequent natural hazards such as cyclones, storms, floods and tornadoes have impelled the government to intentionally externalize the ecological costs arising out of these natural calamities. As a result the government has been allowing migration and settlement in the CHT from the natural disaster affected and prone areas. In such a situation the conflict is likely to continue. Unless and until the government of Bangladesh addresses itself to the enviromental problems in plain areas and stems its tide, the repatriation of Chakmas to their homeland will be a remote possibility. As reports about the Pakistan's military training of north east rebels and insurgents in Bangladesh territory are to be relied on, the Indian Government can encourage CHT rebels morally and materially to the greater disadvantage of Bangladesh. With the changes in the political scenario of both India and Bangladesh, an amicable settlement to the repatriation of refugees appeared imminent. As per the agreement in 1995, 6,000 refugees then in camps went back in two phases in February and March", the situation seemed to change after the Ganga waters agreement between India and Bangladesh and Chakmas became hopeful for a political solution. On 9 March 1997, an agreement was signed between Abdul Hasnat Abdullah, Chief whip of the Bangladesh parliament and Upendra Lal Chakma, leader of the Chittagong Hill Tracts Jumma Refugees Welfare Association. Since then, refugees started moving. But "there are storm clouds on the horizon.[18] In the CHT, the Bangladesh National Party (BNP) and the Jamaat-e-Islami have opposed the Chakmas' return claiming that the accord with the refugees was against the settler's interest. Bandhs were observed on this issue. Will the Bangladesh government show the political will to remove 400,000 settlers from plains in CHT, restore to the tribal people their land and give them autonomy ? As seen before, the environmental scarcity of resources like land, water, forest etc. will remain central to the settlement of refugee crisis. The ever growing population and the need to settle flood and storm affected plain people and pressure on land will be the main stumbling blocks. In CHT a new kind of political turmoil may take place with Chakmas returning and demanding their right to land occupied by plain settlers and the plain settlers refusing it. Unless and until the main environmental problems are addressed, the issues are going to remain unresolved to the chagrin of both Bangladesh and India. Though the conflict, has already been an intra state violent conflict in India, it has never been a violent interstate conflict between India and Bangladesh. In India - the receiving state, the political parties remaining at the helm of affairs particularly Congress and C.P.I.(M) are using the migrants as potential voters. According to a startling disclosure, nearly 1.5 lakh Bangladeshis who still live in that country cross over to vote in West Bengal on polling day. Illegal migrants, concentrated in some pockets of the country have changed political dynamic of certain border areas. The centre estimates that in West Bengal, out of 294 Assembly constituencies, illegal migrants are in a position to sway the electoral results in 52 constituencies and influence the results in another 100. In Assam, the migrants now determine the result of as many as 33 Assembly constituencies. That means the efforts on the part of C.P I.(M) government in West Bengal and of the government that is interested in such vote banks in Assam to stop the flow and highlight crisis will be luckwarm.[19] Border fencing with central government spending Rs. 1500 Crore and West Bengal government Rs. 1,000/- crore per annum has not been effective. This has already become an irritant between the two countries' relation. Policing the 4O96 Kms. long border much of it riverine and murshy has become a near impossible task. In any case, the corruption is rife with each migrant paying a small sum on border to be let through. A border fence is coming up but, irony of ironies, the fence to keep out illegal Bangladesh migrants is being built with illegal labour from Bangladesh. What acts as the enabling circumstances for the continuance of migration is the Indian politicians finding in refugees a reliable vote bank.

India's decision to fence the Bangladesh border with barbed wire to stem the tide of Bangladesh refugees due to environmental degradation in Bangladesh, has already embittered their bilateral relation. The issue of Bangladeshi refugees has already been fought out militarily between parties. Though the issue has been downplayed by some Indian political parties in view of refugees having provided a vote bank, portents of regional separatism in the form of Bodo land, ULFA or son of the soil movements have already been seen in Assam fighting tooth and nail against the Bangladeshi refugees with both the Assam and central governments.

Decreasing land-man ratio, increasing population growth and environmental scarcity and degradation of land sources in Bangladesh will continue to encourage environmental flight of refugees into Indian territory with all their concomitant repercussions on India's economy and security. Given Assam's declining resource base and other adverse environmental condition in other parts, as noted earlier, the refugees will no longer be considered as acceptable. In case of the predicted sea level rise, flight of some more millions of Bangladeshis into Indian territory will aggravate the situation making the prospect of group identity conflict in Assam and other North-Eastern states of India more apparent. Massacre, communal riots, ethnic conflict, involvement of immigrants in a spate of robberies and heinous crimes and rise of centrifugal forces against the flow of refugees will be more frequent with a greater possibility of India and Bangladesh being involved. This would create far reaching implications on India's security, federal structure and unity. India's overenthusiastic concern for maintaining neighbourly relations with Bangladesh may not be stretched too far to ignore its own national interests and put a lid over new security implications arising out of the flow of migrants from Bangladesh induced by environmental scarcity of resources such as land and water and its degradation in the overall context of global warming and sea level rise.

Conflict Management And Conflict Resolution: Approaches

If the two countries go to war due to environmental degradation, the very basis of environmental security will collapse. The removal of the main causes and problems of environmental degradation will enliven the prospects of the management of conflict, by reducing its various social effects like economic decline, decline in agricultural productivity and population displacement. This will further arrest the forces encouraging ethnic and social divides. With the eradication of much of the social effects, the disruption in political and social institutions can be halted. There must be a very clear cut environmental policy and along with determined efforts to implement it, so that a check can be put on the degeneration or environmental scarcity of renewable resources. The first, and immediate step required of them is to take steps to curb spawning population growth, which will enable them to stop the accelerated pace of 'resource capture' and 'resource marginalization'.

It requires not only an unilateral action on the part of Bangladesh but also a bilateral and regional action as the effects of environmental degradation in most of the cases are transboundary. The member countries of South Asia should cooperate among them selves through exchange of experiences of planners, scientists and social scientists to develop a holistic approach for the management to environmental crises and resolution of their effects.

So far as problems of global warming, ozone layer depletion, greenhouse effect and sea level rise are concerned, global action is necessary to solve them.

Peaceful conflict management and conflict resolution depend on the ability of South Asian states to eliminate the environmental problems along with their social effects which have led or may lead to conflicts. What is needed urgently in South Asia is to broadly define a comprehensive security.

Eradication of Enviromental Degradation

In order to solve the problems of environmental degradation within a country, the fundamental task is to arrest the population growth. Population control will decrease the pressures on land, water, forest, atmosphere and ocean for a sustainable development strategy. Along with this, plans, programmes and policies should be adopted to arrest the renewable resources being degraded.

Unilateral Actions

A land use policy reform requires a primary attention based on multi-disciplinary inter-sectoral approaches in order to ensure optimum use of land, protection of land from degradation, reclamation of utilized or degraded land for suitable use and improvement of land for future generation. Environmentally sound agricultural and livestock policies need to be devised for suitable and sustainable use of the land resources. Priority should be given to those coastal lands which are most vulnerable to erosion. Measures are to be taken to arrest land degradation by controlling shifting cultivation or cultivation on the slopes. Plagued by the problems of accelerated land degradation the countries of the region should undertake major programmes to protect and maintain the productivity of their land.

Protection of existing forest and mass scale afforestation programmes should be undertaken to prevent environmental degradation. People's dependence on fuel wood should be reduced "by providing them alternative energy like solar and hydropower. Environmental education is necessary to create awareness among people to preserve the forests and halt deforestation. The crucial role that forest plays in the ecological life of the human and the universe is to be inculcated into the minds of the people. Commercialization of forest should be stopped along with the high consumeristic culture prevalent among the rich and elite mass in the South Asian region. The people should be taught that the symbiotic and integral relation that exists between human beings and forests is crucial to their very existence and survival.

The problems like water logging, decline in water quality, intrusion of saline water from the sea into coastal freshwater aquifers, decline of groundwater tables and agro-chemical, industrial and human pollution of water, should be addressed with determined efforts and strong policies by the governments of the region. The threat that the water resources in the region face is to be removed.

As regards the atmospheric pollution and greenhouse effect, the contribution of South Asian region in comparison to that of the rich industrialized North is minimal. That does not mean, the countries in South Asia do not contribute to atmospheric pollution. Since the coastal areas of Bangladesh, India and Maldives would be seriously affected by sea level rise, appropriate measures should be taken to minimize at least the human and resource loss by constructing new embankments or modifying existing ones along the coast and liver banks. An adaption strategy should also include measures to adapt to the change in spatial and temporal distribution of rainfall and temperature as will occur due to global warming and greenhouse effect. This means it should aim at diversification of crop and employment opportunities, change in cropping pattern and farming practices.

Natural disasters like flood, drought, cyclone, landslides, mass wasting, earthquakes and tornadoes have become associated with the daily life of the people in the region. Human activities and developmental policies which sometimes contribute to the frequency and intensity of these disasters need to be reviewed, losses to human life and property can be minimized by developing early warning, forecasting and relief strategies.

Implementation of Unilateral Actions

Prerequisites for implementing unilateral actions to prevent environmental degradation would require a well planned environmental policy by all nations of the region. Various institutional arrangements and their strengthening are essential for resource management and conservation. Building up efforts and extended support are necessary for research studies in resource management. Cooperation between the government and non-governmental organizations (NGOs) should be built up in order to coordinate joint efforts at mitigating the problem. Exchange of knowledge and experience will be beneficial in finding solutions to environmental problems.

In order to have a strong and effective environmental policy, legal provisions should be made strictly mandatory and need to be updated and revised to face the current problems and present requirements.

Public awareness and participation in the management of resources and prevention of environmental degradation is a must which can be created through environmental education.

Major Constraints

The countries have shown interest in undertaking major programmes to protect and maintain their resources on a sustainable basis. However, their attempts have not always succeeded. So far as land management is concerned, several countries suffer from shortage of research facilities, trained personnel, equipment for surveys and laboratory analysis, lack of infrastructure for micro level planning, data and integrated approaches to land use. An overall perspective of land utilization, protection and reclamation could not be obtained due to partly the sectoral responsibility of government agencies.

In case of water management and its optimal use almost all countries in the region are stymied by a shortage of financial wherewithals to develop their water resources to cater to their domestic and agricultural needs, generate hydro electricity, and to treat polluted water. As regards the problems of deforestation, agencies are weak and understaffed. There is a shortage of equipment and financial resources for fresh research survey and monitoring. There is also lack of data on forest resources to develop improved programmes in the future. There are inadequate policies and laws for involvement of the people and NGOs on forest management.

Regarding measures to control air pollution member countries of South Asia suffer from a lack of trained personnel, monitoring equipments and necessary funds to invest in pollution control measures.

Though there have been attempts at developing effective measures for disaster management in terms of forecasting, warning, rescue and relief by the South Asian countries, these proved to be inadequate due to shortage of finance, equipment and trained personnel.

Regional Actions

As seen earlier, environmental degradation in one country affects the neighbouring countries. Besides, human activities in one state may result in the environmental degradation of other states. So regional efforts and coordination are necessary to prevent environmental degradation. The following steps suggested by SAARC, need serious attention.[20] These are necessary for not only preventing environmental degradation in the region but also for managing existing natural resources on a sustainable basis.

- SAARC member countries should cooperate among themselves through exchange of experiences of planners, scientists and social scientists on a holistic approach to land and water management to develop appropriate land-livestock-"biomass-water systems for the ecological vulnerable regimes like arid, unirrigated, semi-arid, irrigated semi-arid, mountain, flood prone deltaic and coastal regions.
- Cooperation should be prompted among riparian member states for improving water management and optimal use of water resources for various purposes.
- For strengthening forest management and protection in the region a SAARC Forestry and Watershed Programme should be formulated which covers sharing experiences in afforestation and water management, exchange of scientific, technical and management, related information, training for improving human skills and capabilities, sharing of knowledge and forestry research and findings, training in forest survey and monitoring and cooperative arrangements for tackling problems of fire and shifting cultivation.
- Technical cooperation among member states should be established for information and technological transfer programmes in the field of alternate and renewable energy systems, energy conservation and use of waste products.
- A regional technical cooperation programme for pollution control should be developed.
- People's participation in resource management should be encouraged and interaction between environmental NGOs be facilitated. A South Asia NGO forum on environment should be formed.
- A SAARC fund for regional cooperation in the feld of environment should be set up.
- Institutional arrangements in the SAARC region should be coordinated, planned and facilitated for disaster management, forecasting, warning, relief and rescue.

Reduction of Carbon Dioxide : North's Responsibility

As noted, the ethnocentrism of mimetic western paradigms of development based on fossil fuel technology and industrialization and the exorbitant consumption of the rich industrialized North have been perceived in terms of greenhouse effect, global warming and ozone layer depletion, as a result of which there will be sea level rise affecting millions of lives in the South more particularly the South Asian region. Much of the global carbon dioxide emissions stems from the developed industrialized world which constitutes only 27 of the world's all sovereign nations accounting for 43%of the global land area and 20% of global population. The rest of the developing world constituting 80% of global population and 57% of the global land area emits comparatively little of the carbon dioxide. The environmental consequences of global air pollution could be second only to those of a global nuclear war.[21]

Global efforts in the direction of reducing carbon dioxide needs achieving sustained discard which requires over all reduction of the order of 50% from the present world wide emissions levels, that is to the level of the year 1965.[22]

Achieving equitable discard which aims at attainment of the goal of global equity in controlling carbon dioxide emissions, requires the entitlement to each nation of the world of a permissible maximum release based on national area, not on national population, or national wealth or past national arrogation as suggested by some. The land area of the world excluding Antarctica is 133 million sq km. One carbon dioxide release chit for each of these sq km is to be found out, each one permitting the discharge of one 133 million of the total permissible amount. Each nation will then be awarded the number of such one sq km chits corresponding to the size of its national territory. Since many developing nations have not made use of their chits can lease out those on financial terms to those developed nations who want to make use of more than their allotment. This amount derived from lease can be geared to their developmental needs.[23] To reduce carbon dioxide emissions, a fossil fuel use tax should be imposed on the developed world, the revenues collected from this can be used for atmospheric protection. If atmosphere is the common heritage of mankind, then the industrialized North has used it inequitably demanding an equity in burden sharing. Before equity in burden sharing is accepted, equity in sharing the resources must be recognized. To achieve that ideal of equity in sharing the resources requires the distribution of the limited emissions considered permissible by the scientific community taking historical emissions into account, on per capita basis with each human being getting an equal entitlement. To dispel the apprehension that this system -would encourage population growth the per capita entitlements could be frozen on the basis of a population distribution of a chosen year. Thereafter, if population increases, its per capita entitlements would decrease proportionately, if it decreases, entitlements would grow accordingly.[24] The South should resist the industrialized North's finding in the former's part of the ocean a favourite spot for disposal for the latter's toxic chemicals and radioactive wastes. Alternative developmental strategies should be devised which will be very friendly to the atmosphere. Alternative greenhouse gases and CFCs should also be devised which will have little impact on the atmosphere.

The Kyoto protocol on climate change has already run into rough weather with US stressing upon meaningful participation of the South countries without taking into account its own historical emissions. The common and differential responsibility was overlooked. The developed countries through the Clean Development Mechanism suggested by the treaty are committed to reduce carbon dioxide in South countries without having a commitment to reduce the same at their domestic front. So the treaty's fate has already been caught in the mire of US floating the idea of meaningful participation by the South countries as a condition to ratify the treaty and already rejecting the treaty altogether.

Inordinate consumerism of the industrialized North has been responsible for pauperization of the South as well as despoliation of the planet earth. Five per cent of the people in the world consume one third of the planet's resources[25] Intrinsic human qualities and ethical values in terms of modesty, austerity, continence and control of the self should be cultivated and inculcated into the life styles of people of the rich North. "In a fragile biosphere, the ultimate fate of humanity may depend on whether we can cultivate deeper sources of fulfilment founded on a widespread ethic of limiting consumption and finding non-material enrichment.[26] As Arnold Toynbee observed :

> religious founders disagreed with each other in the picture of - what is the nature of the universe, the nature of the spiritual life, the nature of the ultimate reality. Buc they. all agreed in their ethical precepts ... They all said with one voice that if we made material wealth our paramount aim, this would lead to disaster. [27]

While decrying the inordinate consumption and exorbitant life styles of the industrialized North, the South Asian countries should not be impervious to the same consumption and extravagant life styles of their rich elite class which includes bureaucrats, businessmen, technocrats industrialists and ruling class. Inculcation of ethical values of modesty and self control need to be applied not only to rich North but also to the rich classes of the South. Progress of talks on climate change has already been mired in the U.S. economic interest.

Eradication of Social Effects of Environmental Degradation

To remove social effects of environmental degradation, viz. economic decline, population flight and domestic problems and differences is one of the primary responsibilities of a state.

To attain a self reliant economy what is necessary is the adoption of a sustainable development strategy aiming at the fulfilment of not only the present but also the future needs. So while defining development, it is to be viewed, first, in terms of the fulfilment of the immediate and basic needs of the people who are in most need and secondly in terms of the needs of the nature or environment. The anthropocentric view of development is to be replaced by a cosmo-centric view of development which recognizes the symbiotic relationship that exists between human and nature. A restructuring of the patterns of international economic activity is needed to reduce the environmental tension to which humanity is going to be subject in coming decades.

To tackle economic decline states need the attainment of the goal of human resource development through many methods. These are population control, employment generation, health and hygiene facilities, planned urban and rural human settlements, supply of pure drinking water, a mass literacy programme, improvement of transport and communication, and development of weaker sections such as women and children.

To increase agricultural production is an important step in the direction of arresting economic decline which covers crop, agriculture, fisheries, forestry, poultry, livestock. Soil conservation, proper use of manure and rational use of pesticides and irrigation facilities will help increase the agricultural productivity. Selection of crops, suitable to soil and climate, rotation and diversification, selection of improved seeds, maintenance of irrigation equipments and rational utilization of water are necessary to increase food production.

Alternative energy sources should be explored to decrease the people's dependence on wood for fuel. This would also help improve the soil quality and fertility and, biomass extraction from land is reduced.

To retard the process of population displacement due to natural hazards or over exploitation of natural resources, measures should be taken to provide alternate sources of living. This should check rural migration to urban centres and other neighbouring countries.

The ethnic divide arising out of population displacement due to natural hazards or declining resource base or developmental activities can be solved within a country if the environmental refugees are distributed throughout the country unlike the settlement of disaster affected plain people in CHT. If ethnic divide is transboundary, then alternate resources of living and economic opportunities should be provided to bring back these refugees living in a foreign country. There should be cooperation and determined political will between the two countries while negotiating repatriation of refugees.

If resources are redistributed on the basis of equity and needs of the people, land reforms are made, concentration of wealth in one hand is decried by legislation, the existing social divide in South Asia can be removed. A basic human needs approach (BHNA) is necessary to bridge the gap between rich and poor. What Galtung applies in the world context can also be applied to South Asia:

> It is an effort to cut through rhetoric, focusing on what is essential and basic, and to provide individuals and societies with a measuring rod that lowers the focus of social attention downwards unto this last saying this : tell me how much material and spiritual misery there is at the bottom of society you have ... Human suffering, deprivation shall count more and serve to set our priorities straight.[28]

If this occupies a peremptory place in this developmental strategy of the South Asian countries, not only the social divide will be removed but also population displacement intra and inter state can be halted.

As regards the political divide, the possibilities of dictatorial regimes coming to power can be eliminated if provisions for various structural and institutional arrangements in the context of a strong democratic institutional build up are made. These can help strengthen democratic culture and system if power is decentralized and empowerment of people and their participation in the democratic process, administration and development are facilitated.

Regional Initiative Redefining Development

One of the bedrocks of western metaphysics of economic thinking and development has been the policy of exclusion and expulsion of the non-European and non-American participants to the periphery of the world economic structure. This always keeps them at the receiving end and reduces them as charity boys of the North or confines them in a tunnel without exit".[29]

This integrated world economic structure dominated by the industrialized North has led to the pauperization of the South. Problems of environmental degradation, various social effects such as poverty, economic decline and their consequences in the form of conflict actual and potential are some of the major challenges that face the South Asian countries. The aim is to find out alternative development strategy which will change their peripheral status in the world economic structure and make them self-reliant. Instead of defining development in terms of vertical relation with the rich industrialized North which are solely dependent on them, a horizontal relation among the South Asian countries should be allowed to develop and given a premium over and above all other considerations. All efforts should be made to make SAARC more like EEC or ASEAN. Removal of trade barriers, taxes on export and import items are some of the imperatives to ensure economic cooperation among the SAARC countries. Leaving aside their narrow and immediate political interest, long term considerations should be adhered to. These should include providing alternative development strategies which will change their peripheral economic status in the world economic structure, strategies which will make tham self-reliant and provide them an economy with enough strength to meet the immediate basic human needs of the people, those who are in most need without despoliating their nature and environment.

The South countries have imitated the western model of development as their own development. To persist in this kind of belief that another is the cause of development of another has helped only the implantation of western economic thinking on their soil blocking all the alternative roads to development. With a religious surrender to the western paradigms of development, the South countries have led the critics to wonder whether there is 'poverty of philosophy' in the South. To dispel this what is needed of the South is to redefine development in their own historical, social and cultural context. A homo-nature balanced and cosmocentric development should be the basis of re-examining the very logic of having blindly accepted the western model with all its negative consequences. Cooperation among the SAARC countries in this regard should be facilitated to devise the other roads to development in their respective contexts keeping in view the basic human needs of those who are in most need and also equally, the needs of the nature.

To work out such a policy necessitates formation of a common knowledge pool from among the member countries of SAARC which will primarily be concerned with evolving alternative developmental strategies. So long as those who are excluded whether they are poor, women, children, villagers , rural folk, urban poor, indigenous people or tribes from the very process of development, are not empowered and brought to its centre stage, development defined in other terms cannot be worth the name. [30]

Recognition of South's Access to Resources on the Bedrock of Equity

The social effects of environmental degradation in South Asia can be eradicated though international mechanisms like NAM, UN, NIEO and other forums which can put pressure on the rich industrialized North to do something positive for the development of the South. If resources of the earth are the common heritage of mankind, then South should have its due share. So equity in the management of resources whether it is air, sea or biodiversity, should be the bedrock of any negotiation between North and South. The Rio Earth summit went a long way in creating GEF for protection of the environment. A South-South cooperation and solidarity would be one of the basic conditions for exacting concessions from the the North in matters of trade, economics, business and environment.

Comprehensive Security

Security, as discussed, can no longer be confined only to military threats. In South Asia, there persists intra or inter state political conflicts with military involvement India and Pakistan's military involvement over Kashmir and Punjab, Sri Lanka and LTTE armed conflict, CHT and Bangladesh and so on, are some examples of armed conflicts for reasons political, economic and environmental. Even if these conflicts are resolved, the threats as seen above, emanate from the environmental degradation and its disastrous social effects, to the security of peoples. As seen above, some regional political insecurity can be attributed, first, to environmental scarcity of resources and its trans-boundary effects in terms of economic decline, diminishing agricultural productivity and population displacement within a state or beyond its border. This happens when there is disproportionate or overall exploitation and depletion of natural resources being shared by two or more states. Secondly, to the extent of pernicious wastes by transboundary air or water, carbon dioxide emissions by the rich industrialized countries in the Northern hemisphere in terms of greenhouse effects, global warming and ozone layer depletion has been , as discussed earlier, threats to the millions of people in Bangladesh, India and Maldives due to sea level rise. So what is urgently needed in South Asia is a comprehensive regional environmental security system which must satisfy the following prerequisites.[31]

- First, prevention of armed conflict and fulfilment of basic human needs of those people who are most in need.
- Second, the quality of human environment must be protected and any harvesting of renewable natural resources must be carried out on a sustainable basis.

The fulfillment of these above prerequisites for comprehensive regional environmental security in South Asia needs the active cooperation and joint action among its members. If South Asia remains an ecogeograhical region covering seas with their associated drainage basins such as watersheds, catchments areas, major rivers with their associated drainage basins, major mountain ranges, etc. there would have been no problem. The problems about sharing of environmental scarcity of resources, its degradation along with various social effects arise only when various socially determined regions like ethnic, political, linguistic and so on are superimposed upon the ecogeographical region or when there is incongruity between the natural ecogeographical region and the superimposed political boundary which are less stable and more volatile.[32] It is this incongruity and frequent changing of political boundaries on ethnic or linguistic or religion lines, that necessitates active cooperation among the member states to face the challenges posed by the environmental degradation for effective implementation of comprehensive regional environmental security.

References

1. Ronnie Lipschutz, "Environmental Conflict and Environmental Determinism: The Relative Importance of Social and Natural Factors", in Conflict and the Environment, ed, Nils Petter Gleditsch (Dordrecht, The Neatherlands : Kluwer, 1997), pp. 35.50; See also Wenche Hauge and Tanja Ellingsen, "Beyond Environmental Scarcity: The Causal Pathways to Conflict", Journal of Peace Research 35, no.3 (1998), pp. 299-317.

2. Thomas F.Homer Dixon, Environment, Scarcity, and Violence, (Princeton, New Jersey: Princeton University Press, 1999), pp. 180-181.

3. CHT Commission, Life is not Ours, pp. 24, 74-75.

4. M. Abdul Hafiz and Mahid Islam, Environmental Degradation and Intra-Interstate Conflict in Bangladesh, ENCOP Centre for Security Studies and Conflict Research, Zurich/Berne, Occasional Paper No. 6, May 1993.

5. Jumma Peoples Alliance, Special Issue 2, unpublished, document, 25 October 1997.

6. Ibid, and, CHT Commission, Life is not Ours, 1992 update, p. 7.

7. Survival Action Bulletin, May 1992, noted that 1200 people were burnt alive in their homes in the Logang massacre. See also Survival Action Bulletin, January 1994 for reports on the massacres at Mallya (February 1992), and Naniarchar (November 1993).

8. See CHT Commission, Life is not Ours, p 36, and 1994 update, p. 20. See Survival International, "Chittagong Hill Tracts revisited, unpublished field trip report, 18-27 October 1992, on the Tiger Force, Government efforts to utilise the smaler tribes against the Chakma, who constitute 60% of the jumma, deserve further attention. Within the Chakma itself there are also exploitable antipathies.Mey 'Genocide', p. 15, for instance, notes that the Taungchengya clans have their own separate guerrilla force which has at times fought the Shanti Bahini. The latter also has poor relations with the tribally based Mizo National Front over the Indian border in Mizoram. Wolfgang Mey, "Genocide in Bangladesh. The CHT case" Paper presented at the 7th European Conference on Modern South Asia Studies, 7-11 July, 1981.

9. Suzanne Goldenberg, 'Immigrants bear brunt of Assam's culture of mutiny', Guardian. 17 April 1996. More generally, See Nietscbmann, Indonesia, Bangladesh, pp. 96-97: Thomas Eraser Homer Dixon, 'On the threshold: environmental changes as causes of acute conflict', International Security, Fall 1991, pp.76-116 and Richard L Rubenstein, The Age of Triage, Fear and Hope in, an Overcrowded World, Boston, MA: Beacon Press, 1983.

10. Quoted in Tim McGirk, 'Fear-filled return home for exiles', Independent, 25 February 1994.

11. Anti-Slavery Society, Chittagong Hill Tracts, p.27.

12. CHT Commission, Life is not Ours, p. 24.

13. Antl-Slavery Society, Chittagong Hill. Tracts, pp. 27-28: Huq, 'Changing nature, pp. 83-84.

14. M. Mufazzalul Huq, "Changing nature of dominat forces and interventions in the CHT", Journal of Social Studies (Dhaka), 56, April 1992, p. 82. An additional complicating variable in this demographic picture is the 100000 Rohingyas, the Burmese Moslem refugees expelled from Buddhist Burma who have fled into an area adjacent to the CHT, CHT Commission, Life not Ours, 1994 update, pp. 8, 29, has questioned whether the Bangladeshi government might use these refugees against the jumma.

15. Cited in Suzanne Goldenberg, 'Rivalry and corruption cripple the self-help economy', Guardian, 17 February 199 6.

16. See statement of Colonel (retd) Oli Ahmed, the Communications Minister and President of the government created special committee on the CHT with responsibility for talks with the JSS. Bangladesh Times, 31 December 1992.

17. Two foreign firms to explore oil in CHT, Dhaka Observer, 31 July 1995; JSS, 'Situation in CHT, unpublished report, 28 October 1995. Survival International archive, London. The TNCS in question are Shell, Amoco and BHP.

18. Tapas Ray "A step closer to peace: repatriation of Chakma Refugees", Frontline Vol. 14, no. 6, 5-18 1997, pp. 49-51.

19. Times of India, 15 Septamber, 1999.

20. Regional Study on the Causes and Consequences of National Disasters and the Protection and Preservation of the Environment (Kathmandu : SAARC Secretariat, 1992), pp. 205-12.

21. H.L. Ferguson, ed., Changing Atmosphere: Implications for Global Security (Conference Statement, Toronto, 27-30 June 1988), New York : U.N General Assembly Document no.A/c.2/43/2, 3 October 1988, p. 12.

22. M. Grubb, Greenhouse Effect: Negotiating Targets (London: Royal Institute of International Affairs, 1989), pp. 36-40.

23. See Arthur H. Westing, "The Atmosphere as a Common Heritage of Human Kind: Its Role in Environmental Security", Scientific World(London), 34(4), 1990, pp. 5-6.

24. Anil Agarwal and Sunita Narain, Towards a Green World (New Delhi: Centre for Science and Enovironment, 1992), pp. 52-53.

25. "American Excess", Adbusters, Vancouver, Summer 1990.

26. Alan Durning, .."Asking How Much is Enough" in Lester R.Brown et. al. ed, State of the World 1991, World Watch Institute (India), New Delhi, 1991, p. 165.

27. Arnold Toynbee, quoted in Paul Wachtel, The Poverty of Affluence (Philadelphia: New Society Publishers, 1989).

28. Johan Galtung, "International Development", in Roger A Coate and Jerely A. Rosati, ed., The Power of Human Needs in World Society (Boulder and London: Lynne Rienner Publishers, 1988), p. 151.

29. Rudolf Bahro. From Red to Green: Interviews with New Left Review (London: Verso, 1984), p. 211.

30. See John Friedmann, Empowerment: The Politics of Alternative Development (Cambridge: Blackwell Publishers, 1992).

31. Arthur H. Westing, "Environmental Approaches to Regional Security", in his ed., Comprehensive Security for the Baltic: An Environmental Approach, International Peach Research Institute (Oslo) (London: Sage, 1989), pp. 7-12.

32. See L.H, Brown, "Regional Collaboration in Resolving Third World Conflicts", Survival (London), Vol. 28, 1986. pp. 208-20: L.J. Cantori and S.L.Spiegel eds., International Politics of Regions: A Comparative Approach (Engelwood Cliffs, New Jersey: Prentice Hall, 1970).

Bibliography

Primary Sources

Reports/Documents on Bangladesh

A New Millennium : A New Challenge, Proshika Activity Report, July 1999-June 2000, Dhaka, 2000.

An Assessment of Environmental Impacts of Flood 1998 on Dhaka City, IUCN, Department of Environment, Government of the People's Republic of Bangladesh, Dhaka, 2000.

Annual Report of Caritas Bangladesh, 2000-2001, CARITAS Bangladesh Dhaka, 2001.

Annual Report, July 1994-June 19956, Bangladesh Space Research and Remote Sensing Organization {SPARRSO}, Dhaka, 1996.

Asian Disaster Preparedness Center Calamity Report, Asian Disaster Preparedness Center, Bangkok, 1992.

Bangladesh: Green House Effect and Climate Change, Briefing Documents, Bangladesh Unnayan Parishad {BUP} Center For Environment and Resource Studies {CEARS} University of Waikate, New Zealand, UEA, Climatic Research Unit, University of East Anglica, Norwich U.K, Dhaka, 1993.

Bangladesh 2020. A Long Run Perspective Study, Bangladesh Institute of Development Studies, World Bank and BCAS, University Press Limited, Dhaka, Bangladesh 1998.

Bangladesh Action Plan for Flood Control: Achievements and Outlook, Flood Plan Coordination Organization, government of the People's Republic of Bangladesh, Dhaka, 1992.

Bangladesh Bureau of Statistics, Statistical Pocketbook of Bangladesh, Government of Bangladesh, Dhaka, Annul, 1998.

Bangladesh Meteorological Department, 1991 and 1997 Cyclone Reports, Government of the People's Republic of Bangladesh, Dhaka, 1991 and 1997.

Bangladesh: Action Plan for Flood Control, Asia Region Country Department, World Bank Dhaka, 1989.

Bangladesh: A Proposed Rural Development Strategy, A World Bank Study, University Press Limited, 1989.

Bangladesh: From Counting the Poor to Making the Poor Count, A World Bank Country Study, the World Bank, Washington D.C., 1999/2000.

Bangladesh: Green House Effect and Climate Change, Bangladesh Unnayan Parishad Center for Environmental and Resource Studies, Climate Research Unit, University of East Anglica, Dhaka 1993.

Caritas Report on May 1997 Cyclone, CARITAS Bangladesh, Dhaka 1997.

Climate Change in Asia, Bangladesh Country Report, Asian Development Bank Manila, 1994.

Cyclone Damage in Bangladesh, Report on Field Study and Investigations on the Damage Caused by the Cyclone of 1991,UNCRD and UNATI, Nagoya, Japan 1991.

Cyclone, Flood Drought, Environmental Degradation and Mining, Proceedings of International Conference on Disaster and Mitigation, Anna University Madras, 1996.

Cyclone' 91, Bulletin No. 7. CARITAS Bangladesh, Dhaka, 1991.

Deluge in the Delta: Flood 1998, ADAB Activity Report Association of Development Agencies of Bangladesh, Dhaka, 1998.

Flood 1988, Bulletin No. 2, CARITAS Bangladesh, Dhaka, 1988.

Flood 1988, Bulletin No. 3, CARITAS Bangladesh, Dhaka, 1989.

Guidelines for Environmental Impact Assessment, ISPAN, Arlington, USA, 1992.]

Impact Of Tornado on the Process of Migration in Saturia, Bangladesh Institute of Development Studies, Dhaka, 1991.

International Sea Level Rise, National Assessment of Effects Possible Responses for Bangladesh, Unpublished Report to the University of Maryland, USA. 1990.

May 1997, Cyclone, ADAB Activity Report, Dhaka, 1997.

May 1997, Cyclone, Special bulletin No. 3, CRAITAS Report, CARITAS, Bangladesh, Dhaka 1997.

May 19, 1997 Cyclone, Draft Copy Report, ADAB, Dhaka, 1997.

Population Census 2001, Preliminary Report, Bangladesh, Bureau of Statistics, Ministry of Planning, Government of the People's Republic of Bangladesh, Dhaka, 2001.

Regional Study on the Causes and Consequences of natural disasters and the protection and Preservation of the Environment, SAARC Secretariat Report, kathmandu, 1992.

Regional Study On Greenhouse Effect and Its Impact on the Region, SAARC Secretariat Report, Kathmandu, 10992.

Report from the Yokohama World Conference on Natural Disaster Reduction, IDNDR {1990-2000}, and the World Bank, Yokohama, May 23-27, 1994.

Report on Floods of 1998, Disaster Management Bureau, and Dhaka 1999.

Reverine Chars in Bangladesh: Environmental Dynamics and Management Issues, EGIS, University Press Limited, Dhaka, 2000.

The Devastating Flood 1998, Activity Report of ADAB on Flood 1998. ADAB, Dhaka, 1998.

The future for the Small States: Overcoming Vulnerability, Commonwealth Secretariat London, 1997.

Vulnerability: Small States in the Global Society, Report of a Commonwealth Consultative Group Commonwealth Secretariat London, 1985.

World Development Report, Annual, World Bank, Washington D.C., 1999.

World disaster Report, 1994, 1995, 1996, 1997, 1998, 1999, 2000, 2001, International Federation of Red Cross and Red Crescent Societies, Oxford University Press, Mijhoff publications, 1994-2002.

Government Publications, Documents And Non Government Reports

Amnesty International, Unlawful Killings in the Chittagong Hill Tracts (London: Amnesty International, 1986).

Bangladesh District Gazetteers, Chittagong Hill Tracts (Dhaka: Bangladesh Government Press, 1971).

Bangladesh Environment and Natural Resources Assessment, Final report, prepared for the U. S. Development and Environment, Washington B.C. 1992.

Bangladesh JRC, The Ganges Water Issues, Ministry of Water Resources (Dhaka: Government of Bangladesh 1984).

Bangladesh Meteorological Department 1991 and 1997 Cyclone Reports, Government of the People's Republic of Bangladesh, Dhaka 1991 and 1997.

Bangladesh, Ministry of Foreign Affairs, White Paper on the South Talpatty, 26 May 1981.

Bangladesh, Recent Economic Development and Short Term

Prospectus, Documents of the World Bank, Report No. 7596-BD, 13 March 1989.

Bangladesh, White Paper on the Ganges Water Dispute (Dhaka, September 1976).

Comments on the upgraded Indian Proposal (Government of Bangladesh: Dhaka, February 1984).

Cyclone 1997, CARITAS Bangladesh Report, Dhaka, 1997.

Developing the Infrastructure, Report of the Task Force on Bangladesh Development Strategy for the 1990's, vol. 3(Dhaka: UPL , 1991).

Earthscan, Environment and Conflict, Earthscan Briefing Document 40, London: International institute for Environment and Development, 1984).

East Pakistan Id strict Gazetteers: Chittagong (Dhaka: East Pakistan Government Press, 1970).

Environmental Policy, Report of the Task Force on Bangladesh Development Strategies for the 1990's vol.4, Dhaka, 1991.

Foreign Affairs Record, Ministry of External Affairs (New Delhi: Government of India, 1974). May 1974, p. 155, Vol. 20-1974, Vol. 22, 1974.

Fremji K.K. "The Farakka Barrage Project the fulfillment of dream" in Government of India, Souvenir, Farakka Barrage Project, 21 May 1975.

Government of Bangladesh, The Ganges Water Crisis in Bangladesh, Memorandum circulated at the Organization of Islamic Conference. Foreign Ministers Conference in Istanbul, May 1976.

Government of the People's Republic of Bangladesh, Study on the Causes and Consequences of Natural Disasters and Protection and Preservation of the Environment, Dhaka, December, 1989.

India, Lok Sabha, Public Accounts Committee, 196th Report, Farakka Barrage Project, Delhi, January 1976, p.9.

India, Ministry of Irrigation and Power, Preservation of the Part of Calcutta(New Delhi, Government of India Press, 196i),pp. 10-1-t.

India, Lok Sabha Debates, "Indo-Pakistan talks on" the Gangetic basin", 25 August 1959,s2,33, col.4324.

India, Lok Sabha Debates. 16 August 1961 "International Situation, s2, 56, col. 2405-2560.

India, Lok Sabha Debates, "The Farakka Barrage", 19 August 1961, 1961, 62, 56, Col. 32D.

India, Lok Sabha Debates, "Visit of Pakistan" experts to

Farakka Barrage site", 26 July 1968, s4, 18, Col. 2080.

India, Lok Sabha Debates, "Construction of barrage across the river Padma by Pakistan", 31 March 1969, s4, 26, cols. 46.

India, Ministry of External Affairs, The Farakka Barrage (New Delhi: Government of Indian Press, 1976).

India, The Report of Expert Committee on the River Hoogly and the Improvement of .its Head Water Supply, vol.1: Report, (New Delhi, Government of India, October 1952) p. 60.

Managing the Development Process, Report of the Force on Bangladesh development Strategies for the 1990' s, Vol. 11 (Dhaka, UPL, 1991).

Nadik, S.,The State of the World Population 1990 (New York: World Population Fund, 1990).

SAARC, Regional Study on the Causes and Consequences of Natural Disasters and the Protection and Preservation of ,the Environment (SAARC Secretariat, Kathmandu, 1992).

Sen Gupta,R. et al. State of the Marine Environment in the South Asia Seas Region, UNEP Regional Seas Reports and Studies Ho. 123, UNEP, 1990).

The Environment and Development in Bangladesh: An overview and strategy for the future, prepared by the Canadian International Development Agency for Bangladesh Programme, Asia Branch, October, 1989.

Sadik, Nafis, The State of the World Population 1991 (New York: United Nations Population Fund, 1991).

State of India's Environment, A Citizen's Report: Floods, Flood Plains and Environmental Myths (New Delhi: Centre for Science and Environment, 1991).

Task force on Migration (TFM) Internal and International Migration in Nepal(Kathmandu: The National Commission on Population, 1983), pp. 51-73.

The State of India's Environment : the First Citizen's Report (New Delhi.,' Centre for Science and Environment, 1987).

The State of the World's Children 1987 (New York, UNICEF, 1987) The United Nations Population Fund, The ' State of World Population 1992 (New York: 1992).

Towards Sustainable Development: The National Conservation Strategy of Bangladesh, First Draft, Ministry of Environment and Forest, Government of Bangladesh, Dhaka, 1991.

Towards Sustainable Development: National Conservation Strategy of Bangladesh, Ministry of Environment and .Forest, Government of Bangladesh /IUCN, Dhaka. 1991.

The World Bank, Nepal, Politics of Improving Growth and, Alleviating Poverty (Washington, D.C.:W.B. 1989).

UN/ESGAP 'Marine Environmental problems and Issues in the ESGAP Region", Proceeding of the Regional technical Work shop on the Protection of the Marine Environment and related ecosystems, Asian Institute of technology, Bangkok 20-28 Feb.1984.

UNCTAD, Handbook of International Trade and Development Statistics(New York, UN 1987).

UNIDO, Industry and Development Global Report 1987, Vienna, 1987.

United Nations Economic and Social Commission for Asia and the Pacific Marine Environmental Problems and Issues in the ESCAP Region, Protection of the marine environment and related ecosystems, Asian Institute of Technology, Bangkok, 20-28 February, 1984.

United Nations" Environment Progranme, UNEP Profile (Nairobi, 1990).

UN Food and Agricultural Organization (FAO), "New Deforestation Rate figures Announced", Tropical Forest Programme, IUCN News letter August 1990.

World Bark, World Development Report 1988 (New York: Oxford University Press, 1988).

World Bank, World Development Report 1992, Development and the Environment (New York: Oxford University Press, 1992).

World Bank, World Development Report 1987 (New York: Oxford university Press, 1987).

World Bank, Development Report 1992 (New York: Oxford University Press, 1992).

World Bank, Development Report 1995(New York:0xford University Press 1995).

World Commission on Environment and Development, Our Common Future, The Brundtland Report (New York: London: Oxford University Press 1987),p. 290.

Books

Abbas, B.M. The Ganges Water Dispute (Dhaka: University Press Ltd, 1982),

Abboltt, P.L., Natural Disasters (Dubuque, IA: William C. Brown Publisher, 1996)

Agarwal Anil and Sunita Narain, towards A Green World (New Delhi: Centre for Science and Environment 1992).

Ahmad Nafis, A New Economic Geography of Bangladesh (New Delhi: Vikas 1976).

Bahro Rudolf, From Red to Green: Interviews with New Left Review (London: Verso, 1984).

Bain J.S.,India's International Dispute: A Legal .Study(London: Asia Publishing House, 1962).

Barnet R.W., Beyond War: Japan's Concept of Comprehensive National Security (Washington: Pergamon Brassey's 1986).

Baxter Craig, Yogendra K.Malik, Charles H.Kennedy and Robert C.Oberst Government and Politics in South Asia (Boulder and London: Westview Press 1987).

Brown Lester R. et al, ed., State of the World 1991, World watch Institute (India)New Delhi, 1991).

Bryant E., Natural Hazards (Cambridge: Cambridge University Press, 1991).

Cantori L.J.and Spiegel S. L. ed., International Politics of Regions: a Comparative Approach (New Jersey: Prentice Hall, 1970).

Chakma Siddhartha. Proshongo : Parbotyo Chottagram (Calcutta: Nath Brothers, 1392 BE (1985-86).

Choudhury G. W. Pakistan's Relation with India 1947-66 (London: Pall Mall Press, 1964).

Crow Ben, Alan Lindquist and David Wilson, Sharing the Ganges: The Politics and Technology of River Development (New Delhi/Thousand Oaks/London: Sage, 199 5).

Dalby Simon, Creating the Second Cold War: The Discourse Politics(London: Print, 1990).

David L, River basin development for socio-economic growth: general report in UN Development Programme, ed., River, Basin Development: Policies and Planning (New York : UNDP, 1976) Vol.1.

Deudney Daniel H, et al. Contested Grounds (Albany: State University of New York Press, 1999)

EL-Hinnawi Essam, Environmental Refugees (New York: United Nations Development Progranme, 1985).

Enloe C., Bananas, Beaches and Bases: Making Feminist Sense of International Politics (London: Pandora 1989).

Fischer Dietrich, Nonmilitary Aspects of Security: A Systam's Approach, United Nations Institute for Disarmament and Research(UNIDIR) Alder-shot: Dartmouth Publishing Company Ltd, 1993), P. 10.

Franda Marcus, Bangladesh, The First Decade (New Delhi: South Asia Publishers, 1981).

Friedmann John , Empowerment: The Politics of Alternative Development (Cambridge: Black well Publishers, 1992).

Galtung Johan. International Development" in Roger A Coate and Jerely A. Rosati, ed. The Power of Human Needs in World Society (Boulder and London: Lynne Rienner Publishers, 1988).

Garlake, Tersa, Dealing with Disasters, (Dhaka: Oxfam Bangladesh, 2000).

Gilpin Robert, The Political Economy of International Relations (Princeton/ New Jersey: Princeton University Press, 1987).

George P. Castille and Gilbert Kushner, ed. Persistent Peoples: Cultural Enclaves in Perspective . (Tuson: University of Arizona Press, 1981).

Ghosh Partha S., Cooperation and Conflict in South Asia (New Delhi: Manohar, 1989)V.

Giddens Anthony, The Constitution of Society: Outline of the Theory of Structuration (Cambridge: UK: Polity Press, 1984).

Gleick Peter H. "Environmental resources and international security and politics", in E.H. Arnett, ed., Science and International Security: Responding to a Changing World (Washington D. C American Association for the Advancement of Science, 1990) p. 512.

Goldsmith Edward Nicholas Hildyard, "The Social and Environmental Effects of Large Dams", Vol.1, Overview, A Report, to the European Ecological Action Group (ECOROPA) (Cornwell : Wadebridge Ecological Center, 1984).

Grubb M., Green House Effect: Negotiating Targets (London: Royal Institute of International Affairs, 1989).

Gurr Ted, Why Men Rebel (Princeton: Princeton University Press, 1970).

Harrison Paul, The Third Revolution: Environment, Population and A Sustainable World (London/New York: Tauris and Co., Ltd, 1992).

Hassan Shaukat, India-Bangladesh Political Relations During the Awami League Government 1972-75 (Ann Arbor MI: UMI. Dissertation Information Service, 1988).

Hillel D., Out of the Earth: Civilization and the Life of the Soil (New York. The Free Press, 1991).

Hollis H.B., A.L.Powers and M. Sommers, ed, The Conquest of War: Alternative Strategies for GlobaL Security (Boulder, Co., Westview Press, 1989).

Homer-Dixon Thomas F. Environment, Scarcity and Violence (Princeton/ New Jersey: Princeton University Press, 1999).

Horowitz Donald, Ethnic Groups in Conflict (Berkeley and Los Angelas: University of California Press, 1985).

Hoyt E., "Conserving the wild relatives of crops", International Board for Plant Genetic Resources, International Union for the Conservation of Nature and Natural Resources(IUCN), and World Wide Fund for Nature (WF),Rome and Gland, 1988.

Hussain Akmal, Resource Depletion and Sustainable Development in South Asia, Asia Panel meetings of IUCN. The World Conservation Union, Perth-Australia, 26-27 November 1990,

Hutchinson R. H. Sneyd, An Account of the Chittagong Tracts (Calcutta: Bengal Secretariat Book Depot, 1906).

Huxley J. Human Crisis (Seattle: University of Washington Press, 1963).

Iftekharuzzaman and Imtiaz Ahmed, ed, Bangladesh and SAARC Issues, Perspectives and Outlook (Dhaka: Academic Publishers, 1992).

Islam M. Rafique, Ganges Water dispute: Its International Legal Aspects (Dhaka: University Press Ltd, 1982).

Jacobson Jodi L. Environmental Refugees: A Yardstick of Habitability, World Watch Paper, No.86,1988).

Job B.ed., the Security Dilemma: National Security of Third World States (Boulder, Co. Lynne Rienner, 1992).

Johnston, R. J. A Question of Place Exploring the Practice of Human Geography (Oxford: Basil Blackwell, 1991)

Khan H , On Thermonuclear War, edn. 2(Princeton/New Jersey: Princeton University Press, 1961).

Kaldor M., The Imaginary War (Oxford: Basil Blackwell, 1990).

Kaldor M. and R, Falk, ed. Dealignment: A New Foreign Policy Perspective (Oxford: Basil Blackwell, 1987).

Lemarquand David G., International Rivers, The Politics of Cooperation (University of British Columbia and the Waterloo Research Centre, 1977).

Leonard Jeffrey, "Overview", Environment and the Poor: Development Strategies for a Common Agenda (New Brunswick, NJ: Transaction, 1989) p. 7.

Lewin T.H., Wild Races of the Eastern Frontier of India (Delhi: Mittal Publications, 1984),

Linkgreen Goran, et al. ed., Peace Processes in the Third World, Report from the 1991 Advanced International Programme Conflict Resolution, Department of Peace and Conflict Research, Uppsala University, Sweden 1991).

Lundquist J.U. Lohn and M. Falkenmark, ed., Strategies for River Basin Management (Dordrecht: D. Reidel Publishing, 1985).

Mahatab F.U. Effects of Climate Change and Sea Level Rise on Bangladesh (London: Common Wealth Secretariat, 1989).

May Wolfgang, ed., They Are Now Burning Village After Village: Genocide in the Chittagong Hill Tracts, Bangladesh (Copenhagen: International Workgroup for Indigenous Affairs, 1984).

——— Politische System in den Chittagong Hill Tracts Bangladesh (Bremen:Uebersee-Museaum, 1980).

May, E.G. ed. They are Now Burning: Amnesty International, Unlawful Killing, Survival International, Bangladesh Chittagong Hill Tracts Report for 1988.

Milliman John D., et. al., Environmental and Economic Impact of Rising Sea Level and Subsiding Deltas: The Nile and Bengal Examples, Woods Hole Oceanographic Institution, Woods Hole, Massachusettes, 1988.

Mills J.P. "Notes on a tour in the Chittagong Hill Tracts 1972", in Census of India, 1981, Vol.V.Bengal and Sikkim, Appendix-II

Moller B., Common Security and Non-offensive Defense: A Non-Realist Perspective(Boulder, Co., :Lynne Rienner, 1992).

Ohlsson Leif, "Sustainable Development of the Greater Ganga: A Case for Regional Cooperation" in Ibid., ed., Regional Conflict and Conflict Resolution-Case Studies II, Padrigue papers, Gothenburg University, 1991.

Pearce David, Markandya Anil and Barbier Edward B., Blue Print for a Green Economy (London: Earthscan Publications, 1989).

Peters R. and Lovejoy T. ed, Global Warming and Biological Diversity (New Haven: Yale University Press, 1992).

Peterson V.S. ed., Gendered States: Feminist (re)Visions of International Relations Theory (Boulder, Co: Lynee Rienner, 1992).

Phadnis Urmila, S.D Muni and Kalim Bahadur, ed. Domestic Conflict in South Asia, Vol. 1,Political Dimensions (New Delhi: South Asia Publishers, 1986).

Rahman Atiq, Nick Robins and Annie Roncerel, ed, Exploding the Population Myth-Consumption vrs. Population which is the Climate Bomb ? Brussels, Dhaka, Rome-Santiago, July 1993, p. 52.

Rao K.L. India's Water Wealth: Its Assessment, Uses and Projections (New Delhi: Orient Longman Ltd, 1979)

Ray Nishit Ranjan, ed., Saga of Freedom (Delhi:People's Publishing, 1983).

Renner M., "Assessing the military's war on the environment" in L.Brown et al, State of the World 1991 (New York: Norton, 1991), pp. 132-55.

Rifkin J., Biospheric Politics: A New Consciousness for a New Century (New York: Crown, 1991), p. *2.*

Risely H.H., The Tribes and Castes of Bengal: Ethnographic Glossary (Calcutta-Firma Mukhopadhyaya, 1981), vol. 1, pp. 28-29.

Rogge Hohn R. River Bank Erosion: Flood and Population Displacement in Bangladesh (Dacca: Jahangirnagar University, October 1990).

Roger Peter, David Seekler and Peter Lydon, Eastern Waters Study: Strategies to manage flood and drought in the Ganges Bhramaputra Basin, Prepared for the office of Technical Resources, Bureau for the Asia and the Near East, US Agency for International Development, April, 1989.

Rural Poverty in Bangladesh: A Report to the Like Minded Group(Dhaka: UPI, 1990).

Sale Kirkpatrick, Dwellers in the Land: The Bioregional Vision (San Francisco: Sierra Club Books, 1985).

Sneyd R. H. Hutchinson, An Account of the Chittagong Hill Tracts (Calcutta Bengal Secretariat Book Depot, 1906).

Starr Joyce, R. and Daniel C. Stoll, ed., the Politics of Scarcity: Water in the Middle East(Boulder, Westview Press, 1988).

Stockholm International Peace Research Institute, Policies for Common Security (London: Taylor and Francis, 1985)

Survival International, Bangladesh-Chittagong Hill Tracts Reports for 1988: No End to Human Rights Abuses (London: Survival International, 1988).

Talukdar S.P., *The* Chakmas Life and Struggle (Delhi: Gian Publishing House, 1988), pp.47-58.

Validya K.S., "Accelerated erosion and landslide prone zones in the Himalayan region", in J. S.Singh, ed., Environmental Regeneration in Himalaya: Concepts and Strategies(Nainital: Central Himalaya Environment Association, 1985).

Verghese B.C., Waters of Hope Integrated Water Resources Development and Regional Cooperation within the Himalaya-Ganga Brahmaputra-Barak Basin (New Delhi, Oxford University Press, 1990).

Wachtel Paul, The Poverty of Affluence (Philadelphia: New Society Publishers, 1989).

Walker R.B.J. and S. Mendlowitz, ed., Contending Sovereignties: Redefining Political Community (Boulder, Co: Lynne Rienner, 1990).

Weiner Myron, Sons of the Soil: Migration and Ethnic Conflict in India (Delhi: Oxford University Press, 1988).

Westing Arthur H. ed., Global Resources and International Conflict: Environmental Factors in Strategic Policy and Action(Oxford: Oxford University Press, 1986).

Westing Arthur H. Comprehensive Security for the Baltic: An Environmental Approach (London/Newbury Park: Sage, 1989).

Weston B,ed., Alternative Security: Living without Nuclear Deterrence (Boulder, Co: Westview Press, 1990).

Periodicals, Journals And Papers

Abbas B.M., "Floods can only be controlled by measures in India and Nepal", Courier (Dacca), vol. 5, Issue 6 16-22 September 1988, p. 8.

Abbott Elizabeth, "Where waters run brown", Equinox, Vol.10, No. 59, September-October, 1991.

Ahluwalla, N.G. Carter and H.B, Chenery, "Growth and Poverty in developing countries", Journal of Development Economics, Vol.6, No.3, 1979.

Appasamy Paul P, "City of Thirst", Down to Earth, Vol.2, No. 20, 15 March 1994.

Banerjee Ruben, "The North-East: returns to arms", India Today, 30 November 1992.

Baker James, "Diplomacy for the Environment", Address before the National Governors Association, 26 February 1990. Washington D.C. reprinted in Current Policy, No. 1254, February, 1990.

Bhaumik Subir and H. C. Vanlalruata, "Sailo's grand strategy: The former CM has picked up the Greater Mizoram cause to come out of the political wildeness", Sunday, 19-25 June 1988.

Boge Volker, Proposal for an Analytical Framework to Grasp Environmental Conflict", Environment and Conflict Project (ENCOP), occasional Paper No.1, Center for Security Studies and Conflict Research, Bern/ Zurich, July 1992.

Bose Ajay, "Dacca blames India for flood disaster", Guardian, 24 September 1988.

Brock Lothar, "Peace through Perks: The environment on the peace research agenda", Journal of Peace Research Vol. 28(40), 1991.

Brown L. and Wolfe E., "Soil erosion quiet crisis in world economy", World Watch Paper 60, 1991, World Watch Institute, Washington D.C. 1991.

Brown L.H., "Regional collaboration in resolving third world conflicts", Survival (London), Vol.23, 1986, pp. 208-220.

Brown Lester R. and Joci L. Jacobson, "The future of urbanization: facing the ecological and economic constraints", World Watch Paper 77, May 1987.

Bruyninckx Hans, "Environmental security: an analysis of the conceptual problems defining the relationship between environment and security", a paper presented at Budapest on the Workshop on Environment and Security, organised" by the European Peace Research Association, 11-16 November 1993, pp. 1-16.

Buzan Barry, "Environment as a security issue" in Paul Painchaud ed., Geopolitical Perspectives on Environmental Security, Cahier du GERPE, No. 92-05, University Laval, Quebec, p. 24, quoted in 01e Waever, Securitizat on and Desercuritization Working paper 5, 1993, Centre for Peace and Conflict Research, Copenhagen, 1993, P. 14.

Byers Bruce, "Ecoregions, State Sovereignty' and Conflict", Bulletin of Peace Proposals, Vol.22(1) 1991.

CMT. "Beleagured tribals", Far Eastern Economic Review, 6 October 1988.

Chakravarty Ratan Lal, "Chakmas resistance to early British rule", Bangladesh Historical Studies, vol.2, 1977.

Crow B. "Appropriating the Brahmaputra: the onward march of India's rich peasants", Economic and Political Weekly, 25 December 1982.

Crow Ben and Alan Lindquist, "Development of the rivers Ganges and Brahmaputra: the difficulty of negotiating a new line", DPP Working Paper, No. 19 (Milton Keynes: The Open University, February, 1990).

Daily G. and Ehrlich P., "Population, Sustainability and Earth's Carrying Capacity", Bioscience, Vol.42, No.10, 1992.

Dalby Simon, "Ecopolitical Discourse: Environmental Security and Political. Geography", Progress in Human Geography Vol. 16, no.4, 1992.

———"American Security Discourse: the Persistence of Geopolitics", Political Geography Quarterly, Vol.9. 1990, pp. 171-88.

Das Gupta Sumita, "Watershed deals", Down to Earth, Vol.4, No5, 31 July 1995.

Debes Mukherjee, "Farakka Barrage Project a challenge to engineers". Proceedings, Institution of Civil Engineers, London, Part I, Vol.58, February 1975, pp. 67-84.

———"Farakka Barrage Project for the Preservation of the Port of Calcutta", Engineering News of India, October, 1972, pp. 328-34.

Deb Mani, "Assam's patience with Delhi grows increasingly thin", Financial Times, 3 February 1988.

Deudney Daniel, "The case against linking environmental degradation and national security", Millennium, Vol.19, No.3, Winter 1990, pp.416-476.

———"Rethinking the link between environment and national security issues", Perspectives on War and Peace, Centre, for International. Cooperation and Security Studies, University of Wisconsin, Madison Vol.7, No.2, Spring 1990, p. 12.

Dewan R. S., "The jumma representative's statement on the systematic genocide of the helpless Jumma people of the CHT being carried out by the Bangladesh aimed forces", Woeking Group on Indigenous Populations, United Nations Economic and .Social Council, Geneva, 31 July - 4 August, 1989.

Dixon Thomas F.Homer, "Environmental change and economic decline in developing countries", International Studies Notes, Vol.16, No.1, Winter 1991.

———"On the threshold: environmental changes as causes of acute conflict", International Security, Vol.16, No. 2, Fall 1991.

———"Environmental scarcities and violent conflict: evidence from cases"] International Security, Vol.19, No.1, 1994.

Dixon Thomas Homer, Boutwell Jeffrey and Rathjens George, "Environmental change and violent conflict", Scientific American, February 1993.

Durning A., "Poverty and the environment: Reversing the downward spiral", World Watch Paper 92, World Watch Institute, Washington D.C.:1989.

Fallkenmark M. "Water: the silent messenger between cause and effect in environmental problems", Water International(Lausanne, 9(2), 1984.

———"New ecological approach to the water cycle: ticket to the future", Ambio (Stockholm),Vol. 13, 1984.

Farmer B.H., "Perspectives on the Green Revolution in South Asia", Modern Asian Studies, 20, 1986,pp. 175-99.

Finger Mathias, "The military, the nation state and the environment", The Ecologist, Vol.21,No.5. 1991.

Franda M, "Indo-Bangladesh relations", American Universities Fieldstaff Reports, South Asian Series, XX, 16 September 1975.

Ganguly Amulya, "Bangladesh lebensraum", Times of India, 13 July 1992.

Galtung Johan, "Violence, Peace and Peace Research", Journal of Peace Research, vol.8, No. 3, 1969, pp. 167-91.

Ganguly Sumit, "Ethno-religious Conflict in South Asia", Survival, Vol.35, No-2, Summer 1993.

Gleick Peter, "Water and conflict", International Security, Vol.18, Ko.1, Summer 1993, pp. 79-112.

———"The Implications of global climatic changes for international security", Climate Change, Vol.15, 1989, pp. 309-25.

———"Environment and Security: The clear connections", The Bulletin of the Atomic Scientists, April 1991, p. 18.

Gordon Sandy, "Resources and Instability in South Asia," Survival, Vol.35, No. 2, Summer 1993.

Gore Albert, 'Strategic environmental initiative (SEI)" SAIS Review, Vol.10, 1990, pp. 59-71.

Gosselink Robert G., "Minority rights and ethnic conflict in Assam, India", Boston College Third World Journal, Vol.XIV, Winter, 1994.

Hafiz M. Abdul and Nahid Islam, "Environmental degradation and intrainter state conflicts, in Bangladesh", ENCOP, Occasional paper No .6 Bern/ Zurich, May 1993.

Hamilton Lawrence S., "What are the impacts of Himalayan deforestation on the Ganges-Brahmaputra low lands and deltas? Assumption and Facts", Mountain Research and Development (Kathmandu), Vol.7, No.3, August 1987.

Hannan A., "Impact of reduced flow of the Ganges", Paper presented at a seminar organized by the Department of Water Resources Engineering BUET, 23 August 1980.

Hare F. Kenneth, "Climate, drought and' desertification", Nature and Resources, Vol.20, no.1, January-March 1984.

Hassan Shaukat, "Environmental issues and security in South Asia". Adelphi Paper 226, The International Institute for Strategic Studies, London, 1991.

Hassan Shaukat, "Problems of internal stability in South Asia", PSIS Occasional paper No.1, 1988, Geneva, The Graduate Institute of International Studies, June 1988.

Hassan Syed Aziz AJ and Bhumitra Chakma "Problems of national integration in Bangladesh", Asian Survey, Vol. XXIX, no. 10, Oct. 1989.

Hazarika Sanjoy, "India admits failure to cut Bangladesh Influx", New York Times, 16 December, 1992.

———"Bangladesh and Assam: Land pressures, migration and ethnic conflict, Occasional Paper Series of the Project on Environmental Change and Acute Conflict, A joint Project of the University of Toronto and the American Academy of Arts and Science, no. 3, March 1993.

Hossain Syed Anwar, "Ethnicity and Security in Bangladesh", paper presented at a seminar on South Asia's Security in the 1990s: Primacy of its Internal Dimensions, Organized by Bangladesh Institute of International Studies(BIISS), 5-7 January, 1992.

Huda Md.N. and Chowdhury J.U., "Floods and Erosion", paper presented at a Regional Conference on Floods and Erosion, Dhaka, 7-10 September 1989.

Imhoff M et al., "Monsoon flood boundary delineation and damage asessment using space borne imaging radar and land sat data", Photogrammetric Engineering and Remote Sensing, 53, 1986.

Islam Muinul, "Natural calamities and environmental refugees in Bangladesh", Refugee, Vol. 12, No.1, June 1992.

Islam Nahid, "The Ganges water dispute: environmental and related impacts on Bangladesh", BIISS Journal(Bangladesh), Vol.12, No.3, July 1991, pp. 263-92,

Islam Nurul and Md. Humayun Kabir, "Indo-Bangladesh common rivers and water diplomacy", BIISS Paper, No. 5, December 1986.

Islam Syed Nazmul, "The Chittagong Hill Tracts in Bangladesh: Integrational Crisis between Centre and Periphery" Asian Survey, Vol. XXI,No. 12, December, 1981.

Jacobson, Jodi L, "An unnatural disaster", Bangladesh Observer, December 1990.

Johansen, R. G. "Real security is democratic security", Alternatives, Vol. 16, 1991 pp. 209-42.

Kamaluddin S., "Bangladesh-Tribal insurgents try to disrupt Hill Council Polls: Intimidatory Tactics", Far Eastern Economic Review, 29 June 1989.

Kates R. and Haarmann V., "Where the poor live: Are the assumptions correct ?", Environment, 34, no.4, 1992, pp. 5-11, pp. 25-28.

Khan Amjad H., "Flood, problems and prospects - a regional Overview", Keynote address on a Regional Conference on Flood and Erosion, Dhaka, 7-10 September, 1989.

Khan Hamidur Rahman, "Water resources development in Bangladesh: problems and prospects", paper presented at a Regional Seminar on Water Resources Policy in Agro-Socio-Economic Development, Dacca, 4-5, August 1985.

Kiessling Kerstin and Nathan Keyfitz, "The population debate: urgency of the problem", a paper presented at the Population Summit of the World's Scientific Academies held in New Delhi from 24-27 October 1993.

Leffler M.P "The American conception of national security and the beginning of the cold war 1945-48", American Historical Review, Vol.89, 1984, pp. 246-81.

Libiszewski Stephan, "What is an environmental conflict", Environment and Conflict Project, Centre for Security Studies and Conflict Research, Switzerland, Berne/Zurich, Occasional Paper No. 1 July 1992, pp. 1-16.

Lichbach Mark, "An evaluation of does economic inequality breed political conflict? Studies", World Politics, Vol.41, July 1989, pp.431-70.

Lodgaard Sverre, "Environmental conflict resolution", paper presented at the UNEP Meeting on Environmental Conflict Resolution, Nairobi, 30 March, 1990.

Lodhi Abdul and Charles Tilly, "Urbanization, Crime and Collective Violence in 19th Century France", American Journal of Sociology, Vcol.79, no.2, September 1973.

Loffler Lorenz G., "Carrying capacity, schwendbau problem in Sudostasien" VIe congress International des science Anthropqiques et Ethnoloqiques, Paris, 1960, Vol.2, No.1, pp. 179-82.

Majumdar P.P., "Basti Jibaner Gatishilata O Sthabirata", (Bengali) Bangladesh Unnayan Samikka, BIDS, Dhaka, 1992.

Mathews Jessica Tuchman, "Redefining security", Foreign Affairs, Vol.68, no.2, spring 1989.

McClintock Cynthia, "Why peasants rebel : the case of Peru's Sendero Luminoso" World Politics, Vol. 37, No.1, October 1984.

Menon Ramesh, "Mizoram wild dreams -plans to carve a new state", India Today, Vol.,XIII, no. 12,30 June 1988.

Montu Kazi, "Tribal insurgency in Chittagong Hill Tracts", Economic and Political Weekly, 6 September, 1980.

Myers Norman, "The environmental dimension to security issues", The Environmentalist, Vol.6, no.4, V/inter 1986.

Naqvi M.B., "Pakistan cries wolf", Times of India, 2 January 1995.

Nishat Ainun and Chowdhury Shahjahan Kabir, "Water Quality: Problems and Needs for Integrated Control in Bangladesh", paper presented at a Regional Seminar on Water Resources Policy in Agro Socio-Economic Development, Dacca, 4-8,August 1985.

Norse D., "A new strategy for feeding a crowded planet", Environment, 34, no. 5, pp.6-11, 1992.

Pearce Fred, "War over water", Down to Earth, vol2, no. 11, 31 October 1993, pp. 25-28.

Pimental D., et. al., "Environmental and social- costs of biomass energy", Bioscience, Vol.34, no. 2,1992.

———, Conserving biological diversity in agricultural/ forestry Systems", Bioscience,Vol.42, no.5, 1992, pp. 354-363.

Porter Gareth, "Environmental security as a national security issue", Current History, May 1995.

Position paper on the Chittagong Hill Tracts, Bangladesh Institute of International Studies (BIISS), Dacca, September 1987.

Postel S., "Water: Rethinking management in an age of Scarcity", World Watch Institute (Washington), Paper No. 62, 1984.

Quraishee G. S., Climate change and sea level rise in the South Asia Seas region", The Siren (UNEP) ,1988.

Rahman Atiur, "Impact of riverbank erosion: survival strategies of displacees", Bangladesh Institute of Development Studies (Dhaka), 1985.

Ramakrishnan P. S., "Tropical Forests: Exploitation, Conservation and management", Environment and Development, no. 166, 1993.

Ray J.K. "The Farakka Agreement", International Studies, Vol.17, no. 2, April-June 1978.pp. 235-46.

Reddy G.K. "Farakka pact, best India can get in present circumstances", The Hindu, 6 November 1977.

Renner Michael, "National Security: The Economic and Environmental Dimensions", World Watch Institute, 1989.

Repetto Robert, "Wasting assets: the need for national resource accounting", Technology Review, January 1990.

Rizvi, G. Bangladesh: Insurgency in the Hills", The Round Table, 305, 1988.

Rogers Peter, "The volume of cooperation in resolving international river basin disputes", Natural Resources Forum, Vol. 107, No. 2 May 1993, p. 119.

Schendel Willem Van, "The invention of the jummas: state formation and ethnicity in Southeastern Bangladesh", Modern Asian Studies, Vol.26, no. 1, 1992.

Sonwalker Prasun, "Exodus of Bangladeshis to India", Times of India, 6 December 1991.

Sopher David E., "The Swidden/Wet Rice: Transition zone in the Chittagong Hill", Annals of the Association of American Geographers, Vol.54, no.1, 1964, pp. 107-26.

Springer A.L., "Protecting the environment: a new focus for the Atlantic alliance", Proceedings of the Acedemy of Political Science, Vol.38, 1991, pp. 124-39.

Tietelbaum Michael S., "The population threat", Foreign Affairs, Vol.71, no. 5, Winter 1992/1993.

Takeli Sahim, "Turkey seeks reconciliation for the water issue induced by the South Eastern Anatolia project", Water International, Vol. 15, no.4, December 1990, pp. 206-16.

Ullman R.H. "Redefining security", International Security, Vol.8, 1983, pp. 129-53.

Wayne Cornelius Jr., "Urbanization as an agent in Latin American political instability, the case of Mexico", American Political Science Review, Vol.63,no.3, September 1969.

Wendt Alexandar, "The agent structure problem" ,International Organization Vol.41, no. 3, Summer 1987.

Westing A.H., "Environmental security and its relation to Ethiopia and Sudan", Ambio, Vol. 20, 1991, pp. 168-71.

———, "Environmental security for the Danube Basin", Environmental Conservation, Vol. 16, no.4,1989.

———, "Comprehensive human security and ecological realities", Guest Comment, Environmental Conservation, Vol.16, no.4, Winter 1989.

———, "The environmental components of comprehensive security", Bulletin of Peace Proposal, Vol.20, 1989, pp. 129-34."The atmosphere as a common heritage of human Kind: its role in environmental security", Scientific World (London) , 34(4) , 1990.

Widgrin J., "International migration and regional stability", International Affairs, Vol.66, 1990, pp.749-66.

Index

A

Aborginal extermination, 127
Agricultural chemicals use-impact, 70
Agricultual Growth Bangladesh, 147
Agriculture
- Role in economey, 89
- out put of environmental change, 89

Air pollution (South Asia), 72
Alternative
- Security, 15-16
- Energy sources exploration, 266
- Development strategy, 267

All Assam Students Union (ASSU) movement against illegal immigrants, 151
Annual Frequences of heavy rainfall, 77
Asia natural disasters in, 178

B

Baker, James on environmental threats, 26
Balance of Trade deficit-Bangladesh, 108
Bangladesh rifles killing of BSF 2001, 151
Bangladesh
- environmental degradation, 35
- migrations, 35, 105
- Boyce's study, 39
- Population growth, 51, 129
- Soil, 53-55
- deforestation, 59
- Surface water storage, 63
- Sea ports, 71
- formation, 129
- Water Pollution, 71
- Agriculture, 91-92
- Lande use, 92
- Repair and reconstruction, 94
- system, 106-107
- Health state, 109
- Labour force participation rate, 109
- Climatic changes, 130
- Situation since origin, 136
- Influx in India, 152
- Studies on, 162
- Area, 181
- Physical Features, 181
- Support to MNF, 142
- India relations, 142
- Population projections, 146, 162
- Land vulnerability to disastes, 226

Below Poverty line Population
- Bangladesh,145

Bodoand Movements, 151-52
Brahmaputra Right Bank Embankment (BRE), 69
Brundtland Report on environmental degradation, 19

C

Causes of Floods in Bangladesh 1987,1988,1998,198
CFC emission India, 77
Chakma refugees Tripura, 143
- Population growth, 144
- Killings, 144
- Repatriation to CHT, 256-57

Chittagong Hill Tracts (CHT),123-24,251
- Regulation 1900,106
- Atrocities,125
- Polices, 253
- And colonial rule,131
- Developmental Programme, 137
- Decline-blame, 132
- Ershad's division, 252
- During 1947, 132
- Special Status, 132
- Problem Bangladeshi version, 134
- As reserved forest area, 135
- Environmental refusees in, 141
- Issue, 255
- Group vs Group crisis,142
- Liberation,142
- Resettlement in,254

CHTDB (CHT Development Board), 137
CHT People's Association, 140
Clean Developing Mechanism (CDM), 232
Climate change impact, 76
Clinton Administration on National Security, 26
CO_2 emission
- Effect,18, 20, 73
- Industrialised countries, 39
- As theat to developing world, 237
- Reduction by North, 263

Cold war, 13
- And concept of security, 22

Colonisation Bangladesh, 106
Contextual factors of environmental scarcity, 33
Comprehensive Security (south Asia), 268
- Prerequisite, 269

Conflict
- Management/Resolution Approaches, 258

Consumption of commercial energy, 74
Cost (sector-wise) on repairs/ reconstruction Bangladesh, 94
Cyclones (Banglades), 208
- Origin/formation, 209
- Reasons, 209
- Various in tensity classification, 210-11
- Historical perspective, 211
- In 20th century, 212
- Features/impact/loss/ decenage
  —1991, 215-16
  —1997, 217-20

D

Deforestation, 58
- Results, 58
- South Asia, 58
- Bangladesh, 59
- ecological effects, 60
- India, 61

Degradation of environment
- social impact, 24
- Impact on economy, 18

Demand induced scarcity, 31
Democratization of society importance, 16
Disaster
- World Bank definition, 172
- Nature/causes, 172
- Management strategies Issues, 177
- Cyclones, 220-21

Disaster-Development Linkages (Bangladesh), 222
Dixon, Homer
- On land scarcity Bangladesh, 148
- Theroy on migration, 224

Drinking water (Bangladesh)
- Scarcity, 96
- Demand, 96
- Impact on health, 166

E

Ecological perspective (natural disasters), 174
Economic marginalisation, 249
Eco-Fascism, 23
Ecological
- degradation, 68
- Marginalisation, 32-33

Energy Consumption rate, 83
Environmental degradation, 20, 249
- Threats, 16-17, 27
- And national security threats, 17-18
- Eradication, 259
- Effect on economy, 18
- Impacts (social), 24

Environmental security, 17
- As National Security, 20
- Components, 29

Environmental
- Scarcity, 28
  - — Social effects, 251
  - — Sources, 30
  - — And conflict, 87-88
- Conflict, 28, 148, 250
- Linkages, 87
- Refugees, 35
- Resettlement (Bangladesh), 141
- Systemes-interdependence, 39
- change and agricultral, output 89-90
- Induced Refugees, 167

Environment
- Definition, 17
- And security, 30
- Erosion and Population Displacement (Bangladesh), 1992, 103

Ershad's division of CHT, 252
Ethnic
- Conflicts, 34
- Crisis Bangladesh, 105, 250

F

FAO Tropical Forests resource Assessment Report, 61

Farakka
- Ganges Flow, 64
- Ganges water sharing agreement, 65
- Barrage adverse impact, 92
- Diversion effect, 110-13

Fencing of Bangladesh border by India, 257

Fish production
- Impact of degradation,71
- Bangladesh, 92, 95

Flash floods, 194

Flood
- Impact on developing country, 189
- Hazard (Hewitt's analysis), 188
- Plains (Bangladesh), 182

Floods (Bangladesh), 110
- Causes, 110, 195
- 1998, 204
- Impact, 205
- Deaths, 206
- Infrastructural damages, 207
- Economic impact, 207
- Losses (1987-88), 93
- Impact, 187

Floods and cyclones (Bangladesh), 102-103, 190

Flood disasters
- Analysis, 178
- Bangladesh, 184

Flood damages
- Records-table, 200-201
- Types, 187

Forests
- role, 58
- Types-Bangladesh, 59
- Role in Bangladesh, 60
- Area (India), 61

Foreign aid (Bangladesh), 180

Fresh Water scarcity, 62
- Bangladesh, 63
- India, 70

Ganges
- Upstrean diversion to Bangladesh-impact, 65
- Flow reduction-impact, 114-15, 146

Ganges Brahmaputra Meghna (GBM) Catchment area, 182

Ganges Kobadak Project, 91

Genocidal attacks on indigenous People, 126

Geopolitical scarcity (resources), 27

Global warming, 174-245
- Bangladesh, 174

Gorbachev, Mikhail on environment threats, 26

Green house
- Effects, 26
- Gas emissions, 72
- Of developed/ developing world, 238
- Warnimg impact on agriculture, 95
- (study by cynthia Rosenweig and Martin Party), 91

Ground water
- Planning Bangladesh, 65
- Reduction-reasons, 67
- Withdrawal Bangladesh, 75

Group identity conflicts, 34

H

Hazardous events and natural disaster, 225

Health hazards (Bangladesh) and environment degradation, 99

India
- Population growth, 51
- Land degradation, 56-57
- Fresh water scarcity, 70
- Water Pollution, 70-71
- Ocean and sea pollution, 71
- Marine environment, 71
- Climate change, 77

I

Indigenous people (tribes), 126
Industrial Production decrease (Bangladesh), 100
Industrial effluent discharges, 69
Infrastructure damage by Floods (Bangladesh), 204
Ingenuity supply constraints, 239-40
Inland Fisheries India, 72
Institution as prosperity deternisants, 38
Inter/intra state conflicts, 123, 258
Intergovernmental panel on climate change (IPCC), 161
Intra State conflict
- CHT and Bangla People,251

Intervention and adaptation strategies in Bangladesh
- constraints, 243

Interaction of environmental scarcity, 32

J

James Boyce's study (Bangladesh) on food production and prosperity, 38
Japanese Comprehensive security, 15
Jummas (Bangladesh)
- genocide, 124, 126
- Threat to, 124
- Resistance, 129,251
- Treatment justification, 133
- Illtreatment, 138
- Marginalisation, 139
- Movement, 140
- Political mobilization, 140
- Killings, 252

K

Knowledge (lack of) and environmental degradation, 38
Kyoto Protocol, 237, 264

L

Land degradation, 52
- Bangladesh, 53-56
- India, 56
- and productivity loss, 57

Land distribution/ownership problem Bangladesh, 145
Land inundated by flood percentage (1954-98), 199
Land Use
- Conflict over, 52
- Pattern-Bangladesh, 183
- Policy reform, 259

Land scarcity (Bangladesh)
- And poverty, 148

M

Major disasters (Bangladesh)
- Cyclones, Chronology, 213-14
- Floods-impacts, 202-204
- Natural disasters, 185

Major rivers (Bangladesh), 191
Malthusian explanation of poverty in Bangladesh, 147
Mark Cocker's study on German annihilation of Heroro, 128

Markets incentives on conservation, 38
Migrations
- Due to environmental causes, 36
- From Bangladesh, 101, 148
- Causes, 101, 148

Migrations from Bangladesh, 101, 148
- Areas to, 149
- Numbers estmates, 150
- Homer Dixon's theory, 224
- Tenion with India, 237

Military system as polluters, 21
Mining and Soil erosion, 56
Mineral and fossil fuels, 50
MSL (mean sea level) Changes, 161
Mujibur Rehman cooperation with India, 142

N

Natural disaster, 225
- Process, 171
- Definition, 171
- Socio-cultural perspective, 174
- Ecological perspective, 174
- Economice perspective, 175
- Political perspective, 175
- Developmental perspective, 176
- In Bangladesh, 181
- In Asia, 178

National security, 13
- Realist model, 14
- Definition, 22

National Security Threats
- And environmental degradation, 21
- And environmental security, 25

National Sewrits Document (1994), 26
National Security strategy of Engagement and Enlargement, 26
Non Offensive Defense (NOD), 15
Non-renewable resources, 27
- Depletion, 50

North-East insurgent groups aid from Bangladesh, 152

O

Old Meghna Estuarys Flood Plain, 244
- Pump Drainage, 244

Ozone layer hole in, 20-21

P

Parbottya Chattagram Jana Sanghati Samiti (JSS), 124
Permissible marzin of CO_2 release, 263
Physical scarcity (resources), 27
Policy integration, 24
Political economy/development
- Bangladesh, 185-86

Population explosion causes, 49
Population growth
- And natural resources, 38
- And environmental degradation, 38, 49

Population displacement Bangladesh, 101, 105
Population pressure and conflicts, 25
Push and pull theories on migration, 36

R

Radcliffe Award 1947, 140
Rainwater Floods, 193
Realist model
- National security, 13, 14

Realism
- In international politics, 13-14

Refugees form Bangladesh, 245
Refugees as vote banks, 257
Regional initiatives, 267
Relative deprivation and environmental scarcity, 35
Renewable resources, 50
Repatration problems of Muslim Bangladesh, 151
Resource
- Capture, 32-33
- renewable/ non-renewable, 27, 50
- Conflicts over, 27
- Scarcity
  - — Types, 27
  - — Impact, 82

River bank erosion, 54, 184
Bangladesh, 69, 114, 182
River floods, 193
Road construction in Himalayas impact, 68

S

Salinization, 55
SAARC Forestry and Watershed Programme, 262
Sea level rise
- Impact, 18, 245
- Bangladesh, 74, 75, 104, 148
- Area affected, 75
- Physical assets/ infrastructure affected by 1 Meter rise, 97-98
- Impact assessment, 161-62
- environmental/socio-economic implications, 162-67
- Impact on India, 167

Security, 13
- Redefining, 15
- Integration, 24

Shanti Bahini 140, 142
Struggle within Bangladesh, 137-254
Simple scarcity conflicts, 34
- Social effects environmental scarcity, 32
- Environmental degradation
- Eradication, 265

South Asia
- Economic development, 77, 108
- Income distribution, 78
- Domestic problems, 105
- Proverty ,108
- Working population, 109
- Deforestation, 58

Socio-economic scarcity, 28
Soil
- fertility, 52
- Erosion, 52
  - — Bangladesh, 53

South Asia/Bangladesh
- Impact of disasters, 179
- People Killed, 181

South Asia people Killed (1981-2000)
- Natural disasters, 180

Spatial differentiation of flooding Bangladesh, 196
South/North
- Population explosion, 50

- Consumption of renewable resources, 50

State of Forest Report 1995, 61
Structural scarcity, 31
Supply induced scarcity, 30
Surface water, 63
- Storage, 63
- Bangladesh, 63

T

Temporal differentiation of Flooding (Bangladesh), 197
Totalitarian Regimes, 23-24
Total Dissolved Solids (TDS) in Bangladesh, 64
Traditional/environmental conflicts, 22
Traditional concept of National security, 24
Transmigration of people and inter/intra state conflicts, 25
Tripura National volunteers, 143
Types of floods in Bangladesh, 192

U

ULFA agitation, 151-52
UNFCCC (Framework Convention on Climatic Change), 238
UNCHS (Centre of Human Settlement)
- Framework on natural disasters, 173

Unilateral Actions of eradication of environmental degradation, 259
- Implementation, 260
- Constraints, 261
- Regional actions, 262

Upstream Water withdrawal impact, 95
'Us Vs them' syndrome, 25
UV-Brays exposure to, 21

V

Violent Conflicts, 33

W

Warmer Climates/higher seas —Impact, 76
Wars involving environment, 27
Water/wind erosion, 53-54
Water logging
- Impact on land, 54

World Commission on Environment and Development, 19
World Bank Report 1992 on population growth, 50
World Disaster Report 1997-2000, 178